Story Building Blocks II

Crafting Believable Conflict

Diana Hurwitz

DEDICATION

To Norm for supporting my impossible dreams. To Anna and Andrew for inspiring me to dream them. To the Ladyscribes: Sharon Pielemeier, Rita Woods, Kathie Huddleston, Debbie Steinman Cameron, and Janet Skoog for their wise counsel. To all of the psychology professionals for increasing our understanding of the mind and how to heal it. To Carolyn who helped me understand myself: thank you for the gift that keeps on giving, I am eternally grateful.

CONTENTS

Chapter 1 Crafting Believable Conflict 7
Chapter 2 Responses to Obstacles 13
Chapter 3 Internal Obstacles 23
Chapter 4 Sixteen Characters 35
Chapter 5 Childhood 69
Chapter 6 Caregiving 93
Chapter 7 Boundary Violations 119
Chapter 8 Teenage Years 125
Chapter 9 Self Esteem 141
Chapter 10 Young Adulthood 147
Chapter 11 Adulthood 167
Chapter 12 Mid-Life Crisis 187
Chapter 13 Old Age 199
Chapter 14 Knowledge Obstacles 213
Chapter 15 Facts, Fantasies & Lies 251
Chapter 16 Ability Obstacles 265
Chapter 17 External Obstacles 297
Chapter 18 Organizational Obstacles 303
Chapter 19 Disunity Obstacles 317
Chapter 20 Love, Sex & Hate 333
Index 369

CRAFTING BELIEVABLE CONFLICT

Good writers ask, "What if?" Great writers ask, "Why?"

Humans walk around acting and reacting without considering why. They operate based on "programming" put there by their genetic makeup, personality type, the nurturing they received as a child, and the demands of the world they live in. They are influenced by all they see, read, hear, and are exposed to. Few are fully self-aware. Few are deeply introspective.

Characters in your story world walk around and do what you, the writer, program them to do. They may not know why, but you should. Mindless mannequins that enter a scene to do and say things then exit without a valid purpose or motive are a waste of page time. Effectively manipulating the characters' actions, reactions, and motives makes great fiction.

Faulty logic and missing motive are plot holes that cause reader disconnect. The reader growls and shrieks:

"The character would never do that."

"That made no sense whatsoever."

"I guess the script called for it."

At best, readers smirk and continue to read. At worst, they stop reading and never pick up another book you've penned.

Fleshing out your cast with believable motivations makes them feel real. When you provide the characters with believable obstacles, the reader cares if they succeed in every scene.

Thinking writers, or planners, enjoy selecting obstacles before sitting down to write. They use brief notes or full character and plot outlines before typing "Chapter One." This book helps them choose effective obstacles and outcomes for each scene.

Feeling writers, or pantsers, balk at the idea of outlining. They prefer to channel motive based on their understanding of human nature and their life experience. Their characters "write themselves." This book broadens their understanding and helps them review the final draft with a critical eye.

Whether you plan or wing it, you should take a hard look at the finished draft and ask tough questions at scene and overall story level:

1. Did the scene contain conflict?

2. What did my character do or not do, say or not say?

3. Why did he do or say it?

4. Did it fulfill my intention?

5. Was the motivation believable (not necessarily rational)?

6. Does the conflict serve the plot in an effective way?

7. How does overcoming, or failing to overcome, the obstacle lead to further conflict?

8. What does overcoming, or failing to overcome, the obstacle force the character to do next?

9. What is the price for failing?

10. What is the prize for succeeding?

The answers to the above questions are critical when the scene involves the main characters. The answers are important for the rest of the cast unless they are walk-ons who serve minimal to no plot function. Primary and secondary characters should serve a purpose when they appear. It's more effective if they have an opinion on, or stake in, the overall story problem and the thematic argument at the heart of it.

Secondary characters, and their subplots or story threads, should slow down, complicate, or accelerate the protagonist's and antagonist's progress toward their story goal. Secondary characters and subplots that run alongside the main plot as a distraction encourage readers to flip past those pages. Subplot interactions supply the primary characters' motivations. Secondary characters supply the friction in your fiction.

If a story is multilayered with overlapping, parallel, or consecutive story lines, each thread should serve a purpose and come together to form a satisfying whole. Every scene from every layer should contain character conflict, no matter how subtle. When the verbal camera follows the protagonist, love interest, antagonist, and secondary characters, they should have a goal for every scene.

Think of a scene goal as having an object and a verb. The object of the story problem or scene goal can be a:

- Person
- Place
- Thing
- Information
- Situation
- Physical task
- Mental task
- Need
- Want
- Emotion
- Belief
- Prejudice.

Examples are: a magic orb, person, group, room, building, city, state, country, planet, romantic relationship, job, family, friendship, an idea, belief, important clue, or inner peace.

The verb of the story problem or scene goal can be:

obtain it	⟳⟲	get rid of it
hold onto it	⟳⟲	release it
reach it	⟳⟲	escape it
hide it	⟳⟲	reveal it
change it	⟳⟲	keep from changing it
tell it	⟳⟲	not tell it
evade it	⟳⟲	capture it
avert it	⟳⟲	allow it
define it	⟳⟲	obscure it
prove it	⟳⟲	disprove it
evaluate it	⟳⟲	decide it

The antagonist's, or antagonistic forces', overall story and scene goals are to keep the protagonist from obtaining the object. They make the verb difficult or impossible. If a protagonist wants to hold on to someone or something, the antagonistic force wants to take it away. If a protagonist wants to change something, the antagonist wants it to remain the same. When your verbal camera follows your protagonist and antagonist, the reader learns about their motivations and how they navigate your story world.

The friends and foes provide stumbling blocks and step ladders to keep the protagonist and antagonist moving toward and away from their story goals or scene objects. They make the verb difficult or easier. Friends and foes can have goals of their own. When your verbal camera follows the friends and foes, the reader learns about their motivations and how they complicate the protagonist's and antagonist's story world.

In this book, we explore six categories of obstacles used to complicate the protagonist's efforts to solve the overall story problem, vanquish the antagonist or antagonistic forces, negotiate the helping and hindering friends and foes, and solve his personal dilemma.

☯ Internal obstacles originate in the character's own mind.

⚒ Ability obstacles are generated by how he makes decisions and takes action.

▦ External obstacles come in the form of physical restrictions and time.

📖 Knowledge obstacles stem from what he knows, when he knows it, and the type of information he embraces or rejects.

🚶 Organizational obstacles are provided by the society he lives in, the bureaucracies he fights against, and whose authority he relies on.

👥 Disunity obstacles arise from conflicting beliefs, values, and who he listens to or believes in.

One way to use the information presented in this book is to assign each character in your story a mannequin type. This option appeals more to planners. Pantsers can channel the information presented and reference the profiles at the end of the first draft or when they get stuck. Either way, understanding why characters behave and misbehave helps you craft believable conflict.

RESPONSES TO OBSTACLES

To overcome an obstacle, a character must think or act. His response is mild or exaggerated depending on the circumstances. One character attempts to overcome an obstacle in a way that results in success. Another character's attempts result in failure. Your reader navigates the curves created by successes and failures until they reach the satisfying end.

Two characters in a scene can have oppositional goals. The encounter results in success or failure for either or both of them.

If a protagonist needs information, a secondary character prevents him from obtaining it or helps him obtain it. The secondary character's motivations can be noble or malicious.

When the protagonist and antagonist meet, one of them walks away with what he wanted or needed. The other leaves the field defeated. Both could appear to win and the reader later learns that one actually failed. Both could appear to lose.

Use the obstacles and responses that work best for your scene. You can outline them or review your chapters after you've written them. If you can't identify obstacles and responses, you have a scene that isn't earning its page time.

Responses include:

∿ SPEED BUMPS

Speed bumps require your character to power over them or slow down. Use speed bumps when he is on the right path. He overcomes the scene obstacle and continues on despite the interruption. A speed bump can be:

∿ **Mental**: Mental resistance is provided by a habit, like a compulsive tendency to ruminate over a fact that doesn't add up. Other characters discount his concern. He continues to run it over in his mind until he grasps why the facts didn't add up. He powers over it and overcomes the obstacle.

∿ **Emotional**: Emotional resistance is provided by a thought process, such as the belief that a certain suspect is guilty or that a friend is innocent. Other people try to convince the character that he is wrong. He remains steadfast in his belief and is proven correct and powers over their objections.

∿ **Physical**: Physical resistance is provided by a wall that needs to be scaled or a safe that needs to be broken into. He runs into snags that must be addressed before proceeding. When he finally scales the wall or opens the safe, he gets what he needs.

∿ **Tactical**: When aliens land, he prefers to talk first and shoot them down later. Solving the story problem requires him to disregard the characters urging him to launch the rockets.

As long as the character refuses to quit or change his mind, he eventually wins. Speed bumps demand patience, consistency, and steadfastness. This is difficult for characters lacking those qualities. A character may need to develop those qualities to solve the story problem or solve conflict at scene level.

DEAD ENDS

Dead ends force a character to back up and change the direction of his thoughts or the focus of his efforts. They waste time when the clock is ticking. Use dead ends when he is headed down the wrong path to force him to take the correct path. A dead end can be:

Mental: When confronted with a problem, he relies on his native inclinations to decide or take action. When his instinctive approach doesn't work, he must formulate a new plan or take a different action.

Emotional: The obstacle requires him to do something he refuses to consider, like breaking the law. He must backtrack and figure out a way to solve the problem in a way that doesn't break the law.

Physical: He encounters a physical obstacle he can't remove. He can enter a room without an alternative exit. He must go out the way he came in and face the threat or risk exposure. In his race to point B, the bridge is out and he takes a boat.

Tactical: If he tried aggression, he needs to be subversive. If he is too nice, he must be mean. If subtle doesn't work, a direct approach is needed. If brute force doesn't work, he needs a subtler approach.

⌐DETOURS

Detours force him to increase his knowledge, improve his skills, add to his experience, or find new resources to make up for what he lacks along the way.

⌐ **Mental**: Detours condition him to overcome internal resistance to something or someone he has an aversion to.

⌐ **Emotional**: Detours require him to change a belief, prejudice, or opinion.

⌐ **Physical**: He is physically required to go around the object or person. Where he was headed might not be the way through.

⌐ **Tactical**: Detours force him to re-evaluate plans. This is harder for some characters more than others.

Detours give the character a chance to learn something new about the situation, himself, or someone else.

Y FORKS

Forks force him to reconsider his options. Which direction, information, method, or person is the best option?

Y **Mental**: A fork makes him question what the truth is.

Y **Emotional**: A fork causes indecision. It's easier when there is only one action to take or one lead to follow. The more options there are, the more complicated the decision becomes. Some characters freeze when presented with options either because they hate being limited or fear making the wrong choice.

Y **Physical**: A fork compels a character to pick a tunnel, a hallway, or a road. Exit through the window or the door? Hide or run?

Y **Tactical**: A fork limits him to two options. Certain mannequins hate having their options limited and attempt too many things at once. Their energy is diverted into multiple tactics and leads to failure.

✳ TRAFFIC JAMS

Traffic jams force a character to slow down and cool off, to think more rationally, or exercise more caution.

✳ **Mental**: Waiting for a traffic jam to clear gives him time to think or discuss something important with someone while he is stalled.

✳ **Emotional**: Inserting a traffic jam when your character is highly emotional rarely ends in success whether he is dealing with a toddler or a mob boss. It deepens the scene conflict or sets up a complication for a future scene. If the character hurts or angers someone, paybacks are inevitable.

✳ **Physical**: Traffic jams are created by people, places, or things. They force the character to find a way around the obstacle physically. It could be an actual traffic jam, a crowd he must push through, or a herd of cows in the road.

✕ **Tactical**: Traffic jams gum up the works and delay a character's efforts to achieve the scene goal. He must exit the cab, decide to not take the plane, or spend time working on something else until the jam clears.

⌘ CLOVER LEAFS

Clover leafs force a character to step back and analyze things. Some characters are better at analysis than others.

⌘ **Mental**: Clover leafs force the character to examine interconnected facts to unravel a puzzle, a rambling narrative, or confusing evidence. He must sort out which thread is the right thread before taking action.

⌘ **Emotional**: Clover leafs make the character confused about where to turn. There are multiple layers and options and none of them are win-win. This is difficult for characters who don't want to intentionally hurt anyone else. Moral dilemmas are a form of clover leaf.

⌘ **Physical**: Clover leafs make the character lose precious time. He physically goes around and around and doesn't know which way to head.

⌘ **Tactical**: Clover leafs require the character to sift through multiple strategies and pick one. It might not be the right one, but he tries it anyway. He may have to go back and try a different strategy in another scene.

Clover leafs muddy the situation. There is only one way to escape or skirt the problem, but there is no clear-cut path through.

TRAFFIC LIGHTS

Traffic lights force a character to bide his time until the situation changes. This obstacle shoots anxiety to its highest level when the clock is ticking. Some characters use the added time to reinforce their decision or plan; others fall apart.

Mental: He may be burning to do or say something, but the situation doesn't allow for it. He wants to argue, tell someone off, or reveal something, but he must wait until another time.

Emotional: He must wait for the right moment to deliver the bad news, reveal a secret, or drop a clue. He may have to wait until he has the other person alone. Anxiety causes some characters to scatter, some to withdraw, and others to explode.

Physical: The plane may not land for hours. The boss may not be available until five. He may not see his wife again for a week.

Tactical: He realizes that what he is about to do results in consequences he had not considered before. He must pull back until he figures out a different way.

Traffic lights force him to hit pause. He can use the time constructively or destructively.

STOP SIGNS

Stop signs force a character to question whether he is doing the right thing and if he is strong enough to handle the consequences.

Mental: Stop signs make your character reconsider the right action or decision to achieve the goal. Self-doubt makes him more human and accessible to the reader. Something or someone comes along and shouts, "Wait! Are you sure?"

Emotional: A stop sign makes him question whether he is doing the right thing with his life, his relationship, his job, or his place in the world. Someone or something halts him in his tracks and makes him consider other turns. He may take the familiar route or the road less traveled.

Physical: A stop sign can be presented by a person, place, or thing. He has decided on a course of action, but someone or something comes along and physically prevents him from taking action.

Tactical: A character encounters a figurative stop sign that makes him hesitate for a moment before continuing his plan. Will it trigger a bomb or an alarm? Will it be a point of no return? Can he ever go back again if he powers through on his current course? Is it a one-way exit?

☠ COLLISIONS

Collisions turn the character's world or understanding upside down. Collisions make effective inciting incidents, turning points, and climactic moments. A collision annihilates what he has believed or done up to that point.

✗Mental: A character can be confronted by something that changes everything he ever thought or believed: aliens descend, a conspiracy is revealed, or a man turns out to be a woman.

✗Emotional: A character can be confronted by an awareness of something he never imagined: infidelity, abuse, or betrayal by someone he trusted.

✗Physical: Collisions can be actual crashes, accidents, life changing illnesses, or physical realities that harm the character or someone he loves. They act as wake up calls.

✗Tactical: Collisions destroy whatever his plan of action was. He must sort through the rubble and put the pieces together to form a new strategy.

A story filled with obstacles and responses keeps the reader turning pages to see what happens next. Obstacles and responses can flow along the meandering river of a Literary tale, the gurgling brook of a Romance, the quick rapids of a Thriller, or the torrential waterfall of Horror. No matter the genre, it is important to take the reader on a ride they never forget.

In the end, it is the ride and your characters they remember long after they have forgotten your name and the title of your book.

Diana Hurwitz

INTERNAL OBSTACLES

Internal obstacles are supplied by the protagonist's own mind. They are difficult to overcome because most characters lack objectivity and insight into their subconscious motivations. Rarely are characters self-aware enough to know their strengths, weaknesses, and triggers. Friends and foes hold up mirrors so the character can see himself better. Friends and foes reinforce these obstacles or help overcome them. All characters have emotional triggers and cause explosions by pulling other people's emotional triggers.

Internal obstacles prevent a character from achieving his overall story or scene goal due to:

Internal resistance based on temperament to things that go against his natural inclinations.

Fears and phobias that keep him from going where he needs to go or taking the action he needs to take.

Desire for a personal currency that tempts him to do the wrong thing or sidelines his efforts.

Low self-esteem, arrogance, or pride that keeps him from doing what needs to be done or makes him do things that are better left untried.

☯ Psychological factors, such as conditioning, belief systems, mental illness, anxiety, depression, and addiction keep a character from seeing the situation clearly or keep him from making healthy decisions about what needs to be done or said.

Next, we explore the conflicting psychological motivations, needs, and wants of sixteen characters and how they create internal obstacles.

The characters explored in this series are fictional and loosely based on temperament types. Any resemblance to anyone living or dead is entirely coincidental. You may know your temperament type or identify with a character in this book. If you feel I've gotten it wrong or are insulted, reference the terms "loosely" and "fictional."

I have taken artistic license to illustrate how characters with these temperaments might behave. I am not promoting or disrespecting anyone. I prefer the world to have all the colors in the crayon box.

All temperaments have strengths and weaknesses. In a perfect world, they balance one another. Most humans are average, fairly balanced, and make rather boring characters. For the purposes of this book, their behavior is exaggerated. We warp their psyches to make them protagonists, antagonists, friends, and foes.

In this book, I analyze psyches for the sole purpose of crafting fictional characters. I am not a psychiatrist and the information herein is not intended for therapeutic purposes.

Some temperaments reject the theory of temperaments. They don't have to embrace it as a life choice. It is a tool to illustrate how it could work for fictional characters.

Some temperaments take the information personally anyway. They should probably stop reading now.

Some fear this information is too serious. I suggest they keep reading. Learning how to torture your characters is fun.

What defines a character is a complex amalgam of influences. Jung proposed the theory of sixteen men. Researchers Katharine Cook Briggs, Isabel Briggs Myers, and David Kiersey refined our understanding of personality types. Others have contributed theories of enneagrams and astrologic signs.

To further explore the concepts visit:
1) www.myersbriggs.org, the Official Myers-Briggs site
2) www.keirsey.com, the personality test using the official Keirsey Temperament Sorter
3) www.enneagraminstitute.com.
4) www.astrology-insight.com.

Many titles address the concept of temperaments. I was introduced to *Please Understand Me* by David Keirsey and Marilyn Bates in my twenties. If you are interested in learning more about temperaments, I also recommend *Personality Type: An Owner's Manual* by Lenore Thompson.

I gathered information from many sources, used my own observations, and extrapolated them for this book.

Based on the temperament theory of human nature, there are four key traits that create conflict. There are sixteen combinations of those traits. The traits influence how your characters think and navigate the world around them. The degree to which a character relies on one trait or another varies widely. There are extremes at either end of the spectrum.

Each mannequin's temperament falls on one side or the other of introversion versus extroversion, intuition versus sensing, thinking versus feeling, and perception versus judgment. Achieving balance, embracing an alternative point of view, and adopting a new method demonstrate growth.

The traits determine how each character approaches and solves scene obstacles and overall story problems. The following is a short overview of the four battlefields where your mannequins clash.

To illustrate the percentages, we pretend they all live in Tinker Town, population one-hundred. The breakdown is a rough representation and is not accurate for research purposes. There were different breakdowns from varied sources. I chose the breakdown by personality type into gender. Distributions differ in other parts of the globe.

Fantasy and Science Fiction writers can craft a populace built on whatever traits they desire. Temperaments can be evenly pitted against one another. They can be weighted toward one type or another, leaving the minority to rebel or act as the sole voice of reason. The hero and antagonist can be from the minority or majority.

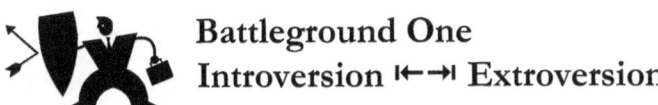

Battleground One
Introversion ⊢←→⊣ Extroversion

Introversion versus extroversion determines how a character obtains information, what energizes him, whose authority he trusts, and whether he turns inward or outward when decisions are made and actions are taken. Introversion is not shyness or social anxiety. Those are fear-based psychological conditions.

Studies suggest extroverts make up seventy percent of the population. However, the breakdown of temperaments by gender resulted in fifty-two percent introverts and forty-eight percent extroverts. It is argued that our public education system, workplaces, and agencies reward extroverted behavior. The extroverts are certainly the ones out there making noise, taking charge, and creating and answering polls. Introverts shun the spotlight, focus on the work, and ignore polls.

A character is rarely one-hundred percent extroverted or introverted. Life situations, careers, and illnesses alter how he engages with the world. Circumstances coerce him to behave contrary to his natural inclination. An introverted expert may be forced to lecture. The extroverted spy is forced to hide and remain silent. These dilemmas provide exquisite torture for your mannequins.

The extrovert is highly social. He shines in the spotlight . His internal battery is charged by interactions with other people. He feels most alone when alone. He prefers to work with teams. His connections are varied and shallow. He is easily bored and prefers to be adequate at many things rather than expert at a few. He is competitive with other people. He

27

communicates better in person than on paper. He consults other people and authorities before making a decision. He acts before he thinks.

At their most noble, extroverts make bold and seductive heroes. As friends, they urge the protagonist to places he normally fears to tread.

As an antagonist or foe, the pathologic extrovert thrives on chaos and is indiscreet. He lacks concentration in routine and long-term projects. He is a fair-weather friend. He loves and leaves romantic partners. He is dangerously competitive. He lives on the edge and needs excitement to feel alive. This places him in dangerous situations. He makes an interesting antagonist or foe. He makes a complicated friend or love interest. He goads and coerces others to do things they'd rather not. He is a bully, con man, business tycoon, or mob boss.

The introvert is not highly social. He shuns the spotlight. His internal battery is charged by solitude and reflection. He feels most alone in a group. He prefers to work independently. His connections are carefully selected and highly valued. He would rather master a few things than perform adequately at many. He is competitive only with himself. He communicates better on paper than in person. He consults his own authority when making decisions then informs people. He thinks before he acts.

At his most noble, the introvert makes an interesting investigator or cop. As a friend, he calls people back to their core values. He helps a protagonist work through how to solve the story problem.

As antagonist or foe, the pathologic introvert lacks spontaneity and is antisocial. He is suffocating in relationships. He makes a prickly friend. He beats almost any topic to death. He can't let imagined wrongs or slights go. He wants to control everything around him. He is the mad scientist or slippery mastermind.

When pitted against one another, extroverts think introverts are dull, quiet, sneaky, unfriendly, snobbish, self-absorbed, socially awkward, and uncooperative. An extrovert can't understand why the introvert is such a boring loner.

Introverts think extroverts are too loud, flighty, hyperactive, unreliable, intrusive, shallow, rude, and bossy. The introvert can't understand why the extrovert is such an erratic friend whore.

This conflict plays out in subtle and overt ways at scene level by forcing one type to interact with his opposite. The character must push past his native inclination to grow. Forcing him to work against his strength creates internal conflict.

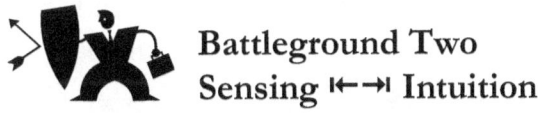 **Battleground Two**
Sensing ⊢←→⊣ Intuition

Sensing versus intuition determines the way a character processes information, the type of information he embraces or discounts, and whether he focuses on what happened or what could happen.

The sensing mannequin relies on sensory data and his perception of what is real. He prefers accepted facts and is not interested in theories of what could be. He bases decisions on what experience has taught him to be true. If it happened before it will happen, and should happen, again in exactly the same way.

The intuitive mannequin projects what is possible. He considers the usefulness of the information. He prefers to theorize and isn't limited to the way things have been done historically. He questions accepted "truths." He considers anything possible and everything negotiable.

When I performed the calculations for Tinker Town, I found a 70/30 split with far more sensing types than intuitive types. The majority of the population relies on what has occurred to define what should happen. The minority dismisses what happened and posits what could be.

When pitted against one another, sensing types can't understand why the intuitive mannequin is such a flighty nut-job. Intuitive types can't understand why the sensing mannequin is such an unimaginative killjoy.

This conflict plays out in subtle and overt ways at scene level by forcing one type to evaluate and reach consensus with his opposite. The character must push past his native inclination to grow. Forcing him to work against his strength creates internal conflict.

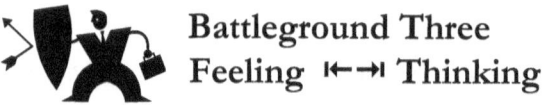 **Battleground Three**
Feeling ⊢→⊣ Thinking

Feeling and thinking determine the decisions a character makes based on the information processed.

A feeling mannequin bases his decisions on the emotional impact. He values consensus, shared morality, and loyalty. He fears breaking connections. He ignores the rational course of action to accommodate people's needs and feelings. He can decide without knowing the outcome up front. He improvises and leaves doors open to future possibilities. He meets internal resistance when asked to plan and commit.

A thinking mannequin bases his decisions on impersonal logic. He values laws, ethics, fair play, and equality. He isn't hampered by connections. He ignores people's needs and reactions to follow the most logical course of action. He prefers to control the outcome. He prefers firm plans with contingency plans. He meets internal resistance when asked to improvise and keep his options open.

When I did the calculations for Tinker Town, I found fifty-nine percent feelers and forty-one percent thinkers. The slight majority makes decisions based on how they impact people. The minority makes decisions based on the best course of action despite the personal cost.

When pitted against each other, feelers can't understand why the thinking mannequin is such a cold and calculating bully. Thinkers can't understand why the feeling mannequin is such an emotional and irrational coward.

This conflict plays out in subtle and overt ways at scene level by forcing one type to come up with a plan of action and see it through with his opposite. The character must push past his native inclination to grow. Forcing him to work against his strength creates internal conflict.

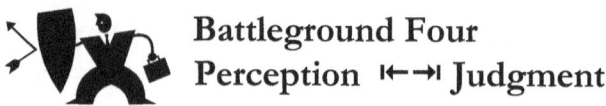

Battleground Four
Perception ⟷ Judgment

Perception versus judgment determines how a character takes action and what he does when he encounters a problem.

A perceiving mannequin is externally forced into completing tasks. He performs tasks the way they have always been done, even if the method isn't rational or effective. He waits until the last minute and does it just good enough. He disregards plans and procrastinates to avoid taking action. He expects things to change and prefers to adapt as he goes. He is less capable of sustained effort and focused attention. He makes popular calls, even if they lack merit. Judgers force him to finish things.

A judging mannequin is internally motivated to complete a task. He approaches a task in the most rational and logical way, no matter how it was done in the past. He completes it on time and to the best of his ability. He sticks to the plan and finds it hard to change course. He expects things to remain the same and prefers to know what is ahead. He has focused attention and is capable of sustained effort. He makes tough calls, regardless of their popularity. Perceivers force him to relax a little.

When I did the calculations for Tinker Town, I found fifty-four percent judgers and forty-six percent perceivers. The slight majority are better at sticking with the long-term plan than improvising as they go.

When pitted against one another, perceivers can't understand why the judging mannequin has to be such a factual control freak. The judgers can't understand why the perceiving mannequin has to be such an irresponsible procrastinator.

This conflict plays out in subtle and overt ways at scene level by forcing one type to work in tandem with his opposite. The character must push past his native inclination to grow. Forcing him to work against his strength creates internal conflict.

↻ Mitigating Circumstances

A character born with a specific temperament is also affected by his level of cognitive and emotional intelligence, native talents, self-awareness, education, physical health, and mental health. He is affected by gender, sexuality, birth order, and childhood wounds. He is externally compressed by his family, poverty level, available life choices, and the restrictions and expectations of the world he lives in. The family or society he is born into may not appreciate his talents or allow his personality type to thrive. Rarely are caregivers and children well-matched. Rarely are couples perfectly matched. Rarely are siblings the same.

There are sixteen possible combinations of traits. When you slide the bar from the extreme ends toward the middle of the scale, you create countless more. When you factor in the mitigating circumstances, the options are endless. All of these differences provide ways for you to customize your characters.

Next, we meet sixteen base model mannequins you can draw on, dress up, and mangle however you like.

SIXTEEN CHARACTERS

When you write a story, you should not introduce sixteen characters in the same chapter. I must break the rule for this book. The mannequins wear name tags throughout to make it easier. When you've reached "The End," you will know them intimately.

The percentages illustrate how prevalent these mannequins are and whether they are more often male than female. If there are numbers illustrating a breakdown by sexuality, I didn't find them. Female and male easily convert to feminine and masculine. I chose androgynous names and refer to them as "he" or "she" based on whether there are more males or females in that category.

As you read about them, keep in mind that every mannequin has a male and female counterpart. I simplified to avoid using he/she, his/hers, and him/her throughout. The mannequins navigate the world the same whether they are male or female. The male Wynn and female Wynn may be faced with vastly different cultural expectations. They may be forced into different gender-specific roles. Even so, they think, decide, and act in ways that are true to their temperaments.

In your story world, you can mix it up, especially if you write Fantasy or Science Fiction. The population of a small American town, English village, or French arrondissement can be made up of the distribution of traits you assign them. You can make the majority introverts or judgers and the minority extroverts and perceivers. Readers won't know the difference. It isn't possible to be historically precise when it comes to the personalities of people who inhabited a location or era. The prominence of traits in the family, town, or planet you design determines whether your characters thrive or wilt in the cauldron you create for them. Choose the traits that work best for your plot.

If you write a tale set in a culture you aren't familiar with, you should study their habits and philosophy to get the details right. One of the weaknesses I see in fiction is the assumption of cultural homogeneity. Differing cultures force your characters to repress different traits.

If you write about a specific historical figure, you should attempt to get his personality right. Otherwise, feel free to improvise and adapt.

We begin with a quick overview of each mannequin. Subsequent chapters teach you how to warp them.

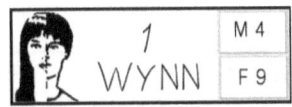

There are thirteen Wynns in Tinker Town. Nine are female. Four are male. Wynn is conservative. She has very strong opinions about what is right and wrong, but will not attend a protest. She looks inward to decide what to do. She won't state her case unless pushed. When life gets tough, she withdraws to weigh the situation. She gains energy from solitude and reflection. People and chaos exhaust her. She prefers to work independently. She prefers small groups of people and is at her best one on one.

Wynn has a burning desire to serve others and needs to be needed. She would rather give than receive. She is loyal, hard working, and taken for granted because she never brags about her accomplishments. She feels it's wrong to seek recognition or to call attention to herself. She won't alert anyone to her problems and distress. She has a few close friends, but won't back them in a fight. She runs for the nearest authority figure.

As a hero, Wynn selflessly helps those in need without hope of reward.

As a villain, Wynn is a simmering volcano of unexpressed needs and opinions waiting to explode.

Ten Ways To Torture Wynn

✎ Involve her in a group project.

✎ Make her speak publicly.

✎ Force her to state her opinion in public.

✎ Force her to become the authority figure.

✎ Violate her sense of right and wrong.

✎ Heap praise on her in public and make her the center of attention.

✎ Explain her good works are actually bad for people.

✎ Insist her point of view is wrong.

✎ Reveal corruption of the authority figures.

✎ Take away her close friends.

There are eleven Francises in Tinker Town. Eight are male. Three are female. Francis relies on his own thoughts and opinions. He prefers rigid guidelines and ignores anything but concrete facts. He is slow to embrace change, especially new procedures. Once he accepts a change, he enforces it. He ignores the personal cost or emotional price tag for others. He hates people who don't keep their word and are inconsistent. He keeps his opinions to himself until asked. When asked, he delivers his opinion no matter how it makes the other person feel. The sensitive types think he is stand-offish and cold.

Francis needs solitude and reflection. People and chaos exhaust him. When confronted with a major decision, he withdraws to ponder. He has a pessimistic outlook. He knows the End Times are coming whether people believe it or not. He feels deep emotion, but isn't able to communicate it. Strangers mistake his aloofness for arrogance and his wry philosophical bent as negativity. His real message is: you can't know which day is the last, don't waste it. Wasting things is stupid.

As a hero, Francis gets things done and encourages everyone to follow the rules.

As a villain, Francis is a controlling commandant who plots revenge and may be driven to take it.

Ten Ways To Torture Francis

🖎 Force him to work in a group.

🖎 Have things change in a way he does not agree with.

🖎 Make the "facts" unclear or change his understanding of "facts" as he knows them.

🖎 Point out he is wrong. Go ahead. I dare you.

🖎 Ask him for his opinion then mock it.

🖎 Force him to work with an unreliable partner.

🖎 Don't allow him to be alone for even one minute during a time of crisis.

🖎 Make him realize his decision had a terrible human cost.

🖎 Have someone he loves walk away because she assumes he doesn't care.

🖎 Take away his close friends and those who agree with him.

There are eleven Nevadas in Tinker Town. Eight are male. Three are female. Nevada is free with his black and white opinions. He looks to authority figures for guidance. He cares about appearances a bit too much. He has a firm sense of right and wrong. He views the world as a dangerous place and feels the need to rescue people. He is hyper-vigilant, bordering on paranoid.

Nevada needs to belong. He is restless when alone. He is stimulated by other people's thoughts and ideas. He embraces group activities and loves to entertain. Social ties are important. He remembers names after one introduction. He wants everyone to be comfortable and involved. Any excuse is a good excuse to celebrate. He clings to tradition and gives generously to charities, his church, or the labor union. He does it to look good. He is easily wounded and wears his heart on his sleeve. He is warm and loving but quick to anger. He likes being appreciated and is hurt if his efforts go unnoticed.

As a hero, Nevada is honorable and works for the common good. He notices problems others miss.

As a villain, Nevada takes on the role of enforcer and sees conspiracies everywhere.

Ten Ways To Torture Nevada:

🏹 Make him realize there are shades of gray.

🏹 Isolate him.

🏹 Convince him there is a conspiracy to throw him off track.

🏹 Have him rescue someone who'd rather he didn't.

🏹 Make him the source of other people's discomfort.

🏹 Have him lose respect for the authority figures.

🏹 Force him to do something that doesn't conform.

🏹 Put him in a situation where he isn't allowed to celebrate anything.

🏹 Make him do something he considers wrong.

🏹 Make his anger threaten a relationship.

There are nine Ardens in Tinker Town. Six are male. Three are female. Arden is realistic, matter of fact, and abrupt. He is interested in the production line for new widgets. He isn't interested in what they are used for. He prefers order and continuity. He has strong opinions about what is normal and what isn't. He makes jokes about people he deems weird or badly behaved. He despises lazy people, particularly if they are put in charge. He is outspoken, principled, and stands up for his beliefs in the face of overwhelming criticism. He won't flatter or bootlick. He treats an equal as an equal.

Arden needs other people to animate him. He prefers group activities. He is drawn to like-minded people in clubs, churches, and service organizations. Belonging is crucial. He has a family crest nailed above his door. He has a fully researched genealogic chart too. Pedigree lends respectability and makes him feel like he belongs to something greater than himself. He enjoys weddings, funerals, reunions, holiday dinners, and birthday parties. He considers attendance mandatory and is irritated by those who don't comply. Genuine friends understand that he means well.

As a hero, Arden stands beside people he values to fight against those doing harm.

As a villain, Arden is controlling and overly judgmental. He bends other people to his will and shoots those who object to the party line.

Ten Ways To Torture Arden

⌘ Tell him he is wrong … then run.

⌘ Force him to influence someone.

⌘ Disorder his world.

⌘ Ostracize him.

⌘ Prove his pedigree has no basis in reality.

⌘ Have his loved ones miss family dinner or an employee miss a production meeting.

⌘ Overturn his understanding of what is "normal."

⌘ Have his jokes about someone come back and burn him.

⌘ Prove his beliefs are harmful or wrong.

⌘ Force him to coax or charm someone.

There are nine Blairs in Tinker Town. Four are male. Five are female. Blair travels to the beat of a different drum. She eagerly embraces the latest fads and starts trends of her own. She is impulsive, spontaneous, and lives in the moment. She is more interested in living life than talking about it or analyzing it. She enjoys the simple moments and appreciates the beauty of the world around her. She is highly sensitive, which makes life a giant Technicolor dream. She needs periods of solitude and reflection because the wonder of it all exhausts her. She is superficial and charming. She draws a crowd to join in the fun. People follow her eagerly. She isn't asking them to, nor does she care if they do. One day she flatters, the next she is aloof and detached. People close to her wonder what they did to upset her. She masks her emotions and avoids ties that bind.

Blair has excellent sensory and motor skills. She is drawn to artistic endeavors. She chafes at restrictions. She is fiercely competitive in sports and games. She isn't a good loser and takes risks others admire (or fear). Structured environments, like schools and cubicles, bore her. She rarely finishes what she starts when a new adventure beckons. She can perform in the big top, but doesn't seek acclaim.

As hero, Blair fights for those less fortunate or suffering.

As a villain, Blair is quite capable of deception and treachery and may lead her followers into danger.

Ten Ways To Torture Blair

🖎 Restrict her options.

🖎 Take away her freedom.

🖎 Have her approach or drop the wrong person.

🖎 Put her in a lose-lose situation.

🖎 Make her conform or die.

🖎 Make the world ugly.

🖎 Take away her alone time.

🖎 Force her to analyze her life.

🖎 Trap her in a committed relationship.

🖎 Have her blithely lead people into danger and force her to stay and fix it.

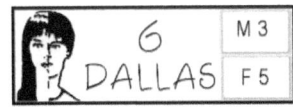

There are eight Dallases in Tinker Town. Three are male. Five are female. Dallas is passionate about things but rarely settles down to master them. She leaves a job or relationship when it violates her deeply held values. She has a keen understanding of what motivates others. Life is a balance of good and evil. Her belief in the innate goodness of people is often self-fulfilling. She is optimistic and shocked when things don't turn out as she hoped. Her emotional life is her life. She paints pretty pictures and hangs them over her windows to avoid looking at a disappointing landscape. People love her sense of humor, but tire of her incessant blathering about feelings.

Dallas is the ultimate people person. She sticks with relationships, even abusive ones. She puts other people at ease. Everyone she meets is a friend. She needs to be with other people to feel alive. Solitude and reflection feel like jail. Her mood varies from moment to moment. She'll start an intellectual discussion then shift to raunchy jokes. She likes wowing the crowd with her antics and stories. She makes other people feel good, but never feels quite good enough. She sits in the front row and watches her own performance.

As hero, Dallas inspires everyone to join in and do what needs to be done in the name of good. She identifies the enemy before everyone else does.

As a villain, Dallas attributes others with hidden motives, questioning their words and actions. Her assumptions are usually negative and inaccurate. Her neuroticism and suspicious nature are toxic.

Ten Ways To Torture Dallas

🖎 Tie her down so she can't leave.

🖎 Violate her principles.

🖎 Have another character reject her.

🖎 Have events conspire to make her doubt herself more than she already does.

🖎 Isolate her.

🖎 Mess up her plans.

🖎 Have someone tell her to stop whining about how she feels.

🖎 Present her with a false conspiracy theory.

🖎 Overturn her negative assessment of someone or make that person aware of it.

🖎 Make her dangerously out of control.

There are eight Hadleys in Tinker Town. Three are male. Five are female. Hadley won't ponder the meaning of life, but supports a good cause. She indulges in pranks, but not in a malicious way. Her opinions are fluid. She switches sides on a whim and flows with the prevailing thought tides. She likes making other people happy. She believes it is better to give than receive. She is uncomfortable when she receives gifts and compliments. She comforts others, whether they need it or not. She lives in the now. She is highly observant and knows what is going on around her.

Hadley loves a party. If there isn't one, she throws one. Her social life is her life. She likes telling stories and having a good time. She is spontaneous, impulsive, and entertaining. Her conversation is sparkling as she flits from topic to topic. She loves everything new, but quickly moves on. She loves people and loves to talk about people to other people. Her wit is touching or biting. She doesn't mean any harm. She is well-liked for her fun-loving and outgoing nature.

As a hero, Hadley picks up on things others miss. She joins the cause and cheers everyone up when things go wrong. She attempts things others fear.

As a villain, Hadley is a dangerous gossip. She is a gadfly who leads you into temptation and leaves you there to suffer the consequences. She rarely stops to calculate the cost of her actions.

Ten Ways To Torture Hadley

🖎 Take away her friends.

🖎 Have thoughtless gossip come back to haunt her.

🖎 Shatter her world with tragedy.

🖎 Have a prank go wrong.

🖎 Tell Hadley her sympathy isn't needed or wanted.

🖎 Silence her.

🖎 Pile on gifts and praise in public.

🖎 Lock her up.

🖎 Have her mistakenly take part in something dangerous.

🖎 Make her actions hurt those she loves.

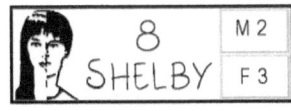

There are five Shelbys in Tinker Town. Two are male. Three are female. Shelby embraces the wonder of the universe and is frustrated when other people don't view life through her rainbow-bright glasses. She would like to buy the world a home and furnish it with love. She sees the good in everyone. She spreads good will and shares her philosophical outlook. She creatively works in the background toward the goals important to her. She spends her life pursuing an ideal job, home, mate, or situation.

Shelby lives more within her rich inner world than in the world itself. She has trouble balancing her desire to help other people with her need for solitude and reflection. She is hard to get to know and may be marginalized. She struggles with her own imperfections while working toward a perfect world. She projects those imperfections onto others.

As a hero, Shelby draws people together to achieve a common goal. She believes everyone has something to contribute. She truly believes good will win the battle against evil.

As a villain, Shelby's definition of good is dangerous. She launches a war in the name of love. She is a toxic enabler and refuses to see flaws in those close to her.

Ten Ways To Torture Shelby

⚑ Force her to work in the foreground.

⚑ Force her to settle for something less than ideal.

⚑ Overextend her.

⚑ Have other people point out her imperfections.

⚑ Have a character she believes to be good betray her.

⚑ Place her in a dystopian world.

⚑ Take away her solitude.

⚑ Have her discount the wrong person.

⚑ Make it appear that evil is winning.

⚑ Accuse her of enabling someone … then duck.

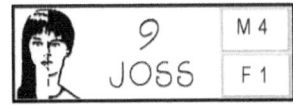

There are five Josses in Tinker Town. Four are male. One is female. Joss isn't interested in the source of the idea. He is only interested in whether the idea works. He is terse and offers one-liners with a flash of humor. He is better at nonverbal expression. He may be viewed as thick-skinned or tasteless. He is not interested in other people's hobbies, theories, dreams, or stories. If he wants your opinion, he'll ask for it. He keeps his opinion to himself. He isn't interested in serving other people and hates mindless routine tasks. He hates sitting still, reflecting, reading for long periods of time, and idle chit chat.

Joss thrives on risk and lives on the edge. He indulges in adrenaline rush activities. He believes he can skate by with a smaller safety margin than ordinary mortals. He hates being tied down. He ignores schedules. He is flexible and spontaneous. He becomes rigid when someone threatens his lifestyle. Killing time makes him anxious. He prefers to be doing whatever he is most interested in. He requires wide personal space in all facets of his life. He is highly territorial. He treats others the way he wants to be treated, which others might not construe as nice.

As a hero, Joss's physical risk-taking makes other people slightly nauseated. He is loyal despite his better judgment. His rash decisions make him vulnerable to predators and can result in catastrophe.

As a villain, Joss is deadly to anyone who crosses him or in support of someone he foolishly believes. He enacts nefarious plans and does not care who it hurts.

Ten Ways To Torture Joss

🖎 Make him rely on someone else.

🖎 Confine him in a cubicle.

🖎 Surround him with people who encroach on his space.

🖎 Have a risky action create a disaster.

🖎 Have him side with someone who is troubled or dangerous.

🖎 Put him in a position where he has to come up with a solid plan instead of winging it.

🖎 Place restrictions on his movements.

🖎 Have someone treat him in a hateful way then point out it is the way Joss treats everyone around him.

🖎 Have him anger the wrong person.

🖎 Force him to kill time and think hard.

There are four Kellys in Tinker Town. Three are male. One is female. Kelly gathers information and uses it to his best advantage. He is realistic and keenly discriminating when he chooses. He never admits to weakness or failure. He admires strength in others. He goes for the shock effect to gain attention. He is crass and outlandish. His senses are on high alert. He thrives on stimulation. He is spontaneous, impulsive, and action-oriented. Life is all about the power, the speed, the risk. It is one long thrill ride. He appears to have an unusual amount of empathy. It's a trick. Every move is calculated to manipulate.

Kelly demands center-stage and feeds off the energy of the adoring crowd. He is lively, resourceful, and entertaining. The moment is the only thing that matters. He knows the best places to be seen and who accepts bribes. He is socially sophisticated and a master manipulator. He may care deeply for someone, but isn't hampered by it. Other characters never know what he thinks or feels. It isn't always complimentary.

As a hero, nothing stands in Kelly's way. He is the ultimate gamer and thrives on beating the competition.

As a villain, Kelly goes for his enemy's jugular. He is the stereotypical sociopath, evil business tycoon, or mob boss.

Ten Ways To Torture Kelly

🖎Figuratively tie his hands.

🖎 Stack the game against him.

🖎 Paint him as weak or a failure.

🖎 Pit him against someone just like him.

🖎 Limit his social outlets.

🖎 Have his outrageous behavior backfire.

🖎 Isolate him.

🖎 Deprive him of material things.

🖎 Have his shenanigans hurt the only one he actually loves.

🖎 Betray him.

The are four Greers in Tinker Town. Three are male. One is female. Greer is the rarest species of mannequin. He worries about being a failure. He second-guesses himself in his desire for competence. He is quiet, analytical, and thoughtful. He hates displays of raw emotion. Emotions should be dealt with logically. Improperly handled emotions are a grenade with its pin pulled. He hates redundancy and incoherence. He seeks to understand the universe and natural laws. He quickly grasps ideas, principles, and behavior. His bomb shelter mind retains it. He is an intellectual snob and grades people on their intelligence. This makes other people hostile and defensive. He doesn't much care. He seeks to understand not be understood.

Greer isn't comfortable in social situations. He enjoys the company of those who share his interests. He isn't nurturing. His quick wit and sly observations diffuse tense moments. He translates complex principles and theories for those less intellectually gifted. He is better on paper than in person. His explanations are detailed. He is offering important information. People should listen. He is charming in a quiet, reserved way. He would be surprised by how much his friends and colleagues like him — and make fun of him. He hates calling attention to himself, but is outspoken when his principles are violated. He is not group-oriented. If insulted, he responds with crushing criticism and is shocked by his outburst.

As a hero, Greer comes up with the solution to the mystery, the cure for the disease, or the weakness of the aliens. He may not convince anyone unless he is highly respected in his area of expertise.

As a villain, Greer designs bombs or plans catastrophes to prove his theories to the dim-witted. He is the hacker who hacks to prove someone's system is flawed.

Ten Ways To Torture Greer

☙ Have him work in tandem with other people.

☙ Make him speak publicly.

☙ Violate his principles.

☙ Force him to work within a restrictive organization.

☙ Have people ignore his sage advice.

☙ Insult his intelligence or competence.

☙ Remove his solitude.

☙ Place him in a chaotic situation.

☙ Give him a problem empirical data can't fix.

☙ Force him to deal with messy emotions.

There are three Taylors in Tinker Town. One is male. Two are female. Taylor is a born leader. She favors cooperation and puts other people first. She automatically assumes people understand her point. She is puzzled and hurt by opposition or questions. This does not happen often because she excels at verbal communication. She is better face to face than on paper. She persuades people to do as she asks. She believes her own hype and views herself as Lady Benevolence. She absorbs the characteristics, emotions, and beliefs of the people around her. Her boundaries are naturally fuzzy. She butts in where she is neither wanted nor needed. She frequently overextends. She neglects herself to fulfill the needs of others. She assumes responsibility for others in ways that aren't appreciated or required. She struggles to separate and say "no." She feels guilty if she has to turn something down or someone away.

Taylor is tolerant and seldom critical. She is trustworthy but overpowering. She idealizes her relationships to a degree no one can live up to. She rarely has intimate friends because she prefers to spread herself around. She places relationships and responsibilities before leisure. She likes intellectual conversation. She isn't drawn to competition or events where people get hurt. She does not handle the fluctuations of a relationship well. She values commitment and loyalty. Transgressions against them are a deal-breaker.

As a hero, Taylor is fiercely protective of friends and loved ones. She is charismatic and confident. She assumes other people will follow her and they do.

As a villain, Taylor is an interfering busy body or toxic enabler. She makes the perfect stalker roommate or girlfriend.

Ten Ways To Torture Taylor

🖎Have her enabling turn dangerous.

🖎 Have her influenced by someone deadly.

🖎 Question her benevolent motives.

🖎 Accuse her of not being as good as she thinks she is.

🖎 Put her in a chaotic relationship.

🖎 Transgress her values.

🖎 Make her plead her case in writing rather than in person.

🖎 Limit her friends or contacts.

🖎 Refuse to follow her lead.

🖎 Force her to be firm.

There are three Cams in Tinker Town. Two are male. One is female. Cam is the most self-confident of all types and is powerfully self-aware. He lives in his own world. He thinks people should be useful. He despises weakness and laziness. He is a perfectionist, but doesn't get bogged down in petty details. He cares if something works, not who came up with it. This applies to methods as well as prevailing social norms. If an aspect of society isn't working, he doesn't understand why others cling to it. He is the ultimate freethinker and immune to peer pressure. He sets high standards for himself, which makes other people feel inadequate. He is oblivious. He expects other people to set their own standards and regulate themselves. He never feels he has achieved perfection. He is a good communicator. He thinks anything is possible and everything is negotiable. He never takes himself, or anyone else, too seriously.

Cam is reserved. The few who know him well find his biting, self-effacing wit endearing. He isn't people-oriented, though he values human life. His powers of observation help him navigate the tricky waters of human emotion. He registers tone of voice, turn of phrase, and facial expression. He is passionate about his loved ones. They are few and carefully selected. He isn't in tune with social rituals. He has little patience with shallow small talk, less for people with materialistic values. He is intensely private, impassive, and misunderstood. He finds humans to be perversely illogical. Once someone has lost his confidence or trust, they don't get it back.

As a hero, Cam does what he thinks he should, regardless of the human cost or emotional arguments against it. He points out things that aren't working.

As a villain, Cam turns his beautiful mind to thoughts of revenge. He knows exactly what makes people tick and how to make them explode. The results would be catastrophic.

Ten Ways To Torture Cam

ᴥ Force him to work in tandem with illogical people.

ᴥ Force him to gauge the emotional ramifications before taking action.

ᴥ Make him take center stage to explain the problem.

ᴥ Partner him with someone he considers lazy or useless.

ᴥ Make him realize human frailty is not the end of the world.

ᴥ Betray him.

ᴥ Question his ethics.

ᴥ Challenge his competence.

ᴥ Punish him for something another character did wrong.

ᴥ Make him have to sell himself instead of the idea.

There are three Morgans in Tinker Town. Two are male. One is female. Morgan is clever, daring, and imaginative. He is equally versed in dealing with people and things. He is optimistic, but does not handle small setbacks or inconveniences well. He greets major setbacks as a challenge. He is enthusiastic and interested in everything, which makes him popular. He is easy to please and a terrific conversationalist. He is confident, open-minded, and prefers life to be open-ended. He is more interested in proficiency than recognition.

Morgan does not suffer fools graciously and doesn't hide it well. He is generally viewed as congenial and charming. He makes friends quickly and bonds closely. He either appears indifferent to the near and dear or surprisingly demonstrative. He prefers his friends to be as clever and entertaining as he is. If you aren't part of his inner circle, you're the audience. He likes playing devil's advocate and offends people who don't view arguing as a sport. His wit is incisively accurate. He is verbally quick and mentally sharp. His perverse sense of humor unintentionally hurts other people's feelings.

As a hero, Morgan forces people to reconsider their actions and beliefs. He argues all sides equally well. He helps people see the full ramifications of what they have done, or plan to do.

As a villain, Morgan is the ultimate devil's advocate. He'll do anything for a truly spectacular show.

Ten Ways To Torture Morgan

🖎 Silence him.

🖎 Have his sense of humor get him in trouble.

🖎 Pair him with a fool.

🖎 Have his indifference misinterpreted so he loses someone special.

🖎 Bore him.

🖎 Trap him.

🖎 Take away his audience.

🖎 Give him a series of small setbacks.

🖎 Have him offend the wrong person.

🖎 Take away his trusted friends.

There are two Lees in Tinker Town. One is male. One is female. Lee is focused on the right and true cause. She believes she lives on a higher plane than other mortals. She is grounded in what is real and what is now, but her beliefs are subject to distortion. She is maudlin and melodramatic. She thrives on structuring other people's lives. She is very persuasive. Others find it hard to decline her plans for them. She is overbearing and can't help meddling. Some follow her adoringly. Others run as far as they can. She is a gift to those who need a guiding hand and an irritant to those who prefer to be left alone.

Lee is the life of the party and enjoys all eyes on her. When the focus shifts, the trouble starts. She'll do anything to pull the focus back to her. She is abrupt and rigid to the point of steamrolling over anything or anyone standing in her way. She rarely takes advice and never asks for it.

As a hero, Lee is decisive, resolute, and courageous. Sometimes it takes Lee to get the job done. She follows the right course of action and won't let anything or anyone stop her. She is a force of nature.

As a villain, Lee is lethal, but arrogance is her flaw. The cronies she mocks and belittles easily turn against her.

Ten Ways To Torture Lee

🖎 Take away her influence.

🖎 Stand up to her.

🖎 Remove her audience.

🖎 Isolate her.

🖎 Question her competence.

🖎 Take away her freedom.

🖎 Force her to work with someone just like her.

🖎 Make her realize she is wrong.

🖎 Hide her backstage.

🖎 Give her an obstacle she can't sweep aside.

There are two Rivers in Tinker Town. One is male. One is female. River genuinely enjoys helping other people. She is a deep thinker who understands how the past, present, and future interconnect. She is eerily perceptive when it comes to the motivations of other people. She is the most spiritual of characters. She may claim to be psychic. She is highly empathetic and aware of other people's emotions. She absorbs other people's distress. She believes in good and evil and prefers to see the good in others. She is not easily fooled. She is equally gifted in person and on paper. She picks up on nonverbal communication. She seeks to understand herself and others. She values integrity and high ideals.

River is selective in her friends. It is important for her to know them intimately and to be known by them. She isn't interested in being popular or famous. She won't join social groups and does not enjoy large parties. She speaks her mind in private to trusted friends. She is naturally suspicious and sees the world as a cruel place. She can appear detached and disillusioned. The distance she maintains is protective. If stressed, she seeks immediate gratification. She yearns to live spontaneously, but rarely does.

As a hero, River is the one with the vision or paranormal ability to save the world. She toils against dark forces to restore the light. Her empathy and insight can solve the overall story problem.

As a villain, River works against anyone she deems a threat to what she considers "good." What she deems "good" might not match up with everyone else's definition.

Ten Ways To Torture River

🖎 Make fun of her extrasensory or spiritual beliefs.

🖎 Paint her as evil.

🖎 Force her to work with a group to succeed.

🖎 Take away her trusted circle.

🖎 Put her in the public eye.

🖎 Dull her intuition.

🖎 Ignore her warnings.

🖎 Have her risk-taking backfire.

🖎 Place her in chaos.

🖎 Surround her with distressed people.

Next, we explore how the different phases of life warp the mannequins. We consider how the different traits create internal and interpersonal conflict.

CHILDHOOD

Childhood is the cauldron in which a character's mettle is forged. Native inclination is dipped in parental, environmental, and societal flames, and comes out something quite different than when it began.

It is simplistic to assume all children were raised by a male and female couple in perfect harmony. Some are raised by relatives, friends, strangers, servants, siblings, aliens, or werewolves (depending on the genre). To expand the paradigm, I refer to those who raise them as caregivers.

Childhood is a time of vulnerable dependence. The infant relies on caregivers to meet basic needs for survival: food, clothing, shelter, and comfort. Each child has specific emotional needs: space versus distance, routine versus freedom, and stimulation versus quiet. The degree to which early needs are met alters his temperament. It matters whether the caretakers are kind, cruel, present, absent, and quick or slow to respond. No two children are the same. No two caretakers are the same.

You may not write about children, adolescents, or young adults. Even so, it is important to understand how early experiences shaped your character, his siblings, and his early cauldron. A plot hole occurs when a child has ideal parents and an ideal home life then suddenly displays imbalances as a teen or adult. This feels false, unless mental illness and catastrophe greatly alter them. In early childhood alone, there are multiple ways to warp your mannequins.

Wynn is an easy baby, unless she is physically ill. As a toddler, she is eager to do the right thing. She won't need more than the basics. If deprived of the basics, she tries harder to please to gain them. She is overwhelmed by too many toys, suffocating attention, and inconsistent rules. Security and routine are extremely important. Caregivers who don't believe in rules, or offer inconsistent rules, make her feel lost. Wynn carries a grudge if she obeys the rules and others break them then get away with it. She carries a grudge if she is punished for something she didn't do. Unfairness becomes a primitive brain trigger. Her anger is passively manifested with small underhanded acts of rebellion or revenge. Once school starts, she conforms and goes along with her few close friends. Barring major life transitions, she clings to her friends for the rest of her life.

Wynn prefers to know what teachers expect so she can be prepared. She struggles with a teacher who favors pop quizzes and last minute assignments. She resists group activities, especially if her best friend isn't involved. When adversity strikes, she is highly introspective. She does not share her dilemma with anyone. If she suffers abuse or bullying, she turns her frustration inward and becomes quietly self-destructive. She won't run to her caregivers or teachers to fix things, particularly if she views them as unreliable. She retreats inside her shell if uprooted or forced to switch schools. A divorce shakes her sense of security to the core. The different sets of rules confuse her. If her caregivers have a tumultuous relationship, it feeds her anxiety and deprives her of her need for routine and safety. She might fail at school and develop anxiety-relieving behaviors.

Francis thrives on order and structure. He fares well in a calm setting where the daily routine is predictable. Indifferent or unstructured caregivers make him anxious and unhappy. He is uncomfortable in new situations and with new people. He clings to the friends he carefully selects. He enjoys group activities, like scouts and camping, because he can prove his responsibility. If caregivers constantly question his competence, he suffers from low self-esteem and becomes highly rigid. He likes listening to stories and looking at the pictures. He prefers good to triumph over evil. He is meticulous and takes care of his things. He tackles his homework before play. He feels lost if his caregivers prefer to play first or ignore his need for structure. He does well in structured classrooms with focused teachers. He struggles with emotionally gooey teachers.

Francis is more at ease when he knows what to expect. He won't thrive if uprooted or passed around. He delights in traditions and holiday celebrations. A divorce disrupts his equilibrium. He misses the family time together. If he has to parent his caregivers, he feels responsible for things at home and responsible for things at school. His attempts to restore order may break him. If he does not receive positive reinforcement for his efforts to be responsible, he turns into a rebellious and self-destructive child. Why be good if no one appreciates it?

3
NEVADA

M 8
F 3

Nevada needs life to be secure, harmonious, and structured. As a baby, he is fretful when passed around or moved about. He is responsible, reliable, and cooperative as long as his need for consistency and personal attention are met. Frazzled, unorganized, or absent caregivers make him anxious and clingy. He seeks the acceptance of other people and works hard to gain it. He aims to please. He does his homework on time and his chores without complaint. He turns willfully obstinate if his values are violated by a sibling, caregiver, or teacher.

Nevada follows the rules as long as they are fair and reasonable. If he feels they are unfair, he speaks out. If he sees other people breaking the rules, he speaks out. He bends himself into knots to please overly critical caregivers and teachers. He becomes resentful and angry when nothing he does works. If his caregivers split up, he speaks out and takes sides. He is furious that they aren't following the rules. In his mind, they should stay together and life shouldn't change. He struggles to conform to all the new situations he is placed in and becomes depressed. If his protests are ignored, he turns against those who make the rules.

Arden is an active toddler. He experiments and is drawn to one new activity after another. He wants to know how things work and disassembles them. He is eager to share what he discovers. Caregivers who limit his options, are absent, impatient, or don't appreciate his voyage of discovery, make him frustrated and angry. He isn't a snuggle on the lap child. He prefers to be on the move. He exhausts an introverted caregiver with his requests for "more" and "again." If denied stimulation, he grows sullen and depressed. He enjoys sports teams or scouts for the trophies and badges. It's important to him to learn to do things correctly. He studies hard to make sure he does.

Arden wants to impress teachers with his cleverness. He interrupts class to do so. He is eager to share his insights with other students and finds it hard to sit at a desk. He doesn't understand why he gets in trouble. He may take a divorce in stride, if it gives him two camps to explore. If it offers restrictions, he becomes depressed and acts out. He enjoys a new neighborhood and school as long as they don't restrict his options and movement. He struggles with emotionally or physically absent caregivers. He may act out to gain their attention.

Blair is a happy baby as long as she is loved and nurtured. Absent, inattentive, or busy caregivers make her feel lost. She needs a solid foundation to feel secure enough to flit. She plays happily by herself and creates her own story world with her toys. She loves fairytales. She is pleasant, quiet, and kind. She resists situations where she is put on display like school plays or pageants. She is drawn to friends, animals, and plants requiring her gentle care. She makes unique and original gifts for her special friends. She is easy to like. Her friendships are fluid and shallow. She leaves wounded introverts in the sandbox to play alone while she is zooming down the slide with someone new.

Blair is artistic, highly sensitive, and a little otherworldly. Insensitive caregivers and teachers who expect her to be logical and precise do more harm than good. She sits in the chair, but her mind wanders. She rebels against caregivers who restrict her free-flowing ways with too much structure. She is frightened by a divorce because it splits her foundation in half. She is anxious when she must choose sides. She resists uprooting or relocation, but integrates if the new situation allows her to bloom. She becomes self-destructive if it limits her options or forces her to be in situations she finds painful.

Dallas is a restless baby. She squirms off a lap as soon as she can crawl and is into everything. Restrictive or overly attentive caregivers suffocate her. She won't enjoy being held, coddled, sat in a high chair, or trapped in a playpen. Nothing is out of bounds. Loose supervision by absent or self-absorbed caretakers could end tragically. She is a danger to herself. She comes up with lots of ideas, most of them impractical or not allowed. She gets in trouble for her vivid imagination. She is the ring leader who gets her siblings in trouble. Other children are drawn to her and sometimes hurt by her fleeting attention. Teachers find her challenging. She isn't happy stuck at a desk listening to other people talk. She is an experiential learner. She forgets homework, colors outside the lines, and resists efforts to make her conform.

A divorce affects Dallas only as much as it limits her. She plays one caregiver against the other to get what she wants. A lack of supervision results in a very wild child. She greets a move as an adventure full of new people and places to explore. She chafes if the new location restricts her movements or options. She may act out and inspire other children to self-destruct along with her.

Hadley is an easy baby. She needs calm, personalized attention. Loud, overly busy, and aggressive caregivers make her anxious and fretful. As a toddler and in school, she is agreeable and enthusiastic. She likes trying everything once. She has deep insights. She delights in everyday joys: a pretty flower, a singing bird, a tasty cookie. She aims to please. She resents a critical teacher or caregiver who orders her to sit down, shut up, and do what she is told. Irresponsible caregivers make her feel responsible for their wellbeing. Rigid caregivers are suffocating.

Hadley brings her favorite teacher an apple. She cares about her friends and wants them to be happy. She is easily led. She blames herself for a divorce. She is torn between her caregivers and does not want either of them to be unhappy. She is depressed when taken away from her friends. She may thrive in the new setting over time, but the initial transition is bumpy. She wilts in a setting where things are grim, regimented, and dull. It negatively affects her self-esteem. She is then drawn to self-destructive types.

Shelby is a quiet baby with a low threshold for excitement. Too much handling, moving around, and chaos make her cranky. She needs calm and consistent nurturing. She cries to escape the torture when caregivers shake her up and show her off. She likes playing by herself, with her toys, or with her imaginary friends. She creates identities for them and comes up with detailed stories about their exploits. She may draw stories on paper. She is a decent student. She gets her work done then spends the rest of the time daydreaming and doodling. She resists being on teams or group assignments. She is highly sensitive to criticism. She finds it hard to stick with tasks requiring extended concentration.

Shelby seems otherworldly. She is easily lost in thought or a hobby. She is reserved in new situations. She bonds with a best friend and is not a social butterfly. She does not handle divorce well. It removes her security blanket and forces her to face things about the world she'd rather not see. She retreats inside her shell if exposed to angry confrontations until peace is restored. She won't enjoy being moved around. She searches for a new best friend to understand and support her. Other kids make fun of her for daydreaming. She may become a loner. Her anger and pain turn inward.

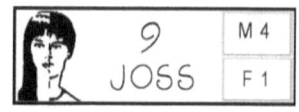

Joss is a quiet, busy child. He accepts structure and concrete rules, but needs flexibility. He asks permission, but finds a way around it if told "no." He grows bored when his options are limited. He is happy to observe on occasion. He takes things apart to see how they work. He doesn't tell anyone what he learns. He makes keen observations and uses the information when needed. He notes flaws and attempts to correct them. He gets lost in his hobbies.

Joss is a good student, but chafes at the restrictions of rote learning. He may bring something else to do while at school. He gets in trouble for not paying attention to the lessons he finds boring. He is a daredevil on the playground. He tries harder to control his world if it spins out of control. A divorce makes him anxious and more rigid. Moving could affect him either way. It could provide a wider field to experiment in or narrow his horizons. The first helps him expand his knowledge and friendships. The second frustrates him and drives him inward. His anger and pain are expressed through rebellious behavior.

Kelly is a freedom-loving handful. He is an active, cranky baby. If his caregivers crave a consistent schedule, they are out of luck. He can't sit still and play by himself. If left to his own devices, he creates chaos. With busy, absent, or inattentive caregivers, he runs wild. Negative attention is better than no attention. He does what he wants when he wants and is frustrated if reined in. He expects his day to be action-packed fun. If bored, he stirs up trouble to make it interesting. He enjoys sports and activities that engage his motor and observational skills. He collects friends and needs the energizing presence of other people. His friends enjoy the fun until they get caught. He isn't easily fazed and likes a challenge. He likes to own nice toys and games. He takes good care of them. Low-key or plodding caregivers frustrate him.

Kelly learns early what works and what doesn't. He manipulates caregivers, teachers, friends, and siblings. He hates being trapped at a desk and is bored by lectures. A divorce is Kelly's playground. He plays one caregiver against the other to get what he wants. He may turn to self-destructive behavior to get attention. Moving around breaks up the boredom and gives him new people to dazzle and dominate. He takes the party with him wherever he goes. Lack of supervision could be tragic.

Greer is a happy baby and eager to explore his world. He plays imaginatively with or without other children. He asks oddball, challenging questions. He enjoys fantasy, mystery, inventing, and thinking. His tastes are atypical for a child. He isn't interested in being the center of attention or on stage. He won't play sports or join clubs. He prefers books and games. If he enjoys music, it is an unusual genre. He is eager to please. Caregivers who can't embrace his quirky intellectualism are suffocating. Overly emotional and messy caretakers make him nervous.

Greer secretly worries he isn't good enough. He wants to be a model student. Not everyone at school gets him. His teachers might not appreciate his questions or observations. He isn't disruptive, but expects to be rewarded for his curiosity. He blames himself for a divorce. The changes create chaos and make him highly uncomfortable. A move causes him to turn inward. Making new friends is hard. He resists leaving his few good friends. He joins the troublemakers as a form of protest.

Taylor is a peaceful baby and needs calm caregivers. Chaotic and unpredictable caregivers make her anxious. She is friendly and values harmony. Pleasing others makes her happy. She takes charge in the playroom and directs the other children. Her feelings are hurt if she senses disapproval or if her efforts are rejected. She overextends herself by playing with everyone. She is talkative and upbeat. Caregivers have to rein her in or she wears herself out to the point of total meltdown. Overprotective caregivers suffocate her. Absent or busy caregivers allow her to spiral out of control.

Taylor likes the routine and social aspects of school. She wants to please her teachers and caregivers. She is crushed by a divorce and the ensuing chaos. She tries to please both caregivers and attempts to make peace. A move is traumatic. Uprooting her from what she knows forces her out of her comfort zone. Her efforts to take charge may not be welcomed in the new setting. She is crushed if the new kids misunderstand her. She tries hard to fit in. If subjected to abuse, she turns inward and self-destructs in a quiet way.

Cam is a quiet, low maintenance child. He won't ask for anything, even for what he needs. He is good because it's important to be good, not to please others. He expects everyone else to be good too: caregivers, siblings, teachers, and friends. A chaotic or highly dysfunctional family pushes him further inside his shell. He spends a lot of time daydreaming and thinking. His questioning of authority and probing questions make adults squirm. He develops his own belief system and does not conform to what others think or want.

Cam is a good student. He loves learning for the sake of learning. At school, he is a loner or has one or two best friends. His reserve makes other children nervous. A divorce makes the world scarier. He carefully weighs which caregiver to trust. He sides with the one who provides the most stability and whose behavior is more in line with what he believes to be right. Moving creates anxiety. It is hard for him make new friends. He may not integrate with the new environment unless he finds someone to bond with. He won't rebel. He'll silently self-destruct.

Morgan is a lively baby. He walks, talks, and gets into everything early. He might do them all a little differently. Caregivers who expect everything to happen on time and in the right way are frustrated. He has a lively, questioning mind. He takes risks and outwits dim caregivers, teachers, or other authority figures. He likes creative projects and follows his unique interests wherever they lead. He takes things apart to see how they work. His penchant for invention is evident early on.

Morgan is outgoing. He likes to orchestrate activities, assign roles, and oversee the progress. Teachers might not appreciate his assistance. The students might not appreciate being managed. He struggles with teachers who expect him to sit down and shut up. He is irritated when things don't go his way and rarely accepts things as they are. He isn't drawn to sports or regimented activities. He struggles with divided loyalty in a divorce scenario. It might drive him to be more of a class clown for attention. A move gives him an opportunity to take his show on the road. He enjoys meeting and organizing new people. They may not appreciate his quirky intellect. He might indulge in outrageous and self-destructive behavior if rejected.

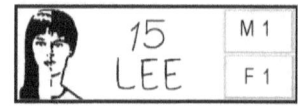

Lee is a high-demand baby. If placed with absent or self-absorbed caregivers, she screams until someone pays attention to her. She proves exhausting to the most attentive caregiver. She knows her own mind from the day she can talk and tells you what she wants and does not want. Caregivers with different plans and goals for her are met with stubborn resistance. She excels at whatever she chooses to participate in. She is in competition with herself not others, but they might not realize it. She wants that pretty red A on her paper. She is a leader on the playground and becomes the enemy of anyone who doesn't follow along. She is the quintessential queen bee. To caregivers with Lee's temperament, Lee is the perfect child. To rigid caregivers, she is a pain. To less intrepid caregivers, she scares them a little.

Lee finds it hard to stay in her seat and not show other people how to do things. Teachers either love her or find her highly irritating. She is deeply hurt by a divorce. She uses her pain to fuel her need for perfection. This results in eating disorders or pushing herself to exhaustion. She is torn in two directions, but sides with the caregiver she is most like, perhaps cutting the other caregiver out entirely for failing her. If relocated, she challenges the reigning queen bee. She either dethrones her or starts her own hive.

River is a quiet baby. She is content to observe the world. A busy, aggressive, or outgoing caregiver makes her cry. She needs peace and quiet to thrive. She lives in a dream world most of the time. Extroverted caregivers drag her kicking and screaming to play groups or to the playground. She sits under the slide and makes up stories about witches that are mean to their children. She has one friend, perhaps two. Her emotional skin is very thin. She feels everything intensely. She cries over injured animals. She avoids group activities and school events with lots of noise and people. She sees the world as treacherous. Trust is vital. She is gentle and hates violence and discord.

River takes her school work seriously and enjoys learning. She hides in the back row to observe. Some teachers appreciate her quiet creativity. Her lack of participation frustrates others. She wants to speak out against bullies, but finds it very difficult. Her stories reveal her deep thoughts and hatred of bullies. A divorce makes the world scarier than it already is. She retreats further inside her fantasy world. It is hard for her to trust again. She might not recover if moving strips her of the security blanket of her best friend. Making friends and fitting in are difficult. She is prone to depression and silent self destruction.

The temperaments of the caregivers and the cauldron in which they are raised result in vastly different outcomes for our sweet sixteen. Each type needed something different and may or may not have gotten it.

Ghosts: Negative experiences and encounters embedded in the primitive brain become triggers: This small brunette person makes me happy and gives me what I want. This big blonde person makes me unhappy and does not give me what I want, or tries to thrust upon me things I don't want. Upon first meeting, the character greets small brunette people with a smile and big blonde people with reserve. This flicker of recognition may be quickly overturned. Every time the child is in the company of negative image people, he is unhappy. When placed with positive image people, he is content. There is no logic to the situation whatsoever. The primitive brain is not logical. It only knows what feels safe and what feels scary. A character could meet a new boss or a friend's new romantic partner and immediately dislike him for no apparent reason. His gut tells him this person is a threat, which may or may not be true.

Favorites: Caregivers, relatives, coaches, and teachers have favorites. They might not admit it. The favored child complements his personality type most or resembles the positive image people imbedded in his primitive brain. The irritating child is his opposite or resembles the negative image people. The child could exhibit behaviors he buried in his shadow self. A child carrying a character's DNA doesn't guarantee a temperament match. Caregivers and children are rarely well matched. If you see a harmonious family, they won the draw. If you see a family full of conflict, they didn't. All of this plays out in the realm of the shadow self for both caregiver and child. It is rarely dealt with on a conscious level. Blended families escalate the conflict potential by adding jealously, resentment, divided loyalty, fear of abandonment, and new temperament clashes.

[ALT] **Introverted Child + Extroverted Caregiver:** Wynn, Francis, Blair, Shelby, Joss, Greer, Cam, and River are introverts. They are overstimulated by extroverted caregivers. They are pushed to attend social situations they don't want to go to. They are annoyed when encouraged to get out and make friends. They prefer playing with one or two best friends and low-octane activities. Extroverted caregivers are bored by reading endless books. They can't grasp why the introvert wants to play on his own for hours at a time. If an introverted child has a mixed family, he gravitates toward the introverted caregivers and siblings and away from the extroverts. An introverted child turns inward and withdraws from other people when the home or school environment is chaotic. He thrives in a calm nest. He struggles with group assignments and hates sharing a room with noisy siblings. He needs advance warning that change is coming and how it will affect him. This applies to new food, a new nanny, or a new bed. He needs encouragement to put himself out in the world to avoid isolation. At best, an extroverted caregiver draws the introverted child from his shell. At worst, the introverted child withdraws and never comes out for air.

ALT Extroverted Child + Introverted Caregiver: Nevada, Arden, Dallas, Hadley, Kelly, Taylor, Morgan, and Lee are extroverts. They are stifled by introverted caregivers. Their caregivers are happy spending hours at home in quiet pursuits. The extroverted child needs to be out and on the move. Inviting one, quiet, well-behaved friend over isn't enough when he can invite twenty rowdy friends. Why play one game when he can play two? He enjoys sports teams, scouts, and play groups. The introverted caregiver finds the social whirl exhausting. If an introverted caregiver has a buddy with a child who is willing to go along, the odds of participating in an activity increased two-fold. An extroverted child acts out when waters get choppy at home and at school. He is energized by a changing routine. He needs his energy reined in and reminders to rest and learn self-care. Getting him to sit through something long and boring requires the carrot of something pleasurable afterward. At best, an introverted caregiver reins in the exuberant child and helps him center. At worst, he escalates the extroverted child's behavior to a firestorm of rebellion and simmering anger.

ALT Sensing Child + Intuitive Caregiver: Wynn, Francis, Nevada, Arden, Hadley, Joss, and Kelly are sensors. They need details and specific answers. "Because I said so," isn't good enough. They aren't happy with, "We'll see what happens. I can't promise." If you talked about it, you promised. The sensing child struggles with imaginative solitary play and prefers structured activities. He needs to know the plan for the next day and struggles with changes in the plan. He drowns in the intuitive caregiver's realm of all things are possible, none are certain. He demands more of the intuitive caregiver's attention than he is able to give. At best, the intuitive caregiver teaches him to go with the flow. At worst, he makes the sensing child extremely rigid.

Intuitive Child + Sensing Caregiver: Dallas, Shelby, Greer, Taylor, Cam, Morgan, Lee, and River are intuitive. The intuitive child suffocates under the rigid rules of the sensing caregiver. The sensing caregiver expects him to do as he is told. The intuitive child frustrates the sensing caregiver with questions like, "Why can't we?" The sensing caregiver answers, "Because I said so." He chafes under a staid unchanging routine. The sensing caregiver is aggravated by his dithering and desire to try things a different way. At best, the sensing caregiver helps the intuitive child become more organized and accountable. At worst, he stifles the intuitive child's creativity.

Thinking Child + Feeling Caregiver: Francis, Arden, Joss, Kelly, Greer, Cam, Morgan, and Lee are thinkers. A thinking child feels suffocated by the emotional and physical closeness the feeling caregiver desires. He wants to be alone to experience the world. He resists family game night. The feeling caregiver can't understand why the child isn't having fun. He struggles with a feeling parent's lack of consistency and predictability. At best, the feeling caregiver tempers the solitary nature of the thinking child. At worst, the feeling caregiver suffocates him enough that he becomes an isolator who fears enmeshment.

Feeling Child + Thinking Caregiver: Wynn, Nevada, Blair, Dallas, Hadley, Shelby, and River are feelers. The feeling child's need for closeness and attention frustrates the thinking caregiver. The thinking caregiver expects him to be self-reliant. The caregiver resents reminding him to finish things and to control his behavior. The feeling child wants to spend time together. The thinking caregiver is bored by the endless games and "let's play pretend" moments the feeling child craves. The feeling child melts at the word "no" and crumples under too much structure and rigidity. At best, the thinking caregiver fosters independence in the feeling child. At worst, the thinking caregiver leaves him feeling unappreciated and abandoned and he becomes a fuser with fuzzy boundaries.

[ALT] **Judging Child + Perceiving Caregiver**: Wynn, Francis, Nevada, Arden, Taylor, Cam, Lee, and River are judgers. The judging child thrives on structure and wants to know what the rules are. The perceiving caregiver's fluid rules change with the circumstances. The judging child can't handle surprises or the change in plans. The perceiving caregiver's admonitions to go with the flow and live in the moment make him anxious. The caregiver's haphazard housekeeping and loose schedule make him anxious. At best, the perceiving caregiver teaches the judging child how to relax and enjoy life. At worst, the perceiving caregiver makes him overly controlling and distrustful of the world.

[ALT] **Perceiving Child + Judging Caregiver:** Blair, Dallas, Hadley, Shelby, Joss, Kelly, Greer, and Morgan are perceivers. The perceiving child is stifled by the judging caregiver's rigid rules and firm expectations. He doesn't understand why the judging caregiver can't relax and take it easy. Why does everything have to be perfect? Why can't they change plans at the last minute if something better comes along? The judging caregiver is irritated by the perceiving child's lack of cooperation, daydreaming, or dawdling. The judging caregiver's organized home and written-in-pen calendar make him anxious. So what if his room is a mess? He knows where everything is. He finds structure suffocating. At best, the judging caregiver provides structure and teaches the perceiving child to focus. At worst, the caregiver makes him more indecisive and frantic.

↺ Each child's personality is affected by multiple factors beyond temperament. The mannequins are based on a relatively average upbringing. Well-matched, internally balanced caregivers, added to a lack of trauma during childhood, result in balanced characters. Even if nothing traumatic happens, some needs and expectations are not met because no caregiver can meet a child's needs every moment of the day.

At any point on the continuum, trauma could strike, a core value could be violated, or abuse could take place. Chaotic and abusive childhoods result in extremes. Children raised in dysfunctional cauldrons typically go one of two ways: they replicate the chaos to one degree or another in their adult lives or they become extremely rigid and controlled to keep the chaos from returning.

Every character, regardless of ethnicity, sexuality, or gender identity, faces similar challenges. Therefore, the cauldron of childhood is crucial in shaping the adult they become. For the sake of crafting protagonists and antagonists, you need a more balanced hero and a more imbalanced villain. Friends and foes can be drawn from the middle or either end of the spectrum.

Diana Hurwitz

CAREGIVING

We've explored our mannequins' needs as children. Barring complications, let's explore the type of caregiver they become. Temperament types react the same whether the character stays at home or works outside the home, whether they are mom or dad, single or married, straight or gay, a genetic parent or nanny. It is important to change it up occasionally. Characters don't have to be orphans. Abandonment is more powerful than divorce or death as a motivational tool. The parents could be shuffled offstage or moved to another city, state, or country for work. The characters may have been raised by servants or relatives, because their parents were self-absorbed or on the go. They may have been raised by wolves or vampires. Do your vampires and wolves have a temperament? Yes.

Nurturing: Wynn is loving and giving, but somewhat reserved. She makes sure her children's clothes are clean and lunches packed. She shows love through tokens and actions. She isn't good with praise, but craves praise for her dedication. She loves holidays. She provides favorite meals, personalized gifts, and lavish celebrations. It stuns her when something she wants her children to have isn't what they would have preferred. She isn't very social, which is a problem for an extroverted child. She becomes structured and rigid when stressed. Wynn doesn't care who made the mistake or caused the problem, she just wants peace restored. She teaches what she considers right from wrong. She expects her children to follow the rules. She feels strongly about conventional behavior and is embarrassed if they deviate from it. She fears ridicule.

Discipline: Wynn finds it hard to play bad cop and avoids direct confrontation. She is possessive of her family. She communicates boundaries, but is weak at enforcing them. Her sporadic attempts to take charge confuse her children. She punishes in subtle ways, such as withholding something they want, or taking away something they value. Wynn represses her displeasure until a core value is violated. Her children are shocked by the violence of the outburst. Her best match is an introverted, self-regulating child. She blames herself for a wild child's mistakes and makes excuses for him to protect him. She reacts fiercely to outside criticism. She is overly protective and involved.

To show growth, Wynn can set firm boundaries, enforce them, and hold her child accountable for his behavior.

At her best, Wynn is remembered as the devoted caregiver who made their home a calm, happy place.

At her worst, Wynn is inconsistent, overprotective, or a toxic enabler.

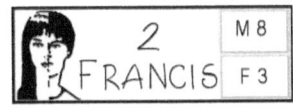

Nurturing: Francis is devoted, but emotionally distant. He puts forth his best effort to raise model citizens and confident adults. He provides financial security, an organized home, and a predictable routine. He makes unemotional decisions. He becomes controlling when stressed. Children who need a little chaos make him crazy. He isn't overly social and dismisses an extraverted child's need to socialize all the time. He expects them to accept traditional family roles. Francis attends performances, school conferences, and sporting events. He isn't big on gifts. He isn't good with praise. He expects his children to be self-regulating and to have the same high standards he has set for himself. Feeling children do not fare well under this caregiver's iron fist. His rigid boundaries and need to be right undermine his children's confidence.

Discipline: Francis has no tolerance for disrespect or rule breaking. He holds his children accountable if they act up at school or elsewhere. He has no trouble assigning punishment. It is his duty to teach his children right from wrong. He avoids confrontation until he explodes, which makes him appear inconsistent. The term "wait until dad gets home" was created for Francis. He fiercely defends his partner and offspring against outside criticism. Turbulence hits when his children are old enough to question his authority. Francis will not tolerate challenges to his alpha position, even if Francis is female.

To show growth, Francis could learn to praise his children. He could apologize for being so rigid and exacting. He could accept that his child's different approach to things isn't necessarily wrong.

At his best, Francis is remembered as the steady hand that kept the family ship safe at sea.

At his worst, Francis is remembered as the brutal family dictator who needed to be right.

Nurturing: Nevada is committed and stable. He prefers life to be orderly and planned. He takes care of his children's practical needs. He is warm and affectionate. He is social and offers a structured, fun environment. He expects them to behave and to honor and respect him. He is critical of what he considers deviant behavior. He is humiliated if his children's actions reflect badly on him. He avoids dealing with an issue until he can't. He takes criticism of his rules and decisions as a personal attack. He is intolerant of everyone around him when stressed. He cares more about how it happened and who was responsible than repairing the situation.

Discipline: Nevada sets clear boundaries, but finds it hard to enforce them. He makes excuses for bad behavior and advocates for his children against outsiders. He struggles with overt confrontation. He punishes his children through manipulation and guilt. These tactics can cause long-term damage to their relationship. When his adolescents turn rebellious, especially if they question the status quo, he won't tolerate their behavior.

To show growth, Nevada could learn to be consistent with expectations and consequences. He learns respect has to be earned not demanded.

At his best, Nevada is remembered for his unwavering dedication and steady home life.

At his worst, Nevada is remembered for being manipulative, harsh, and inconsistent.

Nurturing: Arden strives to be stable and a good example. His priorities place community first and family second. He is big on traditions and expects his family to embrace them with equal fervor. He wants to be admired for his integrity and hard work. He is a fierce advocate for those he loves. He isn't good with praise or loving affirmations. He likes things orderly and planned. He expects his children to be good citizens and to uphold the law. He wants them to be responsible and independent adults. He won't respect them if they aren't. He won't tolerate messiness or dawdling. He has difficulty with the creative bent of the intuitive child. That pairing could turn toxic. He can't relax and go with the flow. He hates changes in schedule. He expects his children to perform well because it is the right thing to do, not for personal gain or fear of punishment. He struggles with a partner and children whose needs are different from his.

Discipline: Arden is a firm, fair disciplinarian and has no trouble with confrontation. He suppresses his displeasure until a core value is violated. His eruptions shock his family. He dishes out criticism, but can't take it. He becomes hypercritical and controlling when stressed. His need for respect is challenged when his children hit the rebellious phase, or if their personalities are so different they don't respect his methods from day one. He overlooks a violation once and is livid if they do it again.

To show growth, Arden learns what is right for him is not what is right for everyone else. He realizes if you want respect, you have to respect others.

At his best, Arden is remembered as dependable and self-sacrificing.

At his worst, Arden is remembered as cold and strict with impossible standards no one could ever live up to.

Nurturing: Blair takes great pride and comfort in her family. She wants to be loved and admired. She is emotionally reserved. She provides a well-tended and comfortable home. She doesn't offer praise, but needs to hear it. She is great with babies and small children. She is easygoing and has realistic expectations. She shows her affection with gifts and makes birthdays special. She gently guides her children and makes suggestions while being respectful of their individuality. She has low social needs, but makes sure her kids have fun. She takes them to parks and on vacations. She allows them to have pets. She isn't overly structured. She changes her mind after plans have been set. She makes emotional decisions and takes criticism of her methods and decisions personally. She is often taken for granted. If she sublimates her needs while she raises a family, she struggles when her chicks leave the nest.

Discipline: Blair hates being an authority. She avoids doling out punishment until her core values are violated. She represses her feelings most of the time, so her outbursts are unexpected. She withdraws and becomes passive when stressed. If her partner provides structure, she goes along with it. If her partner can't provide firm boundaries, or she is a single caregiver, heaven help them. She wants her children to be happy. She makes exceptions to every rule to keep them happy. She feels overly responsible for their mental wellbeing. If they have a bad day, it is somehow her fault. She goes to great lengths to smooth things over. She is a staunch defender against outsiders.

To show growth, Blair could learn to separate and take responsibility for her thoughts and feelings. She needs to master firm boundaries and offer consistent consequences.

At her best, Blair is fondly remembered as the loyal, fun caregiver who put her family first.

At her worst, Blair is remembered as the long-suffering martyr, or the toxically enmeshed enabler.

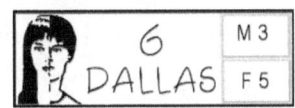

Nurturing: Dallas is highly social and ensures everyone has a good time. Her constant need for stimulation causes problems. Regimented children struggle with her inconsistency. She is affectionate and showers them with praise and loving affirmations. She wants to be adored. Her attempts to make everything "perfect" can go overboard. Her children may have trouble meeting her expectations. She respects their need to be individuals. She lets them explore their interests, but won't make them finish anything. They are embarrassed by Dallas's effusive displays of public affection. She remembers to pick them up from school and makes sure they've had dinner, but routine is not something she thrives on. She goes with whatever suits the moment best. They have sandwiches often.

Discipline: Dallas does not enforce rules until her children violate a core value. She wants to be friends with her children. She crosses the line in her desire to be liked. She relies on her partner to play bad cop and take care of the boring details. Chaos reigns if she is a single caregiver or if her partner can't be the enforcer. She becomes passive-aggressive when anxious and hates confrontation. She takes criticism of her efforts personally. She is more interested in blaming than fixing. She represses her displeasure until she walks away. She might physically or emotionally abandon an unpleasant home life.

To show growth, Dallas could stop being her child's friend and become his advocate. She could work in tandem with her partner instead of against him.

At her best Dallas is remembered as the warm, nurturing caregiver who never let things get boring.

At her worst, Dallas is remembered as the flake who tried to hang out with her children or the one who left them fluttering in the wind.

Nurturing: Hadley is easygoing and highly social. She wants every day to be fun. She thrives on harmony and good will. She is warm and affectionate. She showers her children with praise and loving affirmations. She is hurt if they don't return the favor. She throws big birthday parties and participates in school activities when possible. She encourages her children to try everything. She wants them to have the newest and latest cool stuff. She isn't terribly structured. Some of the routine chores are entirely forgotten. Her children have what they need on a daily basis, perhaps at the very last minute, and held together with colorful duct tape. She keeps them on the move. She thrills extroverted children and slightly alarms the introverts. She handles problems as they crop up, but becomes erratic when anxious.

Discipline: Hadley usually partners with someone who can provide structure and discipline. Chaos reigns if she doesn't. She is not a natural disciplinarian and prefers to be her children's friend. She only punishes them if they violate a core value. She avoids confrontation until she blows. Her children are confused by their normally calm caregiver's fury. Hadley fiercely defends her children when other people criticize them. She takes criticism and objective statements personally. She stands by her children as a buddy rather than holding them responsible for their actions.

To show growth, Hadley needs to enforce healthy boundaries and hold her children accountable for their behavior.

At her best, Hadley is remembered as the beloved, joyful, slightly scattered caregiver.

At her worst, Hadley is remembered as a careless and chaotic enabler.

Nurturing: Shelby is nurturing, but emotionally guarded. She is patient, devoted, and flexible. She passes down her values and wants to be respected. She showers her children with loving affirmations. A turbulent child is a challenge. Shelby is highly emotional and critical when anxious. She needs wide personal space, so she may give a wild child too much freedom. She offers a regimented child room to grow. She listens to her children and respects their individuality.

Discipline: Shelby blames herself when her children don't behave. She looks to her partner to play bad cop. She struggles as a single caregiver to provide firm structure. She avoids confrontation until a core value is transgressed then comes down hard. Her children are shocked to find she can be firm. She fiercely defends her children from outside criticism. She overlooks indiscretions until they reach a point where she can't. She takes objective statements about her children personally. If paired with children she can't connect with, she finds it highly unsatisfactory and may leave emotionally or physically.

To show growth, Shelby needs to learn how to enforce the rules. She needs to view her children objectively and hold them accountable for their behavior.

At her best, Shelby is remembered as a harmonious, nurturing, fun caregiver.

At her worst, Shelby is remembered as the inconsistent, critical, emotionally absent caregiver who abandoned them.

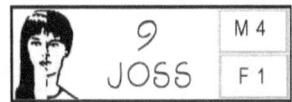

Nurturing: Joss is flexible and easy-going. He hates being controlled and isn't interested in controlling his children. He likes to show off for them. He is emotionally reserved. The rare moments when he tries to get to know his children stand out for them. He has low social needs, though he wants his children to have fun. He places a trampoline in the backyard. He laughs when they slide down the stairway on snow sleds. He tries it himself. He doesn't oversee their day-to-day care. He comments when they display competence. He doesn't offer praise or loving affirmations. He is unconventional and won't care if his kids color outside the lines. If they ask his opinion, he won't tell them who to be or what to do. He listens, but does not interfere, when they bring problems to him. He expects them to resolve problems on their own, like he does. Children looking for firm guidance are confused by their exchanges: "What do you think you should do?" "I think I should do X. Am I right?" "If you think you are."

Discipline: Joss can administer discipline. He usually laughs at his children's shenanigans. He avoids enforcing boundaries until they violate a core value. He punishes with cutting criticism. His partner, if he has one, may resent it. If he is a single caregiver, his children have to pick up the slack. He works best with a self-regulating child. He becomes impulsive under pressure. When his children act out due to a lack of firm boundaries, Joss is worse than they are.

To show growth, Joss needs to be consistent in his expectations. He needs to be more proactive in his advice and guidance.

At his best, Joss is the fun, nonjudgmental caregiver who scolded them with a wink and a nudge and let them experiment.

At his worst, Joss is remembered as the critical and emotionally remote caregiver who wasn't there when it mattered.

Nurturing: Kelly is a big kid himself. He is larger than life and master of the grand gesture. His kids have fun, if being highly social and active is fun for them. He throws lavish parties and encourages them to try daring things. He installs a zip line in the back yard. They are allowed to jump on the beds and climb the walls. He takes them on vacations they can't afford. He isn't fixated on whether they clean their rooms or do their homework. He appreciates their individuality and encourages it. Kelly isn't conventional and doesn't expect his children to be. He freely admits that he doesn't have all the answers. He is good in an emergency. He is poor at stating his feelings. He is uncomfortable if asked "Do you love me?" and turns it into a joke. He won't plan ahead for college funds. He is not structured or organized. He isn't interested in the day-to-day tasks that keep the home running smoothly. He can do them, but they are low on his priority list. He usually pairs with someone who takes care of those tasks.

Discipline: Kelly wants to be his children's friend not their drill sergeant. He drops to their level when it comes to discipline. He forces his partner to play bad cop. If his children violate his personal code of conduct, whatever it is, he shouts at them and may call them names. He becomes excessively impulsive under stress, which is counterproductive when his teenagers are acting out. He may become worse than they are. He fares better with a self-regulating child than a wild child. He may make the most balanced child act out.

To show growth, Kelly would have to be consistent and learn how to use positive affirmations rather than gifts to prove his love. He learns being a parent is more than being a buddy.

At his best, especially if paired with a self-regulating child, Kelly is remembered as a fun-loving, larger-than-life hero.

At his worst, Kelly is remembered as the cold, unreliable caregiver who bailed on his family or ruined them financially.

Nurturing: Greer passes down his love of learning. He needs to be seen as competent and admires his children's competence. He fosters independence of action and thought. He favors rationality and struggles with an imaginative feeling child. He isn't interested in molding his children into his own image. He takes his commitment seriously, but finds the emotional component difficult. He cares and may be proud of his children, but won't say it. He forgets birthdays and special events when he gets lost in a project. He is not a hands-on caregiver. He counts on his partner to handle the day to day running of the home or hires someone. He isn't overly structured or organized. If he doesn't have a partner, his children have to take over.

Discipline: Greer becomes resentful and withdraws under pressure. A wild child who acts out to gain his attention may have the opposite effect. He doesn't offer firm boundaries because he expects his children to be self-regulating. He relies on someone else to provide the structure and discipline. It would take a serious core violation to gain his attention. He ignores emotionally-laden critique about his children and focuses on the functional part. Greer hears they aren't doing their homework. He is oblivious as to why.

To show growth, Greer needs to understand the emotional needs and social obligations of his children. He needs to put his projects a little lower on the priority list.

At his best, Greer is remembered as a loyal, fair, and tolerant caregiver who helped them with science projects.

At his worst, Greer is remembered as the distant, erratic parent who rarely made time for his family.

Nurturing: Taylor puts her children first. She strives to be a good role model and encourages them to make the world a better place. She wants to be appreciated for her goodness and service. Her self-worth is tied up in whether or not her children turn out well. She is strict and has high expectations. She expects them to conform. Deviations from the norm humiliate her. She takes criticism and objective statements about them, and from them, personally. She is warm and affectionate. She lavishes affirmations. She throws special birthday parties and makes sure the holidays are fun and traditional. She provides what they need on a daily basis. She is suffocating to a child who needs space. She may become pathologically enmeshed in her children's lives. She takes responsibility for their emotional health as well as making sure they do everything they are supposed to.

Discipline: Taylor is fiercely loyal and overprotective. She struggles most when her children hit adolescence and rebel. She represses her displeasure until she explodes over a core violation. She understands what makes her children tick and manipulates rather than confronts them. She punishes them in subtle ways: by denying them things they want or making them do things they don't want to do. She hates to argue and becomes rigid and irritable when stressed. She snipes, but never addresses the real problem, which is a lack of firm, consistent boundaries and clear communication.

To show growth, Taylor needs to let her children do for themselves and gain competence. She needs to provide healthy boundaries and constructive feedback.

At her best, Taylor is seen as the benevolent, supportive, loving mother who instilled good values and made holidays special.

At her worst, Taylor is remembered as the suffocating, manipulative, enmeshed caregiver who enforced a hypocritical value system instead of steady guidance.

Nurturing: Cam's goal is to raise his children to be independent, educated, and self-sufficient. He prefers life to be orderly and planned. He is irritated by children who dither or can't take care of routine tasks. He isn't interested in keeping up with the neighbors or doing things just because everyone else is doing them. He won't support his children if they want to. He challenges his children's decisions to make sure they have thought the situation through all the way. He isn't big on praise because he doesn't need it. He offers wise guidance and loving affirmations. His intellectual distractedness may be misinterpreted as a sign he doesn't care. He is passionate for the few he loves. However, he needs his space and expects his children to need space. He has low social needs and struggles with an extroverted child. He shrugs off their struggles with peer pressure. He advises them to be true to themselves and forget everyone else.

Discipline: Cam offers logical critique in the face of emotional outbursts. He is more focused on preventing what happened from happening again than assigning blame. He expects his children to think for themselves and make their own decisions. He expects them to set high standards for themselves. He expects them to be self-regulating and self-motivated. He won't handle a rebellious adolescent well, particularly a sensing feeling one. He views their disobedience as a personal attack or a serious character flaw. He represses his displeasure until a core value is violated. His children are shocked by the violence of his response when they cross a serious line. An out of control wild child loses his respect and may never get it back.

To show growth, Cam needs to understand the emotional and social ramifications his children face in the world. He needs to let them fail because failure is how they learn.

At his best, Cam is the calm, measured parent who encouraged them to succeed, offered wise guidance, and respected their independence.

At his worst, he is remembered as the distant perfectionist who made little time for his children and was easily disappointed.

Nurturing: Morgan is fun and inventive, but inconsistent. Everything is a learning experience. He encourages his children to experiment and think for themselves. He ignores the day-to-day workings of the household. He praises his children for their intelligence and skill. He wants to be admired in that way, too. He fares best with intuitive thinkers. A self-regulating child will do fine. He finds a needy child suffocating. An emotional wild child perplexes him. He may avoid spending time with that child. He spends quality time, but often forgets about his family when he is in full work mode. He is emotionally aloof. He shows love through sporadic grand gestures rather than affection or loving affirmations. He unilaterally plans a move or a vacation and makes disruptive financial decisions. His family finds out after it is too late.

Discipline: Morgan relies on his partner to be the disciplinarian. This is a problem if he does not have a partner. His children may have to raise themselves. He is brought up short when an outsider criticizes his children's lack of discipline. He isn't interested in controlling people and highly resents an outsider's attempts to control him. He sides with his children against the authority figure and encourages subversive acts of rebellion. He avoids confrontation, but enjoys a good debate. His children aren't intellectually sophisticated enough to challenge his logic. Morgan isn't engaged enough to fight, but is critical when confronted. He is scattered when anxious, which is counterproductive if he has an out-of-control teen. Morgan finds permanent commitment difficult. He may physically or emotionally leave a home life turned war zone: a war zone he created.

To show growth, Morgan could learn it isn't his job to debate; it is his job to provide firm and consistent boundaries. He could learn to share how much he cares.

At his best, Morgan is remembered as the adventurous parent who kept their lives from being boring.

At his worst, Morgan is remembered as the disruptive parent who put them all at risk then ignored or abandoned them.

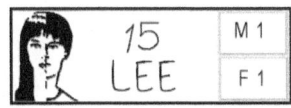

Nurturing: Lee is take-charge, no-nonsense, and emotionally aloof. It is her job to pass on her values and to make certain her children excel. She values independence and competence. She is strict and has high expectations. She has an organized home life. She has high social needs and throws lavish parties. She is materialistic and status conscious, and purchases the latest, greatest toys. She isn't good with loving affirmations or praise. She encourages her children to learn and think independently. She challenges them to understand their position and to defend it. She expects her children to follow her example and to know their place. Lee also expects them to be at the top of their game. She expects them to fall in line socially and academically. Her response is violent if her children let her down or hurt her in the pocketbook. She may not have children at all. Her children respect her competence, but wish she could be a little more loving. A dreamy or introverted child exasperates her.

Discipline: Lee allows her children a mistake once and expects them to learn from it. She frowns on repeat offenses. She represses her displeasure until she snaps. She becomes hypercritical when stressed. She has no trouble confronting her children to the point of bullying. She ignores criticism from outsiders, but hands it out liberally at home. She struggles most when her children hit the adolescent protest phase. She does not take challenges to her authority lightly.

To show growth, she needs to temper her need to control with respect for her children's independence. She needs to let them fail because failure is how they learn. She needs to understand others have a right to do things their way.

At her best, Lee is remembered as the dynamic, hardworking, firm parent they looked up to and admired.

At her worst, Lee is remembered as a harsh dictator. Her children might respect her; they won't like her. A sensitive child may end up hating her.

Nurturing: River is patient, intensely loving, and devoted. She showers her children with loving affirmations and gifts. She is hurt if they don't return the favor. She wants to be admired for her wisdom and desire for harmony. She encourages her children to live up to her high ideals and to make the world a better place. She is vaguely dissatisfied with life because it is never perfect. Her children aren't perfect. She teaches them her version of right and wrong. She supports their individual growth and wants them to think for themselves. She isn't overly social, so an extroverted child is a problem. Her mystical bent embarrasses a thinking child. She overshares all of her feelings, which a remote child finds cloying. She is hurt when her child objects to her effusive displays and incessant emotional temperature taking. She makes sacrifices for her family without question. She may regret the effort if things don't turn out perfectly.

Discipline: River is soft-spoken and gentle unless crossed. She becomes critical and self-absorbed when stressed. She ignores misbehavior until she can't. She buries her displeasure until she erupts. She relies on her partner to play bad cop. This is a problem if she doesn't have a partner or has a partner who can't enforce boundaries either. Firm rules make her children unhappy — and she hates doing anything to upset her children's tender sensibilities. She takes criticism and objective statements personally. She rushes to her children's defense against outsiders. She may go to great lengths to cover up their misdeeds or lack of discipline. She thinks her children are special and misunderstood in a world dismissive of psychic sensitivity. Her children may not be psychically sensitive, but very adept at manipulating her.

To show growth, River needs to learn how to enforce healthy, consistent boundaries, and speak her mind, even if it creates conflict.

At her best, River is remembered as a patient, loving, and inspirational caregiver who truly understood her children at their deepest level.

At her worst, River is remembered as the embarrassing, mystical caregiver who never held her children accountable for their actions.

As you craft your plot, there are many ways to bend and twist the family structure to provide motivation for your characters to behave the way they do.

Stir the Cauldron: If you want your character to have a harmonious home life, match him with children with compatible temperaments and a partner who complements his style. If you want his home life to be turbulent, match him with children with incompatible temperaments and a partner who opposes his style. Place your character in a society or neighborhood full of opposites or one that does not play to his strengths. Assign him a traditional role he is unsuited for.

ALT Daddy Issues: If the daughter has an emotionally or physically absent father, she enters the world seeking male attention in an unhealthy way. If she had a terrific father, no man may ever measure up to him. She could be overly entangled with her father so that no other guy stands a chance. If a male child has a poor role model for a father, he mimics those behaviors in his relationships or vows to be the opposite and goes too far in the opposite direction. If his father was overly critical, his self esteem suffers. He may find it hard to escape from the over-controlling father's influence.

ALT Mommy Issues: If a daughter has an overly critical mother or poor role model, her self-image suffers. She may pick critical partners. She either mirrors the mother's example or strives to be the complete opposite. She may be overly enmeshed with her mother. The guys she dates are offended by her mother's suffocating presence.

If the son had an emotionally or physically absent mother, he may crave female attention in an unhealthy way. For the son, no woman may ever measure up to mama. If he has a neurotic or psychologically unsound mother, he develops a warped sense of what a woman should be. If he is overly enmeshed with his mother, any woman he dates has to compete with her (or her memory).

⌨ Aim the Projector: Characters project things they are afraid are true about themselves, and the things they don't like about themselves, onto others. This is typically someone of the same sex. It can be their romantic partner or children. They may have been criticized for being too thin, too fat, too smart, too dumb, too lazy, too industrious, too sassy, or too quiet. Emotions were either positively reinforced or considered socially unacceptable: inquisitiveness, anger, pride, ambition, quiet reflection, masculinity, femininity, aggression, sadness, fear. Whatever had to be buried resides in the shadow self until it gets a chance to break free or is projected onto someone else. If the negative feelings surface, the character feels anxious and tries harder to hide them.

Repressed emotions can take the form of self-defeating behaviors: addiction, overeating, gambling, lying about where the money goes, hiding "negative" behavior, affairs, sexual exploits, etc. If others view the things he prides himself on— the things he was praised for—in a negative light, he becomes extremely defensive: "I'm not cold and distant; I'm self-sufficient and strong." "I'm not weak; I'm sensitive." "I'm not cheap; I'm careful."

⌨ Triggers: When a basic need isn't met, it creates a trigger in the primitive brain. Characters either overcompensate for their unmet childhood needs or endlessly recreate situations where they are denied them, hoping for a different outcome each time. Whatever they are naturally prone to do, the trigger makes them worse. As a child's world expands to encompass school and the neighborhood, he realizes he can impose his will none of the time, some of the time, or all of the time. He absorbs the rules of the game: when to be quiet and when to be loud, when to give in and when to fight, when to express his nature and when to hide it. Some behaviors are rewarded; some are discouraged. Give the character a child who behaves in ways he was not allowed to. It makes the caregiver overly judgmental and emotional. The caregiver attempts to repress his behavior or secretly revels that the child is getting away with it. This offers an opportunity for growth or tragedy.

ALT Gender Confusion: Children soon notice gender differences and realize they are either physically male or female. There is no room in these pages to debate gender identity issues. However, to ignore them would be a plot hole. Boys and girls are taught what being male or female should look and feel like by caregivers, societies, teachers, and religions. The shape is not always a natural fit. A boy who likes pink princess dolls, or a girl who prefers monster trucks, may cause a stir. Children are not aware of these distinctions until caregivers enforce them. Gender reinforcement is a big conflict if a child's gender identity isn't what society expects it to be based on body parts. It's also a problem when the parent isn't suited to his role. Pair a caregiver whose natural instincts were squelched with a child who repeats the same behaviors.

ALT Switch the Role Model: The same-sex caregiver is considered the most important role model. The female child emulates her mother and looks for someone like her father to complete her. The male child emulates his father and looks for someone like his mother to complete him. This is turned on its head in situations where there is mental and physical abuse or abandonment. It's a massive internal conflict if the caregivers had opposing temperaments.

Absence of a same sex or opposite sex parent obviously interferes with this dynamic. How independent a child is plays a role. If a girl had masculine role models, she may repress her natural feminine instincts. She then finds it difficult to fit in with the girly- females and wants to hang with the guys. If a guy has feminine heroes or role models, he may repress his natural masculine instincts. He then finds it difficult to fit in with the macho-men and is more comfortable with his female friends.

[ALT] Fusers: Temperament types natively struggle with varying needs for connection and space. Experiences during childhood can drive their temperament to extremes. A child raised in a well-balanced home is raised with flexible boundaries. He is able to identify and protect self while feeling connected to, and protective of, others. A child suffering painful or abusive experiences either isolates or tries to fuse with others. He can't let other people in or isn't sure where he ends and the other person begins. Fusers and isolators are a horrible mix for partnerships of any kind. They are often drawn to each other with catastrophic results. The more the clinger clings, the more the runner runs. Some children require connection more than others. If you put them with a caregiver who can't meet their needs, they become clingy. Any child who suffered emotional or physical abandonment can become a fuser.

[ALT] Isolators: If a child needs wide personal space and he is matched with a suffocatingly attentive caregiver, the need becomes exaggerated. Even a child whose basic personality requires close connection can be smothered. He becomes an adult who pushes people away and needs wide emotional and physical distance. He needs the freedom to come and go as he pleases and resists being tied down. Commitment is difficult, if not impossible. He subconsciously sabotages any relationship he forms because he fears engulfment. If he becomes a partner or caregiver, he is an emotionally or physically absent one. Learning how to connect would be a sign of growth.

Abandonment: When a caregiver abandons a child or dies, he leaves a psychological wound that influences the child's life forever. A caregiver who simply disappears leaves the child with the need to understand why. The child fears that he is somehow at fault. Abandonment lowers a child's self-esteem. He grows up fearful. The normal fluctuations in a relationship take on menacing proportions. If someone lets him down, or does not show up, he blames himself. He needs constant reassurance and becomes a suffocating partner or caregiver. Conversely, he might assume that his partner and children will leave him eventually, so why grow attached? It could inspire him to remain steadfast when others are ready to jump ship. He refuses to abandon a child, a friend, or a partner because he know how it feels.

The world is not ideal and children are not always raised in a household with a mom and a dad in situ. Caregivers die, divorce, go to war, give their children up for adoption, enter witness protection, and mentally and emotionally abandon ship. Children are raised by siblings, relatives, adoptive caregivers, foster caregivers, guardians, or total strangers. Make sure you utilize the full tool kit when developing your mannequins.

BOUNDARY VIOLATIONS

This particular form of mutilation deserves its own section. Characters adopt behaviors, coping mechanisms, verbal warnings, and body language to defend psychological boundaries. No one likes feeling violated.

Physical boundary violations are overt conflict. Go to a movie theater and encroach on someone's armrest and you've created tension. The offended party either moves or accepts the situation. He may seethe with resentment during the movie or find passive-aggressive ways to protest. He tosses popcorn or turns on his cell phone and directs the light at his row mate's eyes.

Characters have the right to decide the "who" and "when." You've probably had a conversation with someone who stood uncomfortably close or so far away you didn't think he wanted to participate. Personal space varies from culture to culture. A highly tactile character may touch people when he talks to them. Another character hates touching, and being touched by, strangers. Introverts tend to need wider personal space than extroverts.

When someone infringes on a character's "personal" space, he backs off or pushes the other person away. He finds ways to strike back in hopes of convincing the other person to never do it again. The less empowered the character feels, the more intense his response to a physical boundary infraction. He may avoid the violator in the future. He is certainly less willing to do what the violator wanted him to. If a character ignores physical boundaries, even if he means well, it invokes an anxiety response.

Psychological boundaries offer subtler conflicts with higher stakes. They are the lines separating one person from another. Blur them and things get messy.

Children are warned about inappropriate touching. They are alerted when someone uses inappropriate word choices. Psychological boundary violations are sneakier and children are not instructed in psychological warfare.

Relationships are destroyed when psychological boundaries are murky. A character is hard pressed to vocalize what his psychological boundaries are. However, violations are felt all the way to his core. The violation triggers an explosion. The closer the connection to the violator, the higher the emotional response.

Boundaries are flexible in healthy relationships. A character grows and adapts to allow the other person in, but keep the self intact. He allows people inside his personal space. He permits people to touch him. He gives them access to his deepest thoughts and feelings. If someone uses intimate access to harm him, it is betrayal of the highest order.

All characters are driven to some derivative of fuzzy or rigid behavior, depending on the circumstances. A healthy character tolerates incursions to have a relationship with a rigid person. He becomes a bit rigid when dealing with a fuzzy person. Extreme circumstances force him to exhibit extreme behaviors.

Trap these opposites in a room or a relationship and you have intense conflict. Several mannequins have natural levels of fuzziness and rigidness. They are easily driven to extremes by those who influence the early years. Other mannequins adopt these methods as survival techniques.

Protagonists should fall closer to the healthy end of the spectrum, though they can have their moments. Antagonists fall more toward the rigid end of the spectrum. Providing your antagonist with solid reasons for being rigid makes the character more believable. A fuzzy friend or foe can cause just as much damage as a rigid one. Put a healthy character and unhealthy character together and you have conflict. Put a fuzzy character with a rigid character and you create a very neurotic passive-aggressive dynamic.

Rarely is a character entirely healthy or entirely pathologic. Most fall in the healthy middle of spectrum and that is no fun. Let's examine how using rigid and fuzzy characters causes interpersonal conflict and what constitutes a healthy protagonist.

A healthy character knows where he ends and the other person begins. A fuzzy character can't distinguish himself from the person he forms a relationship with. He uses his partner like drywall putty to fill in his missing pieces. He uses his partner's presence to deflect the emptiness he feels when he is alone. The problem is: no one can heal those psychic wounds for him. A rigid character can't adjust his boundaries to allow the other person in. He ends up in emotionally detached relationships and is incapable of intimacy. He makes a lousy friend or lover.

A healthy character shares personal information gradually in a mutually sharing and trusting relationship. He answers "yes" or "no" to requests and is comfortable when others give a firm "yes" or "no." A fuzzy character over-shares personal information before establishing mutual trust. He can't say "no" because he fears abandonment. A rigid character never shares personal information. He can't say "yes" because he fears engulfment.

A healthy character has a strong sense of identity and self respect. He expects reciprocity in a relationship. He is willing to share responsibility and power. A fuzzy character's identity is defined by what he thinks others want him to be. He is inconsistent. There is no balance of power or responsibility in his relationships. He is either overly responsible and controlling or passive and dependent. A rigid character cannot share responsibility or power. His sense of self is shaky. He is abrupt and easily insulted as a form of protection.

A healthy character knows when a problem is his and when it belongs to someone else. A fuzzy character takes other people's problems on as his own and feels the need to fix them. A rigid character thinks everyone has a problem but him. Nothing is ever his fault. He is critical and quick to blame others as a form of defense.

A healthy character knows what he wants, needs, and feels. He communicates clearly and does not tolerate abuse or disrespect. A fuzzy character is unclear about, or submerges, his wants, needs, and feelings. He defers to other people and is often abused and treated with disrespect. A rigid character has difficulty identifying his wants, needs, and feelings. He rarely admits to having them. He is often disrespectful and abusive.

A healthy character is responsible for his own happiness and fulfillment. He does not feel responsible for other people's happiness and fulfillment. A fuzzy character feels responsible for other people's happiness and fulfillment. He relies on relationships to fulfill him. A rigid character is cut off from his and everyone else's happiness and fulfillment. He has few, if any, close relationships. If he has a partner, they live in separate worlds.

A healthy character values his opinions and feelings as much as others. A fuzzy character relies on other people's opinions, feelings, and ideas more than his own. A rigid character thinks his opinions, feelings, and ideas are the only ones that count.

A healthy character knows his limits and accepts other's limits. A fuzzy character allows others to define his limits or tries to define limits for others. A rigid character has obsessive limits and does not respect or acknowledge other people's limits.

A healthy character is able to ask for help when he needs it and to offer it when appropriate. A fuzzy character offers inappropriate help, but is unable to ask for help when he needs it. A rigid character won't ask for or offer help.

A healthy character does not compromise his values or integrity to avoid rejection. A fuzzy character compromises his values and beliefs to please others or to avoid conflict. A rigid character never compromises, because he is always right.

Characters can fall anywhere on the continuum from normal to pathologic in any of the above ways. Healthy boundary characters make good protagonists and friends. Characters veering toward the pathological end make good foes and antagonists. The conflicts are subtle or extreme. Boundary conflicts result in improved mental health, worsened mental health, or tragedy.

TEENAGE YEARS

The teenage years are a fertile breeding ground for conflict internally, socially, and interpersonally. Even if you don't write young adult fiction, it doesn't hurt to understand how the teen years affected your mannequins.

The young adult fiction category is a money-generating powerhouse. At no other time of life are emotions so heightened, needs so frantic, and the ability to evaluate unacceptable risk so poor. It is a time of discovering who you are and where you belong. A teen tries on identities, plays with accents, dyes his hair, pierces his skin, or changes the spelling of his name. Every generation invents its own form of rebellion, even if it isn't entirely original. Teens live vicariously through other teen characters. Adults relive their wonder years through teen characters. Both have time to read and money to buy books.

Once a child hits adolescence, major circuit switches are flipped off and aren't flipped on until the cause-and-effect motherboard is activated around age twenty-five. Teens decide it's past time to be independent while still physically, financially, and legally dependent on their caregivers. Teens are smugly superior. They question their caregivers' intelligence, politics, religious beliefs, behaviors, and choices. The maelstrom of raging hormones further clouds the teen's immature thinking. Teens are worse than out of control toddlers, because they are much larger and harder to control.

When it comes to our sweet sixteen, if they have a fairly normal life with no specific trauma, their teen years are an extension of how they behaved as children. Let's pretend there are one-hundred students at Tinker Town High.

Wynn wants to be recognized for her dedication. She joins social groups and contributes in her quiet, effective way. She is a follower not a leader. She does not like being the focus of attention. She is emotionally reserved, but purchases presents for her few good friends.

Wynn shares her values by living them. She does her homework and tidies her room when reminded. She encourages cooperation among the students of Tinker Town High. She is more cautious and conservative than her peers. If other students transgress her values, her response is passive-aggressive rather than overt. She gathers loyal friends around her to undermine the transgressor. She is gullible and could be led astray by someone she trusted. She avoids conflict and becomes rigid when challenged. She graduates and does what is expected of her, unless she is turned into a mermaid.

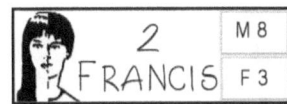

Francis is down to earth and tries to do the right thing at the right time. He thrives on being right and policing other people. He makes a great hall monitor. He is highly social and traditional. If he dates, he chooses judiciously and dates steadily until he is dumped or something major changes. He joins service clubs. He may be selected to run for student council. He may not have enough votes. He could have a part-time job to save for important and practical things.

Francis is responsible and does not ask his caregivers for things. He works hard and meets expectations. If there is a fight, he is on the side of what he perceives to be good. He suffers if you give him the girlfriend from hell. If his upbringing reinforces his rigidness, he could be a bully. If treated unfairly, he rebels. He would prefer to be left alone to follow his path. He finishes high school with a plan for what he wants to do next, unless a tsunami hits.

Nevada cares about other people's feelings and likes to help them when possible. He is responsible and maintains appearances. He volunteers his time and talent in service clubs. He draws people in by being warm, friendly, and concerned. He admires people like himself. He fits in well and participates. The other kids generally like him. Nevada stands up to a bully. He could be a bully. He could assume a hero role, fighting for what is right and helping the oppressed. He graduates as expected and goes on to do what he thinks is the right thing, unless aliens land.

Arden prides himself on his integrity and hard work. He is highly social and belongs to sports teams, the band, or student council. He is suspicious of loners. He is responsible and earns money to save for college or a car. He befriends people who share his values and work ethic.

Arden is on the prom committee and enjoys the special occasions that make high school memorable. He makes a natural hero. He states his opinions openly and won't back down, no matter the opposition. He despises bullies. He attacks when threatened and has friends to back him. If he turns against the establishment, his friends follow suit. Arden finishes high school and moves to the next level with confidence, unless a meteor streaks toward earth.

Blair is quiet, unassuming, and shuns the spotlight. She has her own set of deeply held values and doesn't fit in with the majority. Her quirky fashion sense and refusal to abide by majority rule place her in the artsy clique. She does not seek power over other people because it would require commitment. Those who like her, like her. Those who don't, she won't care.

Blair likes school for its social aspect, but is bored by the classes. Her attention is easily scattered. She could be led astray, or lead others astray, out of boredom rather than malice. She would be an unusual hero. She is usually the quirky sidekick or the unintentionally interfering foe. She has firm opinions. Circumstances could force her to express them, even if they go against the crowd. Blair attends college or embraces a career, unless zombies show up.

Dallas is outgoing, social, and independent. She is a reluctant leader and could be head cheerleader or student council president. Good grades are important to her. She spends long hours talking to her friends about her dream wedding, dream house, choice of bachelor, and her dream job.

Dallas peers behind all the doors and finds it hard to choose one. She hates being limited to one major, college, and boyfriend. If she turns against someone, Dallas is not averse to back-biting or malicious gossip. She is capable of physical altercation if it comes down to it. She is an avenging hero or an aggressive antagonist. Dallas is the first to accept an internship on Planet Zircon as long as she can return to Earth when she gets bored.

Hadley is popular and busy socially. She arranges get-togethers with friends and takes part in as many activities as she can fit in. She is able to laugh at herself and others. Life is an unending party. Hadley dabbles and moves on, particularly if the task requires too much work. She isn't interested in controlling anyone or furthering any cause. She isn't a serious scholar or a focused athlete. She resists anything that requires sustained effort. She is vaguely dissatisfied with everything. Hadley sees everyone as an equal.

Hadley could wear the hero mantle if someone seriously violated her values. It would take something pretty drastic to turn her toward the dark side. She might follow a misguided friend into danger. Hadley makes a good sidekick. She comes up with an original plan of attack to help the hero. She attends college, but struggles with choosing a major. She is easily distracted when the fairy circus comes to town.

Shelby has a bit of a rebellious streak. She is argumentative and firm in her opinions. She enjoys a protest. She prefers a small trusted flock. She is relaxed and fun to be around. Her friends enjoy her sharp wit and unique take on the world. Shelby is considered an odd duck by the rest of the student body. She doesn't care. She does not give up easily once she decides on something. Her approach is mild, so others may not realize her intent until it is too late.

Shelby's path may not be the one her caregivers want her to follow, but she works diligently to achieve her dreams. As a hero, Shelby takes on a corrupt system or an oppressive clique. As an antagonist, if so motivated, she tramples on whoever stands in her way. Shelby forges her own path at college or in the workforce, unless vampires come to town.

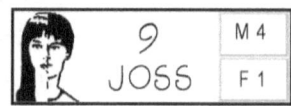

Joss has a couple of close friends and is attracted to people who share his interests or proclivity for physical risk-taking. He likes individual sports where he can challenge himself like high jump or gymnastics. He can't sit still. He is spontaneous and fun-loving, but don't cross him. He won't hesitate to tear an enemy apart verbally, perhaps physically. He takes risks out of boredom rather than malice, which lands him in the principal's office or juvenile detention. He makes an intrepid hero and an unpredictable antagonist. He attends college or enters the workforce on schedule, unless he jumps the next airship to Planet Zircon to battle giant weevils.

School is Kelly's stage. He is there to have fun and learn only what he must to get through it. He makes his caregivers and teachers crazy. He isn't interested in pleasing anyone and is highly manipulative. He either makes top grades to prove he can or flunks to gain attention. He prefers to do things his way on his schedule.

Kelly is action-oriented. Being restricted to a chair and required to listen while someone else talks is torture. He makes smart comments or is disruptive to momentarily shine the spotlight on himself and relieve the ennui. He participates in sports and after-school activities for the social aspect. He quits if he isn't the best. He hates losing. He may work a part-time job so he can purchase the material things he craves, or he scams other students out of their money. Having the best, the latest, and being the most popular are important. He easily leaves things, people, and activities behind when something better comes along. He makes a great wild-card antagonist. He would be an interesting choice as a hero. He attends college or enters the work force unless he is transported to Australia. He makes an impression there too.

11
GREER
M 3
F 1

Greer goes along with the status quo, more or less. He ignores the authorities and rules he does not agree with. He makes friends and leaves them. Those who like him, like him very much. Those who don't, he won't care. His intellectual zeal rubs some students and teachers the wrong way. His intelligence earns him grudging respect. He resents group assignments and avoids group activities. He comes across as self-absorbed.

As a hero, Greer is an intelligent, cool rebel. Other teens follow him because he is so independent, smart, and aloof. He could be an antagonist who destroys the status quo or gets back at a system he disagrees with. He attends college if possible or starts work, unless he has to save the world from a meteor strike.

12
TAYLOR
M 1
F 2

Taylor is well liked and tuned in. She is an active member of social clubs and participates in after-school activities. She is a natural class president. She is the embodiment of school spirit and shares her enthusiasm. She points out what is good in others. She likes the structure of school and supervises group projects. She is a model student when the subject is interesting to her. She seeks recognition from her teachers. Warm, personal teachers like her. Others consider her a brown nose. She takes criticism to heart and works harder to improve. She likes subjects relating to people. She loves independent learning opportunities. She is not a natural antagonist. It would take something truly dire to turn her to the dark side. She is not a natural hero, but would fight on the side of good against evil. She attends college or seeks employment, unless demons invade Tinker Town.

Cam establishes his own rules and style. He is a passionate, intellectual student. Teachers don't appreciate his challenging questions. He sets goals and achieves them to please himself. He has few friends. Trust and respect are key. If they let him down, he is hurt and withdraws inside his shell. He analytically studies the other students from a distance. Peer pressure has no impact on him. He follows his own course undisturbed and is startled if anyone expresses disapproval.

Cam's ability to self-regulate comes across as arrogance. He isn't aware of, or interested in, what other people spend their time doing as long as it doesn't impact him. He would not choose the hero role, but it could be thrust upon him. He could point out a problem no one else is willing to acknowledge. He isn't engaged enough to be the antagonist either, unless seriously violated. If he develops a nefarious plan of action, he is the type to see it through, with or without assistance. He attends college or enters the work force, unless he is tapped to help others understand invading androids.

Morgan is fun loving and easy going. He is clever at bringing people around to his point of view. His few, intense friendships burn out by the time he graduates high school.

He is active in whatever fascinates him: sports, clubs, or student government. He loves a good debate, but avoids interpersonal conflict.

Morgan chafes under the restrictions of rote learning. Tests were not made to measure his capacity. He respects individual teachers, not the institution. Morgan's sharp wit hurts people's feelings. He is not deliberately malicious unless attacked. He can be arrogant. He could be self-destructive if pushed. He is an unusual hero or antagonist. He may shake the peer tree just to see what falls out, for good or ill. He chooses work or college, unless called to war. His friends are hurt when he doesn't stay in touch.

Lee is on the go and takes part in diverse activities. She is team captain, student president, or head cheerleader. She is the social queen bee. She excels at whatever she attempts. She never follows. If someone proves more competent than her, she resents them. She has no problem setting and achieving goals for herself. She finds it hard to conform to someone else's plans.

Lee is self-regulating, which intimidates milder souls. She meddles and tries to control situations she shouldn't. She is fun loving and likes being the center of attention. She is highly competitive. She could be derailed out of boredom. If she took up self-destruction, she'd succeed. She is the stereotypical hero and antagonist. She attends college or enters the workforce, unless she has to wrangle werewolves.

The teen years are difficult for River. If she can't find anyone to trust, she becomes isolated. She prefers a small, intimate circle of like-minded friends. She clings to her best friend as a security blanket. An extroverted friend might encourage her to participate in school activities. She might enjoy it. She may claim to be psychic, but only to those close to her. She hates the limelight and performing in public. She is susceptible to depression and paranoia.

River strives to make good grades and worries if she doesn't. Her perfectionism may wear her out before she moves on to college or work. She tries to be perfect there too. She could be a quiet hero, particularly a paranormal one. She could use her powers of intuition to get back at a system or people who violated her values. If witches show up, she either joins the coven or fights them.

Ways to Warp Your Mannequins

Fences: Caregivers vary in how much freedom they allow. It should be enough to foster competence, but not so much that the teen forgets there are consequences for his actions. A teen tests the strength of the fences that separate him from harm. In a healthy environment, the fences hold. In an unhealthy one, they don't and the teen spins out of control. His native personality, level of familial dysfunction, and mental and physical health play key roles in how far he tests the boundaries and what happens when the fences break. The external compression of the society he lives in, the friends he chooses, and the educational arena he finds himself in play a bigger role than ever.

[ALT] Smash the Stereotype: The stereotype of the teen who is lazy, sleeps all day, takes horrible risks, acts out, is rude, aggressive, slovenly, and irresponsible, is just that: a stereotype. Different personality types handle their teen years in different ways. A teen raised in a nurturing home with well-matched caregivers reacts differently than one raised in a dysfunctional or abusive home. Abused teens are not stereotypical either. A teen raised in a high income household in Boston is not remarkably different from one raised in abject poverty in Mumbai as far as temperaments are concerned. Teens handle financial and emotional impoverishment or excess in many ways. Teens either embrace or reject the role society has assigned them.

[ALT] Emphasize the Exaggeration: Emotions are heightened in teens. Teens feel invincible and believe they'll live forever. They can't imagine being old. They can't grasp long-term consequences. They struggle with hormone rushes, bodily changes, body image distortion, gender identity and roles, social identity, parental pressure, the need to belong and be accepted by peers, but in very individualized ways. Push them to the extremes of their temperaments.

[ALT] Make Them Cranky: Teens need more sleep and nutrients just like toddlers do. Rapid changes occur in their bodies and their brains. They don't take care of themselves. They burn out and push too hard. They don't use good judgment and perform poorly when exhausted.

Rev the Rocket: Teens need varying degrees of structure. They need enough autonomy to become self-regulating, but not so much that they feel they can get away with anything. They need enough responsibility to prove they are capable without taking on adult responsibilities too early. Teens must leave the nest eventually. It frightens them more than it frightens their caregivers. It is easier to leave angry than happy. Teens must build up enough steam to make it out the door. This task is particularly difficult when they are happy at home or afraid to leave it. Leaving people you hate is easier than leaving people you love. Leaving people you feel overly responsible for is a wrenching choice.

The last few years of high school are a buildup for the teen's exit strategy. Caregivers often scratch their heads or become personally offended by the teen practicing to fly. A docile teen who has been perfectly behaved may suddenly flex his independence muscles and cause friction. The caregiver may not know how to handle it. Some mannequins find rebellion harder to stomach than others.

Apron Strings: The level of enmeshment or alienation with the caregiver, and how willing and able a caregiver is to push his chick from the nest, impact how smoothly the transition goes. Suffocating caregivers stifle the teen's attempts to become self-sufficient. Absent, alienated, or abusive caregivers force him to become self-sufficient too early. The teen may plot an explosive exit in revenge. A psychologically broken caregiver is very hard to leave. The caregiving teen nurses pain, fear, and resentment. He feels conflicted about leaving the wounded behind.

[ALT] Switch the Cauldron: The teenage years are affected by where the character lives: small town or big city, urban or rural, socially homogenous or ethnically diverse, religious or secular, crowded or isolated, rich or poor. His experiences are different based on the country, state, city, and neighborhood he is raised in. If he is transplanted at this critical time to a vastly different world, the transition heightens the experience in either negative or positive ways.

A teen is influenced by the household he is raised in: the morals, expectations, roles assigned to him, the behaviors and traits that have been reinforced, and those that were repressed. Changing the household changes the battleground and brings in new opponents and allies.

[ALT] New Role Models: The teen years are a time to question everything, some more vociferously than others. Adding a stepparent or new caregiver sends the teen for a loop. An oppositional stepfamily creates intense conflict. Oppositional caregivers and new siblings introduce a whole new set of influences and restrictions or freedoms. A temperamentally compatible stepfamily could give him the positive reinforcement he dreamed of.

[ALT] Crack the Egg: A teen is affected by his level of physical health, intellectual and emotional intelligence, and talents. Changes in those areas throw a wrench in his plans. Adolescence is a time when psychological pathologies present themselves in addition to body image and identity issues. Teens suffer from depression, eating disorders, learning disabilities, attention deficit, bullying at home and at school, abuse at home or at school, and thoughts of suicide. Teens wrestle with exposure to violence, sex, drugs, alcohol, and social taboos. These challenges affect their young adult and adult lives. Adding these ingredients to the mix sets the stage for your antagonist to strike back or your hero to fight for change.

Rock His World: Teens floating down the lazy river of complacence are capsized when catastrophic events occur or the world turns to war. A teen growing up in Hitler-controlled Germany faced different challenges than one living in war-torn Afghanistan. Teens living in quiet little towns are impacted by tragic events in the wider world. Their heightened emotions make burgeoning political and social consciousness, activism, and patriotism more intense. They rebel and protest. They enter the military early or are frustrated by not being able to. They are enraged by societal restrictions and are eager to break down the walls. They are pacifists or warmongers. If a foreign student joins their school, it can turn their understanding upside down. To expand their worldview, transplant them to a tumultuous part of the globe or bring the world to their front doorstep.

Let Them Fail: Teens learn from their mistakes. Even the best teens make fatal or destructive choices. Families and societies are the safety nets. Give them a safe place to fall or have the safety net unravel.

You can bend or twist your teen mannequins by upbringing, society, or circumstance to intensify age-related issues. Make them count.

Diana Hurwitz

SELF-ESTEEM

Self-esteem is another way to mangle your mannequins that deserves extra attention. A teen needs to feel competent, self-confident, and independent. He needs to know he has what it takes to face the next phase of his existence with a fully-equipped tool kit. He looks to everyone around him for feedback on whether he can. At this phase, the teen relies less on his family and more on his peers, teachers, coaches, and total strangers.

How do outsiders influence your mannequins? A mannequin isn't built in a day. His psyche is made up of layers. The innermost layer is early childhood, the second adolescence, the third young adulthood, the fourth adulthood, the fifth middle age, and the sixth old age. Holes in the inner layers can be healed by the outer layers or made larger. It is important to understand how your adult characters are layered. A hero's journey can heal the holes life created in his inner layers. An antagonist's gaping wound may never be healed. An interfering friend or foe could go either way.

Inferiority Complex: When a teen isn't allowed to master things, he becomes weak and helpless and feels inferior. Any blow to his fledgling self-worth at this stage creates a trigger in the primitive brain that can be pulled by anyone at any point in the future. The hypercritical caregiver, teacher, or coach tells him he is worthless. He doesn't feel as smart, talented, popular, or wealthy as his peers. Proving his worth is a hero's journey. A teen whose wounds never have a chance to heal creates a believable, perhaps sympathetic, antagonist.

[ALT] Question Competence: If the teen grows up with an over-controlling caregiver, he won't gain competence. He needs to know other people have confidence in him. He needs to know he can fly on his own and is so eager to try. Caregivers arrest the teen's development when they withhold that kind of positive reinforcement. Competence triggers trip him up in every facet of his life as he enters adulthood. The teen may not be as good with tests, sports, and managing his time or money as his peers or caregivers. A caregiver, teacher, relative, or coach can question or test his competence. The trigger is very sensitive if competence is the teen's currency. The teen lacking confidence irrationally defers to others. He has low ambition and a pessimistic outlook. Proving his competence is an underdog victory tale.

[ALT] Chips: Chips appear in your character's self-image when people discount what the teen values about himself, belittle his efforts, show their impatience or disgust, or attack the teen when he doesn't share their values. Each teen has his own currency. The feedback he received may not be the feedback he desired. A teen with a dented self-image is jealous and resentful of friends or school mates when they succeed. Later in life, he is resentful of spouses, siblings, bosses, and coworkers. He becomes a bully or indulges in self-destructive behaviors. If a free-flowing child is repressed by a rigid system, his self-image suffers. If a child that needs rigid boundaries is left to float free, his self-image suffers.

[ALT] Miserable Company: Miserable characters go to great lengths to drag others down with them. A self-destructive teen makes a dangerous friend or foe. Oppositional caregivers pull his triggers. Friends pull his triggers. When caring people try to make him feel better, he twists what is said to fit his negative self-image. He can't feel the love other people lavish on him.

A self-destructive character is a poor protagonist in most genres. A literary story could follow the teen's arc from low self-esteem to high self-esteem. Recovery makes for an inspiring coming of age story. A self-destructive character makes a realistic foe, friend, and antagonist. Watching a friend or loved one self-destruct creates an agonizing personal dilemma for a protagonist trying to solve an overall story problem.

Doldrums: Everyone has down days. When a character is biologically (not momentarily or situationally) depressed, he always feels low. Depression keeps him from succeeding in relationships and in life. A depressed teen could be the protagonist in a literary story where he overcomes the problem. Depressed characters should only be used as complicating friends and foes in the other genres. Biochemically depressed characters don't make effective antagonists or heroes, particularly in Thriller and Suspense tales. They can't summon the requisite energy to get dressed much less become lethal. An enraged antagonist? Yes! Mopey? No! Pathetic characters make poor protagonists.

Goalposts: A teen needs to engage in activities that give him a sense of accomplishment and contribution. He might crave competence, status, recognition, fame, or adoration and go to any length to get them. He might obtain it in a healthy way by becoming a top athlete or a violin virtuoso.

He might behave outrageously to gain attention. A teen that can't stand being in the limelight excels in his quiet, competent way and never receives recognition for it. The ones who make the biggest splash, negative or positive, get noticed. Middle of the road teens do great things and have immense talents. They simply aren't jumping up and down shouting "look at me, look at me." They should be heroes once in a while too.

[ALT] **Arrogant and Entitled:** The flip side of low self-esteem is having an exaggerated view of oneself. This happens when caregivers inflate a teen's estimation of his competence. Reality television is jam-packed with these characters. False confidence isn't based on actual talent or ability and is easily deflated. The teen leaves home and realizes he isn't as talented or wonderful as he was led to believe. It is a crushing blow. The realization could make him depressed and self-destructive. If he continues to hold on to the false persona, he ignores all comments to the contrary. He might go to great, potentially lethal, lengths to prove himself to tragic or comic effect.

A character who thinks he is better at something than he truly is attempts to solve problems in a way that creates bigger problems. A character whose pride won't let him admit that something is out of his range can interfere at scene or overall story level. A hero can discard a false persona and embrace his true self. An antagonist can cling to his false persona and become more lethal.

[ALT] **Submersible:** A teen raised by caregivers with emotional problems takes on adult responsibilities too early: for his siblings, the household, and the irresponsible caregivers.

Keeping busy diverts him from the pain and chaos he has no control over. The divided demands of school and home wear him out physically and emotionally. He either acts out as a cry for help or forgets to take care of himself and silently self-destructs. He doesn't have time for hobbies or friends. He is easily led astray. He attempts to heal situations that are better left alone, control situations or people he can't, or fix people who can only fix themselves. This pattern repeats itself in his adult life.

⌨ Overachievers: There is a difference between characters who work all the time to afford fun, because it is fun, or because they are easily bored, and those who stay busy to hide from something they don't want to face. A teen who struggles to say "no" is spread so thin he can't do anything well. He makes careless mistakes. He volunteers his time or agrees to help friends with things that are beyond his capacity. He means well, but. He signs up for too many projects and lets some slide. He makes commitments to friends and can't follow through. Some of your mannequins naturally struggle with follow-through and commitment. Overachievers make interfering friends and foes. As a protagonist, he can show growth by learning balance. He can serve as a well-meaning antagonist.

⌨ Meddlers: A character can be obsessive-compulsive or overly detailed. He feels that no one can do as good a job as he can. He can't delegate. He controls people and information. He is the teen in charge of the prom committee or club fundraiser. He is the PTA member or armchair quarterback who interferes or takes over. He is awful to work with on a group project. He creates crises only he can solve so he ends up looking good. He overrides and oversees everything. He is suffocating and irritating to all involved.

All of these warping methods apply to teens, their caregivers, teachers, coaches, or other adults in your story world. Adults can interfere in the teen's life for the best of reasons or worst of reasons. It can all go tragically wrong.

YOUNG ADULTHOOD

A young adult who wanders the wider world is exposed to influences that are dramatically different from what he has known. Although high school is the time of life explored in most Young Adult fiction, the college years offer more fertile ground for conflict and transformation. A new genre of fiction is targeting the "new adults."

For most North American children, at the end of high school comes the nudge to leave the nest. The young adult must financially support himself. This leads to additional education in the form of technical school, local community college, the move to a larger college and dorm life, joining the military, or entering the work force. His transition is influenced by his physical health, mental health, how he was raised, and whether he can continue to live at home. Dating takes on new meaning. Is this my forever match? Do I want one? Do I have to? What am I looking for? What will I tolerate?

The dating pool in Tinker Town limits him to those he grew up with. Relocating for college, work, or the military broadens his options. Depending on the world he lives in, he experiments with relationships. He falls for fusers and isolators. He falls for partners he is not temperamentally compatible with. His heart is broken at least once. Each mannequin has a particular approach to sex and dating that makes the exploration phase fraught with danger.

A young adult may pass through this second forge unchanged. If he leaves Tinker Town for a while, he can return the same person that left, perhaps with a new hairdo and a few added skills. If nothing major comes along to send the sixteen characters for a loop, they muddle through young adulthood much like they did at home and in high school.

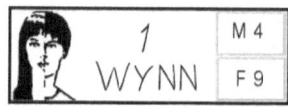

Wynn has no trouble setting short-term and long-term goals. She saves money and plans trips or activities well in advance. She prefers to know her agenda for the day. She anticipates problems. Her backpack carries a change of clothing, an extra pad of paper, a mirror, safety pins, perhaps a stapler. She is useful that way and is happy to assist. She attacks college or work with the same methods that resulted in success in high school. She makes a few friends and settles in a comfortable groove with a partner. Wynn is looking for her soul mate and hopes to find him on the first try. Sex is an emotional bond. She won't appreciate feeling used. She needs to hear "I love you," but doesn't say it.

If Wynn does not attend college, her life easily transitions from school to work or parenthood. If she joins the military, she appreciates the structure and is ever vigilant. She seeks work that is traditional, structured, and allows her to help other people achieve their goals. Depending on her native talents and level of interest, she seeks work that takes advantage of her organizational skills and preparedness. She is easily lured by the exotic. She might travel to other countries and help people there too. They may not appreciate it. She may become their hero.

Francis begins training for a career early. He has no respect for those who can't or won't finish what they start. He defers a permanent relationship until his education is complete or his career secure. He seeks security and an opportunity to prove his worth to an employer or professors. He learns the basics before risking something beyond his skill level. He believes slow and steady wins the race. He may be drawn to an undergraduate degree that leads directly to employment or an apprenticeship. He finds common ground with similar types who have similar goals. He prefers a steady partner, but won't propose yet. Sex is a physical need. He's not a cards and flowers guy. Some partners are offended by his lack of romance.

If Francis joins the military, he finds the bureaucracy frustrating, particularly if he can't respect his superiors. He does his time then gets out. He seeks careers where his attention to detail and desire to work behind the scenes are appreciated. He would not relocate as a first choice, but would if work required it. He resists the lure of the exotic because he thrives on things being the same. It would turn his ordered world upside down. Watching him struggle with it would be fun.

Nevada follows a traditional path. He goes to college if given the opportunity. He plays sports and is a good student. He dates as expected, but won't commit long-term. He graduates on time, probably with honors. He is deemed "Most Likely to Succeed." He tackles the employment field he selects with focus and is a solid employee. He proves trustworthy and is rewarded with raises and promotions. He wants a steady partner. He is a hearts and flowers kind of guy. Sex means he cares.

If Nevada joins the military, he takes it seriously and becomes a reliable soldier. He might make it a career. He seeks work where he can apply relationship-building skills. He would relocate only if work demanded it. He is very traditional and worried about appearances, so the lure of the exotic has less power. If it struck, he would embrace it and make it work.

Arden sets personal and professional goals and diligently works to achieve them. He furthers his education if possible. He belongs to service clubs like Kiwanis or the Masonic Lodge. He has no confusion about which career to choose or which partner to date, even if it turns out to be the wrong choice. A relationship that doesn't work or a job that doesn't fit is a learning experience. He moves on without a backward glance. He won't change his major once he has decided on it. He wants a steady partner. Sex leads to love, but he isn't a romantic guy.

If Arden joins the military, he is attracted to the service aspect of it. He steadily rises in the ranks. He is a firm enforcer. He is also highly critical of aspects that don't work. He seeks careers that allow his natural leadership abilities to flourish. He could be drawn off course by the lure of the exotic. Having his eyes opened to the wider world might inspire him to apply his diligence to international service opportunities.

Blair wants to explore the full menu of life. She wants to travel, to be a painter in Paris, or a dancer in Spain. She won't do any of those things unless someone forces her to stick with it. Her best friend or partner of the moment greatly influences her endeavors. She wants work to be fun and artistic. She fantasizes about "what if." She feels trapped by the restrictions of working life. She is easily bored and quits college with no thought to the consequences. She flits from job to job, perhaps place to place, often leaving her newly-acquired friends stunned by her departure. Blair wants a steady partner. She struggles to settle on just one. Sex is a sacred joining of souls. Some partners are turned off by that. She won't say "I love you," but needs to hear it.

Blair would never voluntarily join the military because she couldn't quit and it is hard work. It would either drain her soul dry or fulfill her need to flit. She seeks careers that allow her to work with and help others. She is easily led by the lure of the exotic. She tries everything once. She hops a plane in a heartbeat. She isn't entirely content anywhere.

Dallas shouldn't commit to anything until she is thirty. She has trouble choosing a major if she opts for college. She may be too eager to start living to suffer the restrictions of a four-year commitment. If she settles down early, she regrets it and ponders the path not taken. Dallas wants a steady partner. She struggles to limit herself to one. Sex means love. She needs to hear "I love you" and isn't afraid to say it. She lives with one foot mentally out the door under the best circumstances. She chooses new and novel ways to spend her time. She tries things on then discards them: an outfit, a job, or friends.

If compelled to join the military, Dallas chafes under the restraints. She is happiest hopping from post to post. She gives her superiors headaches with her inability to stay on task. She finds teamwork unbearable, but respects authority. She seeks jobs that are creative, spontaneous, and fun. She is an idea person and wilts if no one is interested in her creative solutions and plans. She embraces travel and becomes a globe trotter. She is easily led by the lure of the exotic.

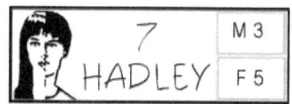

Hadley applies herself to college, but not too seriously. The experience is more social than scholarly. She studies abroad every semester if possible. She is more interested in the clubs, group projects, and parties than the classes. She dates extensively, not exclusively. Sex is recreation. She says, "I love you," but it doesn't mean forever. Her scholarly efforts are good enough, never brilliant. Teachers and students like her.

If Hadley joins the military, she outwardly complies. If she doesn't agree with the rules, she subverts them. Her occasional impulsive move might place her in trouble. She seeks careers that take advantage of her optimism and enthusiasm for motivating others. She loves travel and adventure. She eagerly follows a lover or a friend to distant climes.

Shelby knows what she wants, but it proves elusive. She switches majors, jobs, and relationships until they meet her expectations. She is frustrated with those who dwell on the trivial or oppose her lofty goals. She wants a partner, but is never satisfied with one. Sex is love. She wants to be swept off her feet with romantic gestures. She says "I love you," but it doesn't mean forever. She seeks more than a paycheck and is dissatisfied if the job does not fit her value system. She never feels she has achieved enough and undervalues her contributions.

Shelby would not choose the military, but complies if ordered. She is drawn to the rhetoric of being the best you can be. She falls in line with the regimented schedule. She is easily disillusioned if it proves to be less than perfect. She seeks careers that are creative and allow her to offer support behind the scenes. Her need to try things on makes her a prime candidate for the lure of the exotic. She happily skips across the globe to find the perfect life.

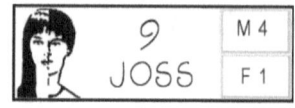

Joss follows the path of least resistance when it comes to a career. He isn't a planner because things rarely happen according to plan. He relaxes while everyone else stresses. He is pragmatic and plays the hand he is dealt. He dates and has a good time. Sex is recreation and he isn't a romantic guy. His partner waits in vain to hear "I love you." He takes advantage of opportunities that arise. He goes to college or applies himself to a trade. He is generally well liked.

If Joss joins the military, he hates the infringement on his personal space and freedom of movement. He enjoys pushing himself to his physical limits. He is the first volunteer to jump out of a plane. He seeks careers that require him to remain calm under pressure and offer instant response. He wouldn't relocate for fun, but work could inspire him to. He would embrace the lure of the exotic because he goes wherever the prevailing tide dictates.

Kelly falls into a career. He favors independence and leaves home as soon as possible. If home isn't restrictive, he might stay there a while so he can spend his money on fun things other than rent. Partners come and go. He is the bad boy people regret hooking up with long term. Sex is recreation and he isn't interested in permanence. His partner won't hear "I love you." Whatever options he explores are exploited to his full advantage. If he has mechanical skills, he may enter a trade rather than attend college. The social aspect of college is a lure. He may follow his friends there.

If Kelly's friends join the military, he follows them there too. He hates the restrictions and possibly ends up in trouble if not AWOL. His innate showmanship gains him laughs from the men, but not from those in charge. He seeks careers where he is called upon to react and solve immediate problems or to use his powers of persuasion. He happily travels anywhere and is highly momentarily distracted by the lure of the exotic. If you give Kelly a cookie, he wants another cookie: first a chocolate chip then a snickerdoodle then peanut butter. He won't settle until he has had them all.

Greer either charts a course and quietly sails toward it or continues to resist and rebel against the status quo. He may focus in depth on a college major or move from one interest to another without explanation. When he feels he has a good understanding or mastery of a task, he looks for another challenge. He doesn't want to be tied down, but would honor a commitment. Sex is physical and he isn't a roses and loving words guy. When he grows bored with a relationship, he moves on.

Greer focuses on his quest of the moment. He seeks careers that make use of his analytical talents and allow him to independently use his imagination and critical thinking. He would not choose the military, but would be highly valued by his superiors. He would hate the confinement and he isn't a team player. He might enjoy moving around. He wilts if forced into a routine job. He points out discrepancies and redundancies. He is intrigued by the lure of the exotic.

Taylor goes to college if possible. If not, she enters the workforce or takes up domestication. She dates as a way to find her ideal spouse. If she goes to college, she chooses a liberal arts degree to explore the humanities. She excels at speech club and joins a sorority. She sets personal and professional goals and follows through. She wants a family someday. Sex means love and she needs to hear and say "I love you."

Taylor is idealistic and wants to make the world a better place. She may be drawn to activism and is easily lured by the exotic. She would not choose the military. If compelled, she ends up in a clerical, medical, or counseling capacity. She seeks careers where she helps others achieve their potential with her quiet leadership. She has no trouble packing a bag and settling in a place where her work makes a difference.

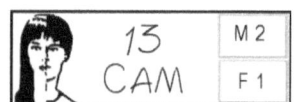

Cam goes to college if possible. He works hard and excels at his studies. He is a loner by nature and makes a few, trusted friends. He is not eager to join the social swing. He may or may not date much. A permanent relationship is not a high priority. Sex is a fascinating experiment. He can say "I love you" if the other person needs it. He is viewed as the studious nerd. He isn't interested in popularity or voting. He doesn't recognize status and isn't interested in being categorized by a clique. If he does not go to college, he continues to educate himself.

Cam chooses the military if it is the only way to get an education. Having to live with a bunch of other people and working with teams instead of solitary tasks frustrates him. He has little respect for authority. He considers rules and regulations illogical and arbitrary. He gets out as soon as possible. He seeks careers that take advantage of his talent for grasping difficult and complex concepts and building strategies. Because he is creative, he is susceptible to the lure of exotic. He isn't risk-taking by nature, but would relocate to do the work he is drawn to. He loves travel because it increases his knowledge of the world he lives in. He wants someone he trusts to go with him.

Morgan goes to college if possible. He works out a flexible schedule and may switch majors more than once. He chooses a job with flexible and innovative tasks. He isn't afraid to take the road less traveled. He hates having his options limited. He dates and feels a little ambivalent about it. He hates being trapped in a permanent relationship. Sex is physical. His partner won't hear "I love you" or receive cards and flowers.

Morgan is easily lured by the exotic. He considers the military an option. He respects authority and goes along with what he is told to do. Trouble sets in if he loses respect for the authority. He focuses on his education and makes the best of a difficult situation until his time is up. He seeks careers that allow him to work independently and express his creativity and insight. He loves the novelty of travel and would not be afraid to relocate on his own.

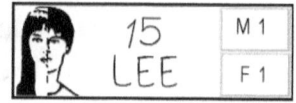

Lee goes to college if she can. She is a natural leader there too. She becomes head of the sorority, the dorm, or teaches for her professors. She has no trouble telling everyone exactly what their major should be or what kind of job they should take. Professors either appreciate her spunk or are highly annoyed by her arrogance. She dates, but does not take it seriously. She may overpower her partner by micromanaging his or her life. Sex is recreation. She isn't romantic, but isn't opposed to material gifts. She may have a part-time job to earn money for the material trappings of success. She ends up managing the business.

Lee fares well in the military, as long as she has a position of authority. She chafes at a lesser position because status is important. She tells the military exactly what it is doing wrong. The higher ups might listen. She seeks careers that utilize her leadership and organizational skills. She has no trouble relocating and finds the lure of the exotic tantalizing. She makes her presence felt wherever she goes.

River attends college if she can. She is an intellectual interested in complex theories. Professors recognize her potential and encourage her. She applies herself diligently to her school work and selects a career early. She won't belong to a sorority or clubs. She makes a few friends and does not seek other social outlets. She may be dragged along by her friends to social functions. She hides behind the potted plants. She dates, but finds it a little scary and fraught with potential rejection. Sex is a deep communion of souls. She seeks a permanent relationship. Her desire for perfection frightens dates away. She needs the words and the flowers. She is vaguely dissatisfied with every facet of life.

River is intrigued by the lure of the exotic and seeks to understand the wisdom of other cultures. She does not fare well in the military. The pace and enforced closeness to others are exhausting. She finds a way to get out as quickly as possible. She seeks careers that allow her idealism and vision to flourish. She isn't the intrepid globe-hopping type. She may relocate to a place that appeals to her spiritual nature, preferably with one of her trusted circle.

Ways to Warp
Your Mannequins

Young adulthood is a turbulent time, no matter which path the character takes. Problems with enmeshment, isolation, social integration or lack thereof, competency, and independence all play out in a new arena and determine whether he succeeds or fails.

This period of breaking free and setting out on his own is rife with life-altering conflict. The mistakes he made during his teenage years in terms of drugs, pregnancy, crime, studies, etc. have an impact on his transition to young adulthood. A young adult who has a successful life despite childhood, teen, or family challenges makes for an inspiring maturation story.

[ALT] Lift Off: The character who stays at home or near home and attends a technical school or local college does not have the same experience as the character who leaves home. A young adult that remains in his hometown, even if it is a suburb of New York City, has a different experience from one that enters the military, attends college in another city, or relocates for a job.

If trapped in Tinker Town, he finds it harder to let his freak flag fly. If he escapes Tinker Town, he is free to reinvent himself. He can choose from all those identities he tried on during high school, or he comes up with an entirely new one. By leaving the restrictions of his hometown and the expectations of his caregivers behind, he is free to express himself however he chooses. He could spiral out of control or become the person he was meant to be.

[ALT] Cages: The young adult who stays at home is subjected to the same prejudices, role assignments, friends, foes, and dating pool as before. You complicate his life by restricting his education opportunities, limiting work availability, and making him work with people he hates. You impose social restrictions that choke him. If he likes groups, make him work alone. If he likes working alone, force him to work in a group. If he likes helping and being useful, put him in situations where he feels useless. If he likes organization and predictability, put him in chaotic, fast-paced jobs. If he likes to be free to explore, trap him in situations where he can't. If he is the type to speak out, silence him. If he is reserved and quiet, force him to speak out. Put him with people he'd rather not room with or work with. Living with roommates in college, or to make ends meet while beginning his career, is a great way to thrust oppositional characters together.

⌨ Paradigms: When he leaves home, he discovers a world filled with people offering different viewpoints, histories, political opinions, religions, and social customs. He may have already been exposed to the wider world through reading, travel, entertainment, and the internet. He might have tried on exotic personas. It depends on the homogeneity of his upbringing. A young adult who has traveled the world is already familiar with the lure of the exotic and would have introduced his friends to it on his return. A foreign student moving to a small American town can have the same effect.

A character trapped in Tinker Town can still have his horizons expanded, unless the town doesn't have a library, cable television, or Wi-Fi. The internet has given the young adult access to the world in a way no other generation imagined. He meets foreigners and those with alternative lifestyles and points of view. It can be enlightening, confusing, or frightening. Caregivers and teachers have very little control over what he is exposed to.

The interesting dynamic is that even though he has the whole world to choose from, he gravitates toward people who think and believe the way he does. He embraces commonality. He is still true to his temperament. He "friends" people that support his outlook and methods. He mocks people who don't agree with him.

⌨ Desire Versus Opportunity: Whether a young adult stays or goes is dependent on several variables: the innate desire to keep things the same or change them, his desire to engage or withdraw from the wider world, financial status, health status, the opportunities open to him, his family history of movement from one place to another, his entrenchment in the community, and whether his world is at peace or at war. He chooses based on a combination of desire versus opportunity. One can work against the other. He may desire to leave and have no opportunity to. He may wish to stay, but circumstances force him to leave. His religion may send him abroad on a missionary trip. His college may allow him to study abroad. His caregivers may send him on a tour of Europe before he attends college.

[ALT] **Broad Horizons:** If the young adult lives in another country, the opportunities and expectations are different than those in small town or big city America. He faces different obstacles in China, Africa, and France. Culture shock either enhances his temperament or crushes it. Francis is still Francis in Boise, Belarus, or Berlin. He may have a different worldview, religion, employment, and social opportunities, but temperaments are universal. An introvert is motivated to avoid crowds whether he works in Sydney or San Francisco. He has the same problems with extroverts in the work place and in social settings. His childhood wounds play out no matter where you plop him.

The desire to explore the wider world takes many forms. He could desire to move from the country to the suburbs, the suburbs to the city, or from a small city to a large one. It could mean hitching the wagon and heading out west to settle on the prairie or to California to pan for gold. It could mean missionary work in Africa or Special Ops maneuvers in Asia. The young adult could switch neighborhoods in New York or backpack across Europe with a friend. He may go to school in France, fall in love with Paris, and decide to make it his permanent home. He might adopt the fashions and accent and marry a Parisian.

[ALT] **Stir the Cauldron:** Consider the cauldron that best suits your character and your story world. What is the thematic statement you want to make about this time of life? How did the choices, or lack thereof, affect your character's trajectory? If you write teen fiction, take a hard look at the demographics, friends, foes, and antagonists you choose. What happens if you make them vastly different from the protagonist rather than from the same town?

If the young adult leaves the family nest, he is introduced to a range of theologies and ideologies. He may study history, sociology, and psychology. These subjects broaden his understanding of the world and those living in it. He may meet people from other cities, states, and countries for the first time. He learns about new traditions, politics, and philosophies. The experience profoundly affects the rest of his life. College is a time when life-long friendships are forged and budding romantic relationships bloom away from the influence of family. The lure of an exotic romantic partner can shake the family tree all the way to its roots.

[ALT] **Feed the Rebellion:** Discovering new things about the world and the lure of the exotic provide intriguing ways to complicate your character's life, especially if he returns home for visits with a new persona. The young adult is more drawn to exploration, fantasy, affectation, and posturing than at any other age. He still has some of the heightened emotions of his teen years. He is idealistic, optimistic, angry, and eager to change what he perceives as wrong in the world.

Until the cause-and-effect chip kicks in around age twenty-five, he continues to make mistakes and decisions that affect the rest of his life. The small flicker of rebellion that made him challenge his caregiver's thinking, choices, politics, and religion during adolescence may flare into a firestorm. He could reject everything he was taught. He may decide his knowledge of the wider world counters what his parents believe.

[ALT] **Home Visits**: New friends and professors have a profound effect on the young adult's thinking. His caregivers and friends back home might not enjoy the "good news." Temperament clashes affect how much this shift alarms the natives. The traditional caregiver won't take it as well as the unconventional or uninvolved caregiver. There are many ways to illustrate the lure of the exotic. He may switch to Jasmine tea instead of coffee in the morning. He can take a baby step or a giant leap toward "different" and "other" belief systems. He could become a socialist or decide his caregivers are horribly provincial. His new ideology creates ripples. If his ideology irritates or threatens the caregiver, he can respond by cutting off your character's financial assistance.

[ALT] **Broken Hearts**: A young adult tests the romantic waters. He learns what works for him and what doesn't. Few, if any, understand temperament differences. He is attracted to partners he ends up hating. They betray one another. The desire for connection versus space, emotional discourse versus logical debate, a tidy house or a messy one, and sex without ties versus permanent bonds affect how well the mannequin plays the dating game. He learns a lot about himself and other people through this process. Getting burned at this stage creates baggage he carries with him into future relationships.

[ALT] Clipped Wings: Some characters never fully grow up or become independent. A character can gain independence then life changes come along to undermine it. He may have to move back in with his caregivers. His caregivers may become aged, ill, or bankrupt and need him to return home. Siblings and friends may have to live together to make ends meet. The young adult can have a child and end up living at home and new tensions arise. The grandchild may become the caregiver's responsibility due to abandonment, war, drug addiction, incarceration, death, or while the young adult regains his financial footing. This leads to new temperament clashes or meshes. Perhaps the grandchild is the child the caregiver always wanted.

Life may not take the path your mannequin's caregivers envisioned for him, or the dreams he had for himself. Children, romantic partnerships, becoming caregivers for others, financial disasters, relocations, health scares, mistakes, and bad decisions create obstacles that alter his steady trajectory and set up conflict for the next phase of life.

Diana Hurwitz

ADULTHOOD

The period of young adulthood shifts to true adulthood. The mannequin becomes the authority he once rebelled against. He must work, build a nest, decide whether to commit, and make reproductive choices. It is time to decide what he wants want to be now that he is grown up. Some struggle with that more than others.

In the normal course of events, if the sixteen characters are on course with no major disturbances, their lifestyle accommodates their temperament. The adult is drawn to certain jobs and may not be able to find them. If trapped in an oppositional career, he finds other ways to act out or satisfy himself. If he remains in Tinker Town, population one-hundred, his options for friends, lovers, and professional roles are severely restricted. Some temperaments take the reins easily. Others flounder miserably.

Wynn settles for whatever comes her way: the first job, first romantic partner, and first apartment. She likes having things decided and isn't looking for new thrills or opportunities. She makes the best of a bad situation whether it is a difficult boss or a difficult spouse. She is loyal to her employer. Hard work is its own reward. She would, of course, like to be appreciated, not thrust into the spotlight. She carries a grudge if her efforts aren't appreciated. Office traditions and the conservation of resources are highly valued. She keeps doing things the way they have been done. She eagerly embraces the tasks she understands. She does whatever she is told without wondering if there is a better way or a better widget. She writes the handbook and notices deviations from it. She notices if someone takes home a stapler. She won't say anything, unless she is in charge of someone's performance review, but she resents it.

Wynn prefers an unchanging workplace. She excels in caring professions and makes an excellent crony. She needs to make other people happy. She may personalize her relationship with her boss to the point of inappropriateness. She sees to his laundry, arranges things in his home, or babysits his children. She isn't good with new bosses. Titles and status impress and intimidate her. She hates being in charge of other people and can't delegate.

Wynn maintains a well-kept, modest appearance. She is offended when people act above or below their station. Everyone should know his place and behave appropriately. She'd make a terrific Victorian housekeeper or butler. She puts work before play and expects everyone else to follow suit. She does not tip the boat. Violations of her standards irritate her, but she squelches them. If pushed to revenge, it is stealthy and passive. She happily shreds papers and hides evidence for the antagonist or protagonist to protect him. If he offends her, she testifies against him and has the correct documentation to do so.

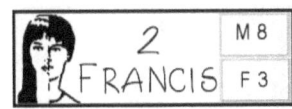

Francis attempts to do the right thing in all things. He feels responsible for upholding traditions and community standards. He takes on additional responsibilities at work. He stays with a job he isn't thrilled with to maintain financial stability. He isn't looking for emotional gratification. He saves for retirement. He fears being dependent on other people and works hard to avoid that fate. He is decisive and steadily navigates the company's shark infested waters with no flourishes. He expects coworkers to pull their weight and has no trouble cracking the whip. He expects his underlings to stay on task and work as a team. His word is his bond and his men are loyal, or they hate him and mutiny. If he isn't in charge, he often goes unnoticed. He could easily become a mob enforcer or police informant. He'd make a great narcotics agent or forensic auditor.

Francis is a good accountant because he won't waste his cash or gamble with anyone else's. He makes a good cop, guard, ranger, or soldier because he is enamored with rules. Some consider him an iceman. He is highly sensitive to criticism and hides his anger until he can't anymore. He hates ostentation and likes uniforms. They are practical and indicative of status. He likes shiny badges. He'll wear a business suit on casual Friday. He doesn't care about frills or fads. He doesn't experiment with food or wine. He enjoys belonging to a men's club, a Moose lodge, or a country club. The other members find him boring or worry that he is a spy.

Nevada takes his responsibilities seriously. He hates working alone. He isn't interested in theories, research, or impersonal debate. He is a nurturing presence at work and in civic organizations. He is an affable host to clients and investors. He loves to head conferences and fundraising dinners. He loves good food, good wine, and sparkling repartee. He kneels before the powerful. He covets status. He is helpful and hardworking and often put in charge. Others look up to him and wish him well. He is the ultimate networker. He has an extensive contact list for everything. He is conscientious, concerned with appearances, and owns a tuxedo. He listens to other people's opinions. He can sell anything because he sells himself not the product. Nevada calls a client by his first name and remembers the names of his kids. He knows what type of wine he prefers and where to get the best hookers. He makes clients feel like he is there for them. He is best at face-to-face interaction. He makes a great minister, teacher, or coach.

Nevada notices when the natives are restless and talks them down before it becomes a riot. He does not rock the rescue dinghy, unless something dire occurs. He is stung when those who matter don't appreciate his services. If he turns against his superiors, he can induce mutiny. He cross-pollinates with his negativity and destroys morale with predictions of doom. He jumps on the phone or internet and spreads malicious rumors. He makes a terrific CEO or swindler. He wants to be a mover and shaker, particularly if he isn't. That won't stop him from pretending or attempting to make it so.

Arden takes his responsibilities seriously. He is punctual and follows through. He is socially adept and well thought of. He is equally effective at organizing personnel or a fundraiser. He makes rules and enforces them. He wants the job done and he wants it done right. He has no patience with those who lack attention to detail. He won't listen to excuses for why the job didn't get done.

Arden considers someone an authority based on his experience and knowledge, not his title and position. He is highly judgmental. His coworkers make fun of him behind his back, particularly the irresponsible ones and creative types. He is abrupt, but isn't generally malicious. He is focused on the widgets and the production line, not how someone came up with the widget, or what he intends to do with it. He'd make a great bomb builder or nuclear reactor foreman.

Arden is willing to sacrifice his time or his life when required. He balances his work life with his civic duty. He'd be a natural cop, guard, or soldier since those roles incorporate both. He is oblivious to the emotional cues of the people around him. He enjoys the office parties, retirement dinners, and rah-rah sessions. He sees himself as a great guy. He'd be confused by how many people he annoys. He is what he appears and nothing more. It takes a truly tumultuous inciting event to disrupt his daily existence and turn him to the dark side. He would be an effective antagonist if he turned against the people, company, or country he worked for. He'd know just how to make the nuclear reactor melt down or the most disastrous target for the chemical weapon.

Blair works behind the scenes, pursuing her quirky agenda. She enjoys helping others meet their goals. She isn't interested in being in charge. She is persuasive if she believes something is in another's best interest. Her motto is "live and let live." She is irritated by people who behave badly and stands firmly against them to support the victim. She has an artistic temperament, even if she doesn't work in the arts as a dancer, painter, or contortionist. Her work largely goes unnoticed unless, by some miracle of You Tube, she becomes famous.

Blair is hedonistic and impulsive. She never plans and likes flying by the ribbon hung from the ceiling. The long hours she spends strumming her guitar are fun. Everything else she has to do is boring. Her art feeds her soul. She doesn't care if it pays the rent or pleases anyone else. When injured, exhausted, or dying, she finds a way to make a vase.

Blair's senses are set on high all the time. She learns by experimenting and isn't interested in reading about her passions. She hates arguing and walks away from an unpleasant conversation. She rarely finishes school or seeks an advanced degree. Regimented work and lectures are boring. Corporate drudgery isn't her thing. She is happy communing with nature or photographing lions in Africa. She is well liked because she is optimistic and happy. No one ever truly knows her. It's hard to paint her as an evil antagonist. If she decided the world needed to be destroyed, she'd find an artistic way to do it. She may work in a restrictive role until middle age and indulge in her true loves as hobbies. She will be very dissatisfied.

Dallas changes careers at least once and is versatile enough to do it. She keeps her friendships fluid and is the ultimate social butterfly. She is fun to be with. Life is a dramatic play and everyone should play. She stands in the front row and watches everyone perform onstage. She starts projects and completes them only when coerced. She makes too many commitments and bails on some of them. She gains a reputation for being unreliable or a flake. This would be a disservice. She is a shrewd judge of character and sniffs out underlying motives. She immediately catches anything out of the ordinary. She fears other people read her motives as easily as she reads them. That isn't usually the case. She makes a good CIA analyst until she ignores information that counters what she believes.

Dallas is great at organizing events and leaving her assistant to finish them. She's a natural spokesperson or corporate "face." She truly believes what she says during the one minute commercial. She is charismatic and works people into a froth then walks away. She could instigate a riot or a flash mob. She is normally on the side of good rather than evil. She likes to arrange meetings and social events, but lacks the planning capacity to pull them off. She needs an assistant who is good with pesky details. She is great at spearheading a foundation then leaving it to flounder. She has a wide network of contacts. She thrives on face time. She ignores the rules and is impatient with detractors. She is a toxic employee if she turns on her employer. She may not design a pipe bomb, but she will have the media on site in seconds to expose someone. She can smile and lie as her team breaks open the safe.

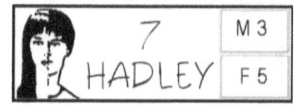

Hadley lives a charmed life. Even when things go wrong, she is upbeat. She lands on her feet, seemingly without effort. She believes the sun will come out tomorrow and, for her, it usually does. She makes every day feel like a party. She relates to people of every age and stage of life. People feel good around her and she feels good around other people. She hates being alone. She refuses to let other people and situations bring her down. She makes a terrific negotiator. She can't sit at a desk. She makes everything sound exciting, even when it isn't. She rallies the employees. She chats about the latest fashions, the best restaurants, and the current fads at the water cooler. She injects her good will, or ill will, like venom. She controls morale.

Hadley ignores problems and refuses to admit defeat. She turns a defeat into a win if it kills her. She is horribly impulsive. She humors the authorities then does things her way. She has a talent for public relations and is clever with spin. She'd make a great politician or drug mule. She develops highly personal relationships with her clients. She makes them feel special. She has common sense, even if she is allergic to planning and thinking ahead. She's calm in a crisis. She doesn't have time to analyze the past. She isn't interested in all those nitpicky details the bean-counters worry over. She talks an angry client into a good mood or a man down from a building ledge. She'd be a great hostage negotiator. She only cares about the knowledge required for the task at hand. She's no expert. She makes a good teacher, social worker, nurse, drama queen, or diva. If she turned to crime, she'd be a swift-talking grifter, a madam with a steel corset, or a sociopathic identity thief.

Shelby is calm and pleasant and makes few demands. She has strong values and suspects people who do not share them. She is congenial until someone violates her principles. She is harsh and rigid to those who do. Her still waters run submarine deep; she doesn't let people close enough to swim them. She is an idealistic loner. She is willing to sacrifice herself and her time for "A Cause". She is frighteningly aware of the evil in men's souls. She'd make a good profiler or spy. Her intuition is usually dead on. She fights on the side of good, but may flirt with evil. She has a talent for interpreting symbols and creating them. She'd make a great archeologist or cryptographer.

Shelby has no interest in lofty theories or detailed analysis. Nitpicking facts make her cranky. She'd rather work alone, but can work with others. She hates interruptions. Hypothetically speaking, she'd rather you didn't hypothesize. She wants you to get to the point. She focuses on the emotional subtext of the situation. She intuits how the people around her feel and uses the information to her advantage. She is tuned in to subtle body language cues and turn of phrase. She catches what they don't say. Corporate drudgery isn't her thing. She could be an effective writer because she understands what makes people tick. She may never indulge in the nitpicking drudgery it takes to edit and revise the book. She works for the greater good, which is a relief. If she turns her talents to the dark side, she plans global destruction. She manipulates people into doing things for her by appealing to their emotions.

Joss seems relatively laid back and mellow. Insubordinate is a good word for him. He isn't interested in structure for himself or others. He ignores rules and regulations. He is loyal to his band of brothers, but disdains his superiors. He makes a wild card soldier, spy, or cop. Employers admire him for his expertise. He thrives on risk and likes beating the odds. He makes each move skillfully without the prep work. Some admire that about him. Most just move out of his way. It can be tragic if they don't.

Joss indulges in high octane adventures, like climbing the Empire State Building with sticky gloves. He'll do it during his spare time if he can't make it a career. He is easily bored, but technically brilliant. He was born with a tool belt strapped to his hip. He makes a great stunt man or contract killer. He'd be equally skilled with knives, guns, and poison darts. He rides a high while the adrenaline lasts then crashes. He bides his time when he must, but it makes him antsy. He makes a great Special Ops soldier or a fireman who free dives on weekends.

Joss is a loner by nature. He likes hanging out with equally skillful mavericks. He is a man of few words. He has the least developed verbal skills of all the mannequins. He isn't stupid; he just won't tell you what he knows. He isn't interested in research, widgets, production, bean counting, or debate. You want him to do something? Pay him and get out of the way. He does what he wants on his schedule, in his way, and no one else's: even if his orders come from the Pentagon. Things get interesting if he goes rogue.

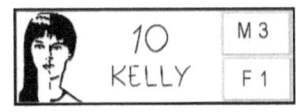

Kelly seeks high physical, intellectual, personal, or financial risks and high yields. He looks for loopholes, special niches, or other unusual opportunities to invest in. He makes a great internet mogul. He is willing to play by the rules to achieve his ends if necessary. He balances work with his free time. He is never boring and not entirely trustworthy. He likes being the man of the hour who rushes in to save the day. Life is a game and he likes to win. He cheats if necessary.

Kelly is a wheeler and dealer. He knows who to bribe, where to get the best hookers, and what his clients' secret fantasies are. He uses other people's motivations against them. He is hypersensitive to micro-expressions. He can sell the client or convict him. Everything he does is for the show whether it's in a courtroom, a film studio, or for the benefit of a rival mob boss. He appears empathetic. It is a ruse to snare you. He remembers all the information he gathers about people, places, and things.

Kelly never apologizes or explains. He may have grandiose delusions and start a business. It fails unless he has a partner who can handle the day-to-day running of the operation. He will drive that partner crazy. He makes an excellent drug lord, counterfeiter, forger, bank robber, or con man. He is unpredictable and amusing and people follow him willingly. He could sell real estate on Mars. He likes to travel and work alone. He is everyone's buddy, but no one really knows him. He bails on negative situations, even if he created them.

Greer is the ultimate absent-minded professor or nuclear physicist. Once he understands a thing, he doesn't share the insight. He won't speak up in groups. He has a sharp mind and a facility for language, on paper not in person. He notes inconsistencies and contradictory statements, no matter how much time passes between them. His recall is excellent. He quickly grasps ideas and systems. He focuses on the path beneath his feet, neither worrying about the forest nor the trees. He isn't impressed by status and titles. He only cares what you know and when you know it. He has no time for illogical, redundant, or inefficient mortals. He is an intellectual snob, which irritates those he needs to persuade.

Greer's goal is to solve the mystery of the universe, but he is out of touch with the people around him. He isn't looking for praise, consensus, or credit. He could be a math or science professor. His students might not like him. He won't care about being popular. He explains his wealth of knowledge in very dry, highly detailed ways.

Greer prefers to work alone without interruption. He would be a very detailed serial killer. He could solve the mystery of black matter, invent a new type of bomb, or cure cancer if left alone and given the resources. He goes quietly mad if assigned to an assembly line or customer service job. He'd argue over the quality of the oil being used and the correct temperature to deep fry potatoes. Then he'd insult the customers. If he turned to the dark side, there is no end to the havoc he could wreak behind the scenes.

Taylor struggles to balance her ideals against the need to earn a living. She takes her community's values or religious dictates very seriously. She is confused when others don't share her zeal. She is loyal, committed, and responsible. She likes public speaking and flow charts. She prefers work that is one-on-one and service based. She is a popular people person. She likes teambuilding and may be put in charge. Work should be fun, so she sends her team on nature survival workshops. She facilitates the office party and brings in cake for birthdays. She is a charismatic corporate leader or a cult guru. She butts in where she is neither needed nor wanted. She idealizes people and is easily disappointed in them. She is seldom critical, but when she turns on you, she turns all the way.

Taylor sways people's opinions. Her intuition is keen, her logic faulty. Pesky facts have no bearing on what she is trying to sell. She isn't hampered by evidence. She spouts a theory and convinces other people to believe it. She makes a great defense attorney, prophet, or politician. She is excellent at reading people and guessing their hidden motives. She is a master of spin, media management, stage, and screen. She makes a great actor, agent, or publicist. She would make an excellent pharmaceutical salesperson or arms dealer. She plans ahead and is reliable. She thrives on complex situations that require her to juggle data. She could falsify ledgers or do insider trading. She has a knack for placing people in the right job and makes an excellent corporate recruiter. She organizes on the run, can pull together last minute meetings, or whip up an instant dinner party. She wants it all to be fun.

Cam is intent on achieving his goals. He works hard and loses track of the rest of his life in favor of it. He sets challenges for himself and meets them. He is motivated, confident, and independent: qualities his boss both admires and finds suspect. He can rest easy. Cam does not aspire to become CEO. That would involve voting, schmoozing, and public speaking. He hates that garbage. People so rarely do what they are supposed to. They slow him down and get in the way. He may seem cold or standoffish, but his still waters run Marianas Trench deep.

Cam sneers at status, rank, credentials, titles, and popularity contests. The work is either good or it isn't. The idea is logical or it isn't. He has little use for incompetent people. Impassioned arguments leave him cold. He hates meetings, company slogans, and what he deems rah-rah or woo-woo crap. He is a competent spy or contract killer.

Cam plays by the rules if they support his objective, otherwise he considers them suggestions. He wants his inbox empty. He makes certain all the counterfeit bills have been cut, stacked, and banded at the end of day. He sees tasks through to completion whether he is wiring a security system or finding ways around one. He points out long-term consequences and system defects. He makes people a little nervous. They fear he can actually see inside their souls. To some extent, he can. He simply isn't interested enough to bother. Humans are like specimens pinned to velvet: attractive, intriguing, and foreign. He could easily annihilate them for their imperfections and start over with DNA manipulation.

Morgan sees connections between unrelated topics and potential for widgets that others ignore. He is action-oriented and works hard to achieve the desired result. He grasps the means and the end. Ideas count only when they make pirated electronics better. He isn't interested in inventing or marketing the latest smart phone. He leaves that to other people.

Morgan enjoys getting his hands dirty and seeks acclaim. He is interested in everything and everyone which makes him a great film director. He doesn't care how things have been done in the past if they don't work. He looks for ways to improve the special effects makeup or reconfigure the camera angles. He understands both the operational and the social workings of a company. He makes a great CEO or mob boss.

Morgan views competence as power and has little respect for the incompetent. He would argue with the President if he disagreed with him. He is a thrilling conversationalist and loves a good debate, which makes him an effective political talk show host. He drops a project midstream to focus on another. He annoys his financial backers and film crews when that happens. He likes outwitting his foes and using the rules of the game against them. He likes beating the odds. He might be reduced to teaching instead of world domination. He makes the administrators cringe, but finds a way to humor them out of firing him. If he turns against the powers that be or the boss that questions his competence, revenge is swift. He is above all persuasive and he has followers to back him up when he switches television stations.

Lee ends up in charge of the soup kitchen or the country, either works. People may not like her much. She goes after what she wants and usually gets it. She has no problem running over other people in the process. She works hard and forgets to play. She micro-manages the other software pirates. She grasps the general idea and relies on summaries to make decisions. She makes a powerful world leader. She needs cronies to help her achieve her goals. She is tolerant of the way things have been done, as long as they get the desired result. If they don't, she unilaterally does things her way. This makes the other human traffickers furious. She hates inefficiency and knows just how many kilos fit in a box of baby diapers and how to work within the bureaucracy to make sure she is not caught crossing the border.

Lee hates gooey emotional stuff. She doesn't care which type of bubonic plague you have contracted; she expects you to work. She has short term goals (take over Manhattan), midrange goals (take over New York), and long-term goals (take over the planet). She makes an impressive courtroom attorney or small country dictator. She thrives on material success and wants that corner office. She may resort to embezzlement to make sure she has the creature comforts she desires. She throws lavish, catered dinner parties at her multiple mansions. She won't care if you like her as long as you show up. She might be too busy to make an appearance, but she'll find a way to make you regret it if you don't.

River invests time in causes she deems worthy. She focuses on her version of the greater good and lives to serve. Her insight and hard work payoff in the right environment. She prefers to exert subtle influence behind the scenes. People come to her, she does not go out in the world to them. She is vulnerable and hides behind a protective facade. She makes a powerful oracle or witch doctor. She understands complex issues and complex people. She is highly sensitive to emotional cues and subtext. She has a vivid imagination and a good memory. She is an intuitive artist, musician, writer, and poet, but not a good public speaker.

River absorbs the emotional energy of other people. She may profess to have psychic abilities. If religious, she makes a good nun, priest, or martyr. She picks up on body language and spots a liar in nothing flat. She makes a personal connection with the people she works with and prefers to work one on one in the confessional. She makes a good therapist or social worker, though she may find it too depressing over the long haul.

River is open to the idea of aliens, ghosts, angels, and deities. She has deep powers of concentration. She has a talent for problem solving and anticipating needs. She sees inside the heart of the person she is helping and hears what they don't want to say. She thrives on giving and receiving praise. She is an effective charlatan or medium. For the most part, River fights on the side of good. If she turns against those in power, she silently and effectively works against them with a voodoo doll or a spell or two. She influences other people to follow her.

The transition to adulthood or maturity is defined by certain benchmarks. The benchmarks vary widely and depend on the culture in which your character lives. In modern North America, an adult is expected to have a job that pays for basic needs, such as food, shelter, clothing, utilities, transportation, and WiFi. Unless your character is independently wealthy, indefinitely sponging off of other people is considered a sign of immaturity or outright sociopathy. There are mitigating circumstances that could prevent these benchmarks from being reached.

Addictions: Alcohol and drug dependency complicate even the most intrepid character's trajectory. The addiction could begin because of an illness, injury, or harmless experimentation. He could be addicted to sex, gambling, Facebook, or World of Warcraft.

Disabilities: The level of native intelligence plays a big part in how your character's temperament flourishes. If he is the intrepid sort and has to overcome being a paraplegic, he finds new ways to succeed. The more independent he is, the harder he fights or resists assistance, graciously or not so graciously.

Unemployment: Lack of income can turn even a straight-shooting character toward a life of crime. In Science Fiction and Fantasy, you can have fun with this. What type of work is available on planet Zircon? If it is a mining colony and your character hates drudgery, he causes trouble to relieve the boredom or tries to figure out a way to hop the next space shuttle home. He may be willing to lie, cheat, bribe, or kill.

[ALT] Hitching Posts: Marrying and raising a family when your character is temperamentally unsuited for it places some mannequins firmly in hell, others in limbo. Others settle in and enjoy the ride. Pair opposites and you can have a little fun at their expense.

[ALT] Saddle Bags: Give him loved ones or friends that require his care. This is particularly amusing if he isn't naturally suited to be a caregiver and he can't afford nurses and nannies.

[ALT] Roommates: Relying on friends to help make ends meet is an opportunity to put oppositional temperaments in the same nest without the rapture-inducing blinders of sex.

[ALT] Unique Cauldrons: In your Historical, Fantasy, or Science Fiction world, your characters have unique communities. The definition of who lives with whom is open to invention. Perhaps females and children live together and males live separately. There were polygamous rulers and those with harems. Oppositional sister-wives or harem girls are explosive. Some societies had no concept of "marriage." Children belonged to the collective rather than the individual. Have fun with it. Place thirty people in a remote village or space station and the options for partnerships and friendships are severely limited. Oppositional pairings are guaranteed.

⌨ Criticism: Caregivers often expect their children to be a mirror image, or a better prototype, than themselves. Bosses expect their employees to behave in specific ways. Friends are drawn to each other, but misunderstand one another. Characters compromise when they want and need the same things. They part ways when their needs aren't expressed in the same way.

⌨ Geometry. Love triangles are common in Romance. Friendship triangles are featured in young adult fiction. Romantic, platonic, or toxic triangles and quadrangles create exciting plot complications.

To grow, your character must learn to appreciate characters with different wants, needs, and approaches. He must stop being irritated and disappointed every time the other character veers from the script. To solve a story problem, he might have to rely on another character's strengths. Attracting and repelling characters offer satisfying friction to your fiction.

MID-LIFE CRISIS

Midlife is another major turning point for the mannequins. Some sail through it calmly, content with the choices they've made, delighting in their day-to-day life. Others are once again obsessed with the paths not taken and the imperfection of the choices they have made. If more or less stable, we can expect our sixteen characters to continue down the road of life in a predictable pattern whether they are spies, housekeepers, or vampires.

Wynn ponders a little more and finds the study of human nature fascinating. She takes part in activities that force her to be more visible. She grows more comfortable with accepting praise for a job well done. She even reaches a point where she can let other people take care of her once in awhile. She learns to decline when people ask for help. She could become disillusioned with the way the world has turned. She may secretly hunger for a dream not realized, like the desire to assassinate her boss and take over. She may find the courage to dream again and become a nun. She has clung to her lifelong partner, but may be highly dissatisfied.

2 FRANCIS

M 8
F 3

Francis branches out a little and takes up a hobby. He collects things or learns a useful craft. He enjoys a few leisure activities. He leaves some of his seriousness behind and lets someone else worry about the future. He has deferred vacations, luxuries, down time, and other joys long enough. He grabs the gusto he forgot about. He finds kicking the traces and roaming free difficult. His martial approach to marriage probably drove his partner off, his children too, if he had any. He has a very long list of the ways life has let him down. If his complacence is blown apart, he may take off, anxious but intrigued. He might admit to being wrong. Nah, just kidding.

3 NEVADA

M 8
F 3

Nevada has matured. He suspends his criticism and enjoys life a little more. He may relax and tease. His ex-partner and children wonder why he couldn't have been nicer while they were around. He takes up hobbies that require imagination and creativity. He pays more attention to his needs and wants. He learns to take better care of himself. He enjoys travel and reading technical books in a professional field of interest, like rifle manufacturing. He plans for retirement so he can enjoy it. He avoids situations that cut him off from other people. He may have been hurt and disappointed by his loved ones. He may not have earned the respect and appreciation he desired. He may break free and try something different before it is too late, like salmon fishing. He may leave behind the people who have let him down.

Arden becomes more in tune with the emotional reactions of others. If not, he becomes a gruff old man. The tight rein on his emotions either loosens or strangles him. He decides he missed out on things. He travels or does something just for fun. He is frustrated when the people around him aren't logical or controlled. His romantic partner has dumped him and moved on. He realizes his loss too late. His children may be distant and his friends too busy to stay connected. He won't ponder too long on what could have been or could be. He remains in his tired groove or learns how to build a better bomb from the internet.

Blair abandons the restrictions adult life has placed on her. She changes jobs, leaves her family, dumps her partner, or has an affair. If financially sound, she opts for early retirement. She longs to follow her bliss. She still doesn't know what her bliss is. She is eager to tread those paths not taken in the hopes of finding something more satisfying. If she has been repressed and stuck in a rut for a long time, she becomes self-destructive and bitter. She does something tragic to shake things up and hopes for a better alternative.

Dallas maintains her youthful enthusiasm and bon vivant lifestyle. She is the perfect candidate for a midlife crisis. She looks forward to early retirement because it brings a new set of options. If she can afford to explore her bliss, she does so. If she is bankrupt or physically disabled, she considers suicide because her options have dwindled and there may be more options on the other side. She dabbles in art classes or other crafty hobbies. She realizes how important a few of her friends are, if she has any left. If she has been repressed and stuck in an unhappy situation, she finds a way to change it before it is too late. She has an affair, undergoes plastic surgery, or turns subversive.

Hadley sails on through. She loves her family, loves her work, and is loyal to both. She nurtures her close friendships and is still the life of the party. She encourages people to embrace life rather than plod through it. She is loyal and predictable. To break her at midlife would take something truly catastrophic. She is usually the encouraging friend in fiction and may encourage someone to change his life with tragic results. She is a sparkling, witty conversationalist. If affluent, she dresses well and lives well. Even in poverty, she finds a way to make a new sarong out of curtains and to throw a party on her tiny balcony.

Shelby decides to increase her mastery of intellectual interests. She might seek an advanced degree. She explores the sensual side of her nature and could have an affair. She explores new social situations and new contacts. She overextends herself and becomes emotionally drained while trying to fulfill her passions before it is too late. No matter how wonderful her circumstances are, she is in search of something slightly better. She may use the mid-life crisis to reinvent herself.

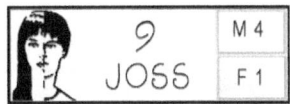

Joss breaks free of the restrictions hampering him. He lets go of friends and family to make it happen before it is too late. He retires early, especially if his work has been dull and draining. If work meets his needs, he resists retirement as others try to force him out. He feels he has not yet mastered his art. He develops the discipline to finish what he starts. He devotes his leisure time to other fulfilling hobbies or he becomes bitter and twisted. He probably doesn't have a lifelong partner. He may choose a newer model if he does.

Kelly is a prime candidate for a midlife crisis. He most likely chose a partner that was good with details and long-term planning. The partner has kept him focused and curbed his impulsiveness. His partner either leaves him or is shocked when he bolts. He may realize the lack of deep relationships and attempt to form a few. If life is boring, he finds a way to make it fun. He travels or takes up a new risky hobby. He retires early if he can and spends the rest of his days in pursuit of a good time. He might take up with a younger partner for the novelty, but grows bored with her too after a while.

Greer has learned to speak up and share his knowledge. He has learned to balance his inner world with his outer world. He indulges in activities for fun rather than to improve a skill. He has been so focused on work that he let everything else slide. His kids have grown up and moved on. His partner may have moved on too. He embraces his sensual side too late. He might sell up and move to an exotic locale if it is work related. He dies at his desk, unless something drastic comes along to derail him and change his focus. Otherwise, he has a quiet mid-life rebellion and ponders how things used to be.

Taylor takes a little time for herself to meditate or write journals. She changes careers, turning away from the pursuit of financial gain to find a more soul-satisfying endeavor. She plans for retirement, but stays where she has friends and family. She isn't one to break free and roam the world alone. She could seek a new relationship if she felt her attempts to make her spouse happy weren't appreciated. If children have been her focus, she struggles with the empty nest. She has a wide social base and could embrace something different, perhaps missionary work in Zambia.

Cam achieves a little balance. He is more social and does things for pleasure rather than gain. He is happy with what he has accomplished. He learns new things and takes time to explore hobbies. He travels and is thrilled by new experiences. He may embrace a little rah-rah or woo-woo. He won't have a midlife relationship crisis unless his partner betrays him. If his partner left, he would figure out a way to cope with it, but spend time analyzing how it all went wrong. He takes on new challenges if the old ones have gone stale. He might dream of moving to a foreign country, He won't, unless it is work related or someone comes along to push him into it.

Morgan's experimentation could get out of hand at midlife. He destroys his career and ruins everything he has worked for up to that point, personally and professionally. He might learn to balance his priorities and make self-improvement a goal. He takes up hobbies like gardening, painting, or reading the classics. He won't do any of it half-way. He won't consider the needs of those around him when he jets off to an ashram in India. His midlife crisis could be a quiet awakening or a flaming rebellion.

Lee always feels vaguely unsatisfied with her life. Has she accomplished enough? Is she good enough? She switches gears and tries something different. She takes up a hobby and pursues it with gusto. She takes a vacation and doesn't come back. She would hate diminished circumstances. She could realize her mistakes and try to mend fences. It is probably too late to repair the relationships with the people she drove away or to distraction. She sails into the unknown before it is too late. She takes her drive and her approach with her and meets with the same results. She may find herself in charge of a clinic in Guatemala.

River continues her quiet, satisfying pursuits. She switches careers if she doesn't feel her values are reflected by her employer. She takes time to write a memoir or indulge in new age hobbies. She stretches herself to make new friends and try new things. She learns to exert herself a little more and is more confident as she ages. She uses her intuitive powers for the greater good. She attends a spiritual retreat in New Mexico or visits a Buddhist temple in the Himalayas. She may retire early to do missionary work.

Ticking Clock: At midlife, things happen that shake your mannequins up. They turn fifty and suddenly there are less days ahead than behind. Those who thrive on options panic. Those who gave up fun, or put their wants and needs on the back burner, decide to do things before it is too late. Even characters content with their lives feel a slight quickening of the blood. They want a life full of options again.

Money Matters: From the time your mannequin flew the nest, he needed to make money to survive. Midlife is a time when he is downsized at work or replaced with a younger model. His security is threatened again. How will he live if he can't work? If he can't do what he is good at, what now? He panics when his job and ability to support himself are taken away or reduced. It hurts the mannequins that weren't good with long-term planning more than the ones who were.

[ALT] **Dump Him**: A divorce not only messes with his security and self worth, it messes with his money. Whatever path he was on comes to an abrupt end. He must reconfigure the plan. This is easier for some more than others. He must revisit the challenges of building a new nest and deciding whether or not to find a new partner. His decisions impact his children, friends, and family in painful or hilarious ways. He can use the opportunity to do what he always wanted to without the restrictive anchor of his partner. He may find a new partner and encounter a whole new set of temperament oppositions. His children take sides when their family foundation is shattered.

[ALT] **Scare Him**: Nothing makes him consider mortality quicker than a health scare. A change in health status threatens his ability to make enough money to retire or to support his family. It either draws him closer to his loved ones or sends him reeling in the opposite direction.

[ALT] **Death Visits**: During this time of life, his caregivers, friends, children, partners, bosses, or coworkers may die. It changes how he navigates and views his life. Does it derail him or make him stronger? Should he make peace with those he hurt before he dies? Does he need closure? Did he get it? If not, how does that change his point of view? How does death complicate his world?

[ALT] Opportunity Knocks: In midlife, your mannequin enters a heightened emotional state reminiscent of adolescence. The awareness of the wider world and the lure of the exotic come knocking once more. He questions all his choices and wonders about the paths not taken. He may decide to explore them. He makes massive changes to his life and either blooms where he was wilting or destroys all he had built. He may relocate and feel at home in the place he should have been all along.

[ALT] Face the Mirror: His body has aged. Inside he is still the person he was in his twenties. It shocks him to realize he is "an old person," particularly when the younger generation makes a point of emphasizing it. The hot stud or gorgeous knockout during high school and college is no longer looked upon as desirable by all the young things he sees on the beach. Some characters struggle more than others. Most indulge in a little nostalgia for how things used to be and dream of how it could still be. How do the physical changes affect him? He may greet this transition with wry, self-effacing humor or complete and utter mental meltdown. He may have plastic surgery or suddenly decide to get fit. The transition is affected by how stable his self-image is, how satisfying his job is, and how happy his home life is. Tweak any of those parameters and you set him on a fictional journey of discovery or destruction.

[ALT] New Roles: If your mannequin loses his job, he may choose a new career or corporation. A new career or position leads to a new boss, coworkers, and temperament clashes. He may have been at the top of his game. He may be shifted to a slightly lower, or much lower, company rung. He must prove himself once again. He may be patronized by the youngsters. He can prove he still has what it takes or realize he is past his prime.

Forced Retirement: Your character was either prepared and moves to the next challenge or it hits him unexpectedly. If he can financially afford to retire, what does he do with his time? If he can't afford it, how do reduced circumstances impact him? What does it force him to do?

Move In: An independent character is suddenly required to share space with his children or other family members. He is back to the old temperament oppositions, except the roles are reversed. How does the shift in the balance of power affect him? Tensions run high. The child who didn't get what he needed is suddenly faced with making sure the caregiver gets what he needs, to comic or tragic effect.

The passage through middle age was either calm or bumpy. The mannequin remained the same or changed drastically. It is time to enter the final round of the game.

OLD AGE

The twilight years mark the final major transition for our sweet sixteen. How the mannequins handle this last phase is determined by their temperament types, support systems, financial situation, available options, and physical and mental health. If life's gentle swells never become a tsunami and they have weathered the minor tempests, our mannequins end their days as they began them: in sync with their temperament.

Wynn reflects on all that she has done. She needs to believe that her efforts were appreciated. She is depressed if her lifetime achievements go unrecognized. She grows a tad selfish. She decides that she has spent her life doing for others and it is time for them to do something for her. They are confused by the request. She has never needed them before, why now? She remains committed to her family, if she has one. Family is very important to her. She encourages her children to be good citizens and to follow the rules. She is a pleasant, if maudlin, resident of Tinker Town Elder Home. Her family might forget to visit. She won't feel appreciated.

Francis regrets all that time spent working, especially if it distanced him from his family. He tries to reconnect or rebuild what was sacrificed. He takes time out for himself and tries to enjoy the time left. After all, he saved up for it and now has money to play with. He encourages his children to work hard and save their pennies. He encourages them to smell the roses since the world has not ended as yet. He hates Tinker Town Elder Home. Everything they do is wrong and he tells them how to fix it. Francis may end up right, but he ends up alone. His children might not visit.

Nevada needs to believe that he was a good citizen and his efforts were appreciated. He becomes emotional at a retirement party where people list his good deeds and accomplishments. He laughs at the gentle ribbing. He seeks retirement situations where there are lots of people and outlets for him to still be useful. He enjoys time spent with his family and clings to the traditions he valued. He encourages his children to be good sports and to care about their community and families. He finds restrictions and limitations very difficult. He would shoot himself if he had to live in Tinker Town Elder Home. He becomes sullen because status doesn't really matter in the elder home.

Arden wants people to remember him as a good, hardworking man. He needs to feel that his diligence and responsibility have been appreciated. If he is still connected to his children, he encourages them to work hard and play smart. He eagerly helps them achieve their goals and is frustrated if they don't seem to have any. He finds restrictions difficult. He applies himself to whatever he thinks he should be doing. He is a cooperative, if grumpy, resident of Tinker Town Elder Home. He strives to meet expectations and minds when his children don't visit.

Blair ponders the paths not taken. She spends her final years trying to become who she should have been, despite the cautions of her friends and family. If she is still connected to her children, she encourages them to experiment and try everything. Life is short. Don't waste it. If placed in Tinker Town Elder Home, she is bitter and hateful because it restricts her freedom. Inside, she is still the free spirit who longs for adventure. The confinement means slow death. Her children may be too busy living life to come back and visit her.

Dallas basks in her former glory. She reminisces about all the fun things she used to do and bemoans the paths not taken. She makes a frenzied attempt to try all the things she never got around to and hangs on to her youthful persona. She grows depressed if limited financially or physically. She hates being dependent on other people and chafes at being responsible for aging relatives or partners. Being confined to Tinker Town Elder Home horrifies her. She either does everything she can to avoid it or kicks and screams at being locked up. The other residents tire of her endless stories. They make fun of her designer muumuus and sparkly house slippers. Some secretly covet them.

Hadley looks back with fondness. She won't second guess or question her decisions. She surrounds herself with family and friends. She may wear herself out cheering up characters that have experienced the slings and arrows of fate. She encourages her children to have a beautiful life and to enjoy each day. In retirement, she is the bright spot in other people's lives. She is the lovely old person that earns the smiles and accolades of the staff at Tinker Town Elder Home. She spearheads the social activities. She may tire of being the one to keep her chin up while everyone else moans. Her children visit often if they can.

Shelby reflects on all she has done. She needs to believe that her life has made a difference. She realizes she has not achieved all that she planned and wants to accomplish the bucket list items left unchecked. She is very attached to her children if she has them. She encourages them to follow their dreams too. If she finds herself in Tinker Town Elder Home, she is either bitter and angry because the world has let her down or she continues to fight the good fight. She mails handwritten letters to the editor of the local paper or takes up internet blogging.

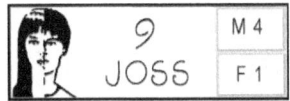

Joss has time to focus on his interests in retirement. Rather than slowing down, he speeds up. When others are playing sedate games of golf, he takes up bungee jumping or parasailing. He chafes against physical or financial restrictions. The last thing he wants is to be bored. He wants to go out in a blaze of glory. If committed to Tinker Town Elder Home, which is his idea of hell, he looks for ways to escape it. He resents whoever or whatever put him there.

Kelly hypes the glory days. He grasps whatever remaining gusto is available based on his health and means. He may have alienated those close to him. He seeks out ways to still feel relevant. He hates fading into obscurity. If jailed in Tinker Town Elder Home, he works his charm on the crowd. He stirs the pot just because he can. It won't be peaceful. Death to him is the final round of poker. He is anxious, yet slightly interested in what follows. He hedges his bets with a conversion to religion. He invests in cryogenics, if he can afford it, so he can have another spin of the wheel.

Greer is philosophical about his ride being nearly over. He has achieved a solid understanding of the way the world works and may attempt to pass some of what he has learned on to his children or total strangers. He is fascinated by all that he has yet to learn. He continues to read, ponder, and research in retirement. If compelled to live in Tinker Town Elder Home, he hates the fabricated social outlets and prefers to stay in his room. He isolates himself against the pain of being abandoned and hides in his research.

Taylor looks back with satisfaction at all the people she helped. She wants to leave the world a better place than how she found it. She nurtures her grandchildren, even if they don't appreciate her. Her relationships are everything. She takes advantage of retirement to volunteer. If she finds herself in Tinker Town Elder Hall, she finds a new outlet for her mothering skills. She may feel betrayed by those she spent so much time caring for who have left her behind.

Cam looks back and wonders what it was all for. Nothing changes. The world continues to spin in the same tired way. He wishes for a brighter tomorrow, but isn't optimistic. He encourages his children to deal with the world the way it is rather than the way they wish it were. He expects them to do what they are supposed to because they want to, not because someone is forcing or threatening them. He continues to challenge his mind. If placed in Tinker Town Elder Home, he hates the confinement, the rah-rah, and the woo-woo. He seals himself in his room and reads books and finds joy in solitary pleasures like puzzles or solo Scrabble. Illogical and emotional residents make him cranky. He may take classes to learn something new. It is for the joy of learning, not the social aspect. He may figure out a way to escape the mortal coil if no one visits.

Morgan yearns to be free. His mind requires a challenge. He may or may not have ties to his children. If he does, he encourages them to think big and or go out in a blaze of glory. If jailed in Tinker Town Elder Home, he causes trouble. He won't be able to help himself. The rules are stupid. The routine is ridiculous. He should be allowed to do what he wants when he wants. He may seek an audience to expound his criticism of the place to if no one visits.

Lee can't handle confinement. She hates the reduction in status and power that aging brings. She works until she drops. If she ends up in Tinker Town Elder Home, she micro-manages them too. She is the loud, pushy resident everyone tries to avoid. She listens to their tales, tells them to stop whining, points out what they did wrong in life, and how they could have avoided it. She makes suggestions for how the home could be run more efficiently. She bullies and cajoles the other residents into doing what she wants them to. They run when they see her coming. Her children don't visit often, if at all.

River feels she has seen too much. She withdraws from life and seeks solitude or has become more interconnected. If she has children, she is intensely loyal and loving. She guides them based on the wisdom she has gained. They may find her mysticism hard to relate to. If she is plopped in Tinker Town Elder Home, she is exhausted by the misery around her. She listens to the war stories and offers insights to help people come to terms with the meaning of their lives. She wants to heal the wounds inflicted. She retreats for days at a time to recuperate. Her children don't visit because they hate seeing her suffer.

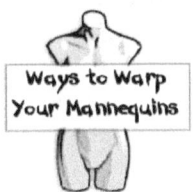

Marginalize Them: In many cultures, the elderly are shuffled aside and treated as near-children once again. They are smiled upon and patted on the head and called "sweet." Unfortunately, the elderly individual is still very much vital, in mind if not in body. Few of them appreciate being called "dear" or "sweet." Some withdraw and reflect. Others go out fighting. Their opinions are considered outdated. Their wisdom is discounted. Society tends to disengage with them and vice versa.

Revitalize Them: The "baby boomers" have redefined what old age looks like. They live and stay active longer.

Some choose to end their days napping by the fire, a book or newspaper lying on their laps, or the television blaring their favorite program. They regale the younger generation with stories of the good old days. The younger generation usually ignores them. Their interest in the stories might not kick in until they are over thirty, and that is often too late. Give the retiree a new challenge to keep him young. Give him a young person interested in his stories.

[ALT] **Autonomy:** Safety and security once again become areas for conflict. Health and psychological fears rear their ugly heads, if they haven't already. The relationships he has maintained and lost take on new poignancy. Who will care for him if he returns to an infantile state? What kind of caretakers will the people he must rely on be? The roles are suddenly reversed. The intuitive child may be the sensing caregiver's enforcer. The extroverted child may be charged with the introverted caregiver's well-being. It can go horribly wrong all over again.

[ALT] **Abandonment:** What if he has no one left to care for him? Friends may have to step in when family is nonexistent, so may strangers in the guise of guardians, nurses, or nursing home staff. Oppositional trait wars occur between residents, nurses, doctors, orderlies, and patients in Tinker Town Elder Home. He now must fight for independence and to prove his competence like a young adult. Elder rights and elder abuse are serious issues. They could feature in a Literary, Horror, or Science Fiction tale. Life and death are the ultimate stakes.

[ALT] **Immobility:** Paralyzed, ill, injured, and elderly characters have their mobility compromised. They face a different set of challenges. Mobility limitations make some feel incredibly vulnerable. It fuels others to break free of the physically imposed bonds. They learn how to play wheelchair basketball. If you cannot walk, you cannot outrun a predator or a zombie. Characters who need wheelchairs to get around can't function in places where they can't use them or don't have access to them. They must navigate the world around them in creative ways. Characters without arms use their feet. Characters without feet use their arms. They sometimes rely on other people in ways they hate.

ALT Illness: Some characters with health issues suffer from depression and withdraw from life. Others take your breath away by not only overcoming the challenge, but teaching us all lessons about living. The important thing to remember about using these elements is the "why." Don't put them in for melodrama or a sympathy vote. Put them in because they are the overall story problem, contribute to the overall story problem, are an obstacle for a character in a scene, or create conflicts between characters.

ALT Mismatches: Children have to make tough choices for and about their caregivers. The conflicts they had with each other as children and young adults add poignancy to an already conflict-fraught issue. Children may have differing ideas of how things should play out. Siblings who have managed to avoid each other for decades are suddenly faced with united cause. They have different approaches to it. Do they turn off life support or keep hoping? Do they move their caregiver in or put him in a home? Who takes him on? Who resents the whole issue?

Bowing Out: The ultimate conflict rears its ugly head: end of life. Thematic arguments in this category are intensely personal and heated. Do people have the right to choose the time and circumstances of their death if they are terminally ill or simply miserable and alone? Is it ever okay to pull the plug? This overall story problem or personal dilemma creates intense conflict. Characters on opposite sides of the question can have extreme opinions. Doctors make tough decisions every day. Sometimes they win the battle for life. Sometimes they fail. Thematic questions about death make intriguing stories. Paranormal Horror, Science Fiction, and Literary tales pose the question, "What happens after we die?" Scientists probe the question. Religions seek to provide the answers. Characters take opposite sides of the argument. Some argue there is life after death; others argue there isn't. Characters lie, cheat, steal, or kill to prove their side of the thematic argument.

Send Off: How will your mannequin deal with wills, trusts, and plans for his funeral? Does he prefer cremation or burial, a lavish send-off or a quiet goodbye? Family, friends, and life partners may have vastly different opinions on the subject. They may oppose the mannequin's wishes. Last minute romances cause heated arguments between characters and their siblings, offspring, business partners, and anyone who feels he has a say in how a character spends his twilight years.

Do children have the right to feel entitled to their parent's stuff? Does it make a difference if the "stuff" is a million dollars, a derelict fishing shack on a lake, or their father's ratty old sweaters? All kinds of ugly stuff from the shadow self is dredged to the surface during these discussions.

Characters form attachments to weird things. If the caregiver had a poor relationship with his children, he may resent their attempts to grasp whatever he accumulated. What does a character owe his children? His ex-wife? Distant relatives he has not kept in contact with?

[ALT] **Enter Eternity**: How far is your mannequin willing to go to live forever? Humans experiment with genetic tinkering, enzyme manipulation, and artificial intelligence. Can scientists scan what makes us "us" into a computer? Could we live forever in cyber-world. Should we? Do we want to? If no one dies, the planet grows overcrowded in a hurry. Do we have to regulate reproduction? If we are no longer able to reproduce, what happens to our world? If our planet dies, where does everyone go?

If we can live forever on earth, is there any need for heaven and hell, gods, or religion? If we never die, what does that look like and feel like? Does consciousness live on after we die? Are there ghosts? If so, there are trillions. Is the energy from our bodies transferred to inanimate objects for others to "read"? Can we exist apart from our bodies? Can we travel outside our bodies? These questions offer thematic arguments, overall story problems, and complications to any genre.

Our sweet sixteen have weathered the storms, thrived or failed, lived, and died. However, we haven't explored all the ways to torture them quite yet.

Diana Hurwitz

KNOWLEDGE OBSTACLES

Speaking is our single most important tool: the one thing, in addition to opposable thumbs, that gives us an evolutionary advantage. People don't use it wisely, which is good news for fiction writers.

At each stage of the story problem, you have to decide what your character knows, when he knows it, how certain he is, and how hard it would be to convince him he is wrong.

Knowledge obstacles prevent understanding and communication in the form of:

📖 Missing information.

📖 Conflicting ways of obtaining information.

📖 Receiving the same information, but interpreting it differently.

📖 Conflicting information.

📖 Inaccurate information.

📖 Inability to understand the information due to language differences.

📖 Inability to deliver an important piece of information.

📖 Knowing something he doesn't want to acknowledge.

📖 Communicating what he knows.

📖 Who he chooses to tell.

📖 How he chooses to tell them.

How do your characters communicate? Do they ask questions or give orders? Do they listen to answers or brush them off? Higher education teaches characters to think and debate, rarely does it teach them to get in touch with their feeling side. When it comes to our sweet sixteen, each could strengthen his weak side.

| 1 | M 4 |
| WYNN | F 9 |

What: Wynn relies on obvious facts and what has been historically proven. She resists new theories and ideas that counter what she believes. She has strong opinions about the way things should be and gives advice accordingly. She values her opinion above everyone else's and becomes angry when challenged. She believes people are essentially good and may not recognize malicious intent. She sorts through information and retains what is relevant to the people and situations that are important to her. She has accurate recall of those impressions. She remembers the way something was said and the emotional impact of it. Wynn seeks positive feedback from others. If she doesn't get it, she becomes depressed and questions her self worth. When her self-esteem plummets, she stops listening. The world becomes unfair and dangerous. She can be gullible. She ignores problems until they become toxic. She grows isolated and relies on the few who support her opinions.

Who: Wynn relies on her inner circle. She endows people with thoughts and feelings they don't have. She suspects hidden motives and agendas, even when dealing with blunt and open characters. She develops vague feelings of impending disaster. Negative impressions build up and she turns against people without them knowing it. Wynn communicates best with Wynn, Francis, River, Nevada, and Blair. She fights most with Morgan.

How: Wynn puts other people at ease. She searches for the right thing to say. She seeks win-win solutions. She has a hard time saying "no" and hates conflict. She is a naturally fuzzy communicator. She tells you what she feels, asks for and delivers sentiments, and is focused on whether the information is good or bad. She wants you to agree. It doesn't matter what the problem is, she wants you to understand how she feels about it. She wants you to acknowledge that she is upset. She is more interested in rehashing the emotional impact of the problem than solving it. She slowly sizzles until she combusts. She is afraid of her own negative emotions. She blames people for things that go wrong based on who they are or because they do things differently than her. She makes outrageously harsh and selfish judgment calls when threatened. She justifies her own inappropriate behavior when called on it. Her suspicion and paranoia can spiral out of control. At her most extreme, she is toxically narcissistic. She shocks others with the violence of her repressed emotions and the grudges she holds.

What: Francis defends facts and traditions, even if they later prove fatal. He isn't interested in intangibles or theories of what could be. He has a steel-trap mind for nitpicky details. He suspects any information that runs contrary to what he thinks he knows. He favors honesty and integrity. He expects catastrophe to strike and ignores theories to the contrary. He relies on societal rules to keep chaos at bay. Failure and accusations of failure infuriate him. He blames himself when things go wrong, but dares anyone to say so. His response is irrational and exaggerated. He relies on his own store of knowledge rather than brainstorming. He is judgmental and dismisses other people's thought and opinions before he has even heard them.

Who: Francis relies on his trusted circle. He withdraws to reflect before talking to anyone. He rejects people he considers incompetent or dishonest. He is uncomfortable with praise and immune to flattery. He won't offer praise in return. Francis communicates best with Francis, Cam, Wynn, Arden, and Joss. He argues most with Hadley.

How: Francis has poor emotional intelligence. He follows the rules and is suspicious of people who don't. He communicates with precision and is a good listener, but is limited by his rigid viewpoint. He tells you what he thinks, asks for and delivers objective opinions, and is focused on whether the information is true or false. He doesn't care how you feel about it. He isn't interested in exploring why he is upset. He wants you to focus on what he thinks about the situation. He is more interested in solving the problem than listening to an emotional rehash of it. He might accept constructive criticism from someone he respected. He handles conflict in a remote, intellectual way. He gives orders. He is blunt and factual. Emotional arguments make him more fixed in his opinions. He has a deep-seated need to be right. He views conversations as win-lose and he wants to win.

What: Nevada trusts facts and what has been historically proven. He resists theories and conjecture. He recognizes patterns and grasps philosophy, but this is not his strength. He has a talent for reading other people. He accepts alternative points of view. He views himself as a good person and seeks approval for his selflessness. His self-esteem suffers if he doesn't get it. Calling him selfish is a declaration of war. He gathers specific details about other people and uses the information to make judgments. He shifts to accommodate those around him. His values are based on what other people think. He doesn't think for himself. He ignores the mistakes of those he cares about. He has trouble seeing the big picture and understanding that actions have consequences. He tries to control people who don't want to be controlled.

Who: Nevada wants to talk things over as he thinks them through. He won't question the prevailing authority and avoids direct conflict. He sides with the majority, even if they are wrong. He dismisses the input of anyone he considers inappropriate. He attributes people with feelings and motives they don't have. He is susceptible to superstition and media manipulation. He is narrow-minded and judges people based on arbitrary superstitious beliefs. He limits his contacts to people who agree with him. Nevada communicates best with

Nevada, Arden, Taylor, Hadley, and Wynn. He argues most with Greer.

How: Nevada's good nature makes him popular. He has a talent for storytelling. People discount him as a foe. He is overly sensitive and imagines slights where none is intended. He uses guilt to manipulate people. He ignores problems until they reach critical mass. He tells you what he feels, asks for and delivers sentiments, and is focused on whether the information is good or bad. He cares if you agree. It doesn't matter what the problem is, he wants you to understand how he feels about it. He wants you to acknowledge that he is upset. He is more interested in rehashing the emotional impact of the problem than solving it. He reacts rashly and emotionally in situations that require calm and logic. He shuts down if someone points out his faulty logic. He meets opposing opinions with amused indifference or open dismissal. He continues to fight after the other person has lost interest. He justifies transgressions even if they are harmful to others. He is very dangerous that way. Nevada is wounded when confronted with cruelty or indifference.

What: Arden relies on concrete facts and what has been historically proven accurate. He has excellent recall and is an excellent strategist. He relies on his own thoughts and opinions. He points out flaws in the system. He won't ponder and theorize. Questioning his work ethic or integrity means war. He ignores communication that isn't clear and firm. If he does something he shouldn't, he goes to great lengths to hide it. When anxious, he grows more fixed in his opinions. He shuts out the evidence he does not agree with.

He clings to being right. He ignores the emotional content of a conversation. The more emotional someone becomes, the less they influence him. He ignores information that does not support his own views.

Who: Arden likes to talk things out as he thinks them through. He relies on his trusted circle. He rejects information from those he considers incompetent, inefficient, weak, or lazy. His focus on the collective good blinds him to the needs of the individual. He becomes toxically judgmental and closed-minded when anxious and cuts off those who don't agree with him. Arden communicates best with Arden, Lee, Nevada, Kelly, and Francis. He argues most with Shelby.

How: Arden is free with his opinions, but stingy with his emotions. He doesn't realize that his opinions come across as unfeeling. A character must approach him with a calm, rational argument. Arden fiercely defends a plan or idea once he adopts it. His switch confuses the people he once agreed with. He tells you what he thinks, asks for and delivers objective opinions, and is focused on whether the information is true or false. He doesn't care if you agree. He isn't interested in exploring why he is upset. He wants you to focus on what he is thinking. He is more interested in solving the problem than listening to an emotional rehash of it. He ignores personal criticism. He enforces rules, even if they are damaging or wrong. If someone does something wrong, he isn't interested in emotional explanations as to why. He isn't open to appeal.

What: Blair relies on facts and isn't interested in debating theory. She takes life very seriously. She is sensitive to other people and grasps the intricacies of behavior and motive. She retains information about the people around her and uses it to manipulate them. She prefers hunches to facts. She is flexible and deferential until violated. She isn't interested analyzing what happened before or what could happen in the future. Her insights are lacking in that way. Her view of reality is based on preconceived notions, so she doesn't have a balanced view of the truth. She blames other people for problems and sees herself as a victim.

Who: Blair prefers to think things over before she talks about them. She confides in her inner circle. She suppresses her emotions and blows up out of proportion to the trigger. She sneers at people who lack self-control. She has strong opinions about what is right and wrong. She dismisses people who disagree with her and they become her enemies. Blair communicates best with Blair, Joss, Shelby, Hadley, and Wynn. She argues most with Lee.

How: Blair shuts down and withdraws when she faces opposition. She justifies her behavior by finding fault with the person who challenges her. She does not accept responsibility for her mistakes. Invasion of her personal space makes her rigid. She can be overly critical and cynical. She is a good listener, but poor at expressing her thoughts and feelings. She is hard on herself and considers criticism from someone else unjustified. She often hears criticism where none is intended. She tells you what she feels, asks for and delivers sentiments, and is focused on whether the information is good or bad. She cares if you agree. It doesn't matter what the problem is, she wants you to understand how she feels about it. She wants you to acknowledge that she is upset. She is more interested in rehashing the emotional impact of the problem than solving it.

What: Dallas isn't interested in how things are as much as how they could be. She recognizes patterns and how things interconnect. She eagerly shares her insight. She is a global learner and thinks close is close enough. She prefers theories and is not limited by facts. She is a keen observer. She analyzes motive. She is sensitive to other people's needs. She quickly picks up on the heart of the conflict. She may evaluate the facts incorrectly. She struggles with sustained effort and persuasive arguments. She ignores long-term consequences. Dallas is a master manipulator. She is also easily manipulated. She usually gets what she wants. She resents anyone that tries to control or label her. She grasps what is and isn't socially acceptable and uses it to her advantage. She is a good judge of character.

Who: Dallas likes to talk things over as she thinks things through. She consults her wide network of friends. She shuts down anyone who opposes her. Dallas communicates best with Dallas, Hadley, Morgan, Shelby, and Taylor. She argues most with Francis.

How: Dallas appears focused on the person in front of her, but she is intensely aware of what is going on in the background. She tells you what she feels, asks for and delivers sentiments, and is focused on whether the information is good or bad. She wants you to agree with her. It doesn't matter what the problem is, she wants you to understand how she feels about it. She wants you to acknowledge that she is upset. She is more interested in rehashing the emotional impact of the problem than solving it. She can talk her way into, or out of, anything. She avoids conflict and takes criticism personally. She represses anger for the sake of peace or acceptance and explodes at inappropriate moments. She blames her problems on other people and uses faulty logic to bolster her side of the argument. She justifies bad decisions. She hates being judged, though she is very judgmental.

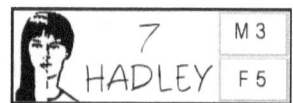

What: Hadley relies on facts rather than ideas. She isn't overly logical or analytical. She won't participate in deep, philosophical debates. She isn't a deep or long-range thinker, so her advice may not work. Hadley avoids conflict and takes criticism personally. She thinks every negative comment or practical bit of advice is an attempt to rain on her parade. She shuts out cautions and possible complications. She staunchly defends whatever she believes. Her views today might not be her views tomorrow. She ignores information that is counter to her shifting beliefs. She ignores the facts that make her uncomfortable. She may adopt extraordinary opinions that have no basis in reality. When anxious, she sees the world as a dark and dangerous place full of people out to get her. She may cut herself off from people who care about her if they disagree with her actions.

Who: Hadley likes to talk things over as she thinks them through. She talks problems over with everyone she comes in contact with. She is open to the opinions of strangers. Everyone she meets is a friend until they criticize her. She is sensitive to the emotions of the people around her. She recognizes, and can sometimes head off, interpersonal conflict before it becomes a serious problem. She also gets emotional cues wrong. Hadley communicates best with Hadley, Kelly, Dallas, Blair, and Nevada. She argues most with Cam.

How: Hadley tells you what she feels, asks for and delivers sentiments, and is focused on whether the information is good or bad. She wants you to agree with her. It doesn't matter what the problem is, she wants you to understand how she feels about it. She wants you to acknowledge that she is upset. She is more interested in rehashing the emotional impact of the problem than solving it. When confronted, she blames the world at large, the blue sky, or the family dog instead of her own behavior and choices. She bluffs with bull. Her rationalizations are shallow. She prefers to do a thing rather than listen to a lecture about it.

What: Shelby seems absent-minded, but spends a lot of time thinking things through. She evaluates not just what is, but what could be, preferring the idealized version over reality. She prefers theory over fact. She relies on intuition to guide her. She runs from conflict. She rates information based on how it feels, not whether it is factually correct. She dismisses impersonal arguments and intellectual debate. She views herself as fighting for good and right and dismisses any comments to the contrary. Her objectivity is poor because she is overly idealistic. She ignores information that counters her belief system or her belief in another person. She ruminates over slights, real or imagined.

Who: Shelby prefers to think things through before sharing them with her small circle of trusted friends. Shelby communicates best with Shelby, Blair, Greer, River, and Dallas. She argues most with Arden.

How: Shelby seeks win-win solutions. She is an active listener with a talent for assessing motive. She tells you what she feels, asks for and delivers sentiments, and is focused on whether the information is good or bad. She wants you to agree with her. It doesn't matter what the problem is, she wants you to understand how she feels about it. She wants you to acknowledge that she is upset. She is more interested in rehashing the emotional impact of the problem than solving it. She can't handle criticism and sometimes hears it when none is intended. She blames herself for everything. She justifies her behavior when others point the finger at her. She represses her feelings and erupts at inappropriate moments.

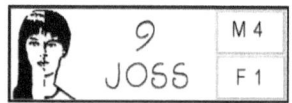

What: Joss is rational and analytical. His logic is fuzzy. He believes what he believes and won't listen to opposing views. He rejects anything that doesn't support his understanding of how things work. He makes impartial decisions quickly and easily. He is highly aware of the physical environment, but blind to the emotional landscape.

Who: Joss prefers to think things through before saying anything. He confides in his trusted inner circle. He ignores sources he does not respect. He ignores people who behave contrary to social norms. He avoids conflict and surrounds himself with like-minded people. He suspects those who behave or think differently of having malicious motives. He can drift toward paranoia, seeing opposition and criticism where none is intended. He thrives on freedom and risk. He won't listen to anyone who tries to corral him. Joss communicates best with Joss, Greer, Kelly, Blair, and Francis. He argues most with Taylor.

How: Joss is a man of few words. He is terse and to the point. He tells you what he thinks, asks for and delivers objective opinions, and is focused on whether the information is true or false. He doesn't care if you agree. He isn't interested in exploring why he is upset. He wants you to focus on what he is thinking. He is more interested in solving the problem than listening to an emotional rehash of it. He keeps his feelings buried and erupts inappropriately when opposed. He is more comfortable acting than talking. He won't indulge in lengthy philosophical debates. He turns cold in the face of emotional outbursts.

What: Kelly observes other people closely to find out what makes them tick and manipulates them accordingly. He grasps motive and is hypersensitive to nonverbal cues. He adds other people's perspectives and opinions to his mental database so he can use the information later to his benefit. Rules are suggestions and everything is open to interpretation. Anyone who says otherwise is a fool. His interpretations of things outside his understanding may be bizarre. He is subject to odd superstitions or flights of fancy.

He comes up with convoluted explanations to prove his beliefs are true. It's difficult to convince him he is wrong.

Who: Kelly likes to talk things out as he thinks them through. He knows a lot of people. No one really knows him. He does not care what other people think or feel about him or his choices. Thinking people bore him. He is immune to criticism. He considers the source and rarely respects the source. He embraces opposition just so he can defeat it. Kelly communicates best with Kelly, Morgan, Hadley, Joss, and Arden. He argues most with River.

How: Kelly is blunt. Some take that as honesty. It isn't. It is a tactic to make weaker individuals doubt themselves. He can talk himself out of trouble. In every conversation, his goal is to win. He tells you what he thinks, asks for and delivers objective opinions, and is focused on whether the information is true or false. He doesn't care if you agree. He isn't interested in exploring why you are upset. He wants you to focus on what he is thinking. He is more interested in solving the problem than listening to an emotional rehash of it. He can be a verbal bully or sweet and charming.

11 GREER M 3 F 1

What: Greer favors precise data and descriptions. He catches contradictions in statements no matter how far apart they are uttered. He has a unique form of intellectual scanning and recall. He sees things clearly and reaches for a logical explanation as to how and why. He picks apart accepted belief systems when they don't work or aren't helpful. He is easygoing until someone violates a core value. He becomes rigid in the face of opposition.

Who: Greer does not trust easily. It doesn't take much to lose his respect. He considers the source and rarely respects the source. He ignores people who are vastly different. He is overly suspicious of their motives. He relies on a select few and could find himself entirely cut off from them. Greer communicates best with Greer, Joss, Morgan, Shelby, and Cam. He argues most with Nevada.

How: Greer is so focused on gathering information, he may not appear to be listening. He pushes for more detailed answers. He lacks the interpersonal skills to convince others and has weak emotional intelligence. He tells you what he thinks, asks for and delivers objective opinions, and is focused on whether the information is true or false. He doesn't care if you agree. He may correct someone, or be sorely tempted to, if their proposition is faulty. He isn't interested in exploring why you are upset. He wants you to focus on what he is thinking. He is more interested in solving the problem than listening to an emotional rehash of it. He shuts down in the face of emotional outbursts. His sarcastic observations feed the flames. He is abrasive and rude. If it isn't rational or logical, it isn't true. He is immune to criticism. He represses his emotions and blows up out of proportion to the trigger.

What: Taylor's intuition is keen, but she often ignores it. She figures out people's triggers and uses them to get what she wants. She is harshly self-critical and rejects criticism from an outside source. Her need to avoid solitude makes her willing to accept ideas she would otherwise object to. Taylor embraces paranormal explanations. She won't listen to theoretical or logical arguments. She prefers to see things as she wants them to be instead of how they truly are. Her objectivity is weak. She sits on moral high ground and refuses to listen to anything that negates her self-image as a benevolent crusader or savior.

Who: Taylor likes to talk things over as she thinks them through. She has a wide network to discuss things with. She is petulant, paranoid, and manipulative if opposed or when someone lets her down. She communicates best with Taylor, Nevada, Lee, Dallas, and River. She argues most with Joss.

How: Taylor tells you what she feels, asks for and delivers sentiments, and is focused on whether the information is good or bad. She wants you to agree with her. It doesn't matter what the topic is, she wants you to understand how she feels about it. She wants you to acknowledge that she is upset. She is more interested in rehashing the emotional impact of the problem than solving it. She has strong thoughts and opinions, but keeps them to herself to avoid conflict. When she does speak up, she does so clearly. She agrees to whatever makes everyone happy rather than that which is most effective.

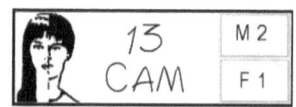

What: Cam is insightful, observant, and mentally sharp, though he rarely advertises it. He sees things for how they are, not how he wants them to be. Belief systems are subjective. They can be utilized or disregarded. He has a talent for brainstorming, generalizing, classifying, and summarizing. He sees connections others miss. He has keen deduction and intuition. He is an expert in the fields that interest him, but ignorant of those that don't. He is self-critical and not open to external criticism. He rejects what he considers woo-woo and irrational explanations. If someone calmly states his case, Cam evaluates it. He may change his mind if the logic is persuasive enough. He won't care if his opinion is popular.

Who: Cam prefers to mull things over before commenting. He listens only to the few he trusts and respects. If he can't trust those around him, he grows isolated. He prefers discussing things with other rational beings. Cam communicates best with Cam, River, Francis, Lee, and Greer. He argues most with Dallas.

How: Cam has a talent for explaining complex theories when he bothers. He comes across as terse and arrogant. His objective commentary alienates those who see criticism where it isn't intended. He tells you what he thinks, asks for and delivers objective opinions, and is focused on whether the information is true or false. He doesn't care if you agree with him. He isn't interested in exploring why you are upset. He wants you to focus on what he is thinking. He is more interested in solving the problem than listening to an emotional rehash of it. Emotional outbursts leave him cold. He keeps to himself and has a long fuse. When he blows, it is lethal. He prefers people to clearly articulate what they think and want. He doesn't seek praise. He offers it if he is impressed. He bases it on fact, not feeling. He is derisive and sarcastic if opposed.

What: Morgan is open to possibilities. He shrewdly predicts what comes next. He is analytical and enjoys complex challenges. He takes in data and applies it to the world around him. He is rational, objective, and logical. He evaluates people and situations and comes up with solutions. He learns all he can about things that interest him and ignores the rest. He decides whether it is useful or not. He comes up with a practical insight just when someone needs it. He does not look before he leaps, so his advice may not be the best in all situations.

Who: Morgan has a narrow circle of friends. He rejects the input of those he does not respect or care about and they are the majority. He listens to all sides and takes the position that makes the most logical sense. If he distrusts the people around him or finds himself in a sea of illogical beings, he withdraws and shuts down. Morgan communicates best with Morgan, Dallas, Kelly, Greer, and Lee. He argues most with Wynn.

How: Morgan has a quick wit and enjoys debate for the sake of debate. He defends those he cares about, even if they are wrong. He isn't in touch with his emotions and has weak emotional intelligence. Emotional outbursts leave him cold. He tells you what he thinks, asks for and delivers objective opinions, and is focused on whether the information is true or false. He doesn't care if you agree with him. He isn't interested in exploring why you are upset. He wants you to focus on what he is thinking. He is more interested in solving the problem than listening to an emotional rehash of it. He ignores the emotional factors. He is argumentative if he feels no one is listening. He is immune to praise and flattery and won't give it. He is arrogant, boastful, and scathing to those who oppose him.

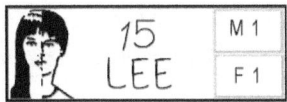

What: Lee has a talent for classifying, generalizing, and summarizing data. She thinks on her feet and comes up with fresh ideas. She isn't interested in the emotional content of a conversation. She considers her ideas superior to most and isn't open for discussion. She enjoys a lively debate, mostly so she can prove her point.

Who: Lee likes to talk things over as she thinks them through. She has minions not friends. Overly emotional people give her the creeps. She won't respect or listen to them. She rarely considers anyone else's opinions and shuts down anyone who disagrees with her. She is highly responsible and dismisses those who aren't. She dismisses people she needs to listen to. She could be conned by someone who appears to support her. She believes those who don't agree with her are plotting against her. Lee communicates best with Lee, Taylor, Arden, Morgan, and Cam. She argues most with Blair.

How: Lee gives advice to help people through a rough patch. She won't listen to them whine. She tells them what she thinks, asks for and delivers objective opinions, and is focused on whether the information is true or false. She doesn't care if they agree with her. She isn't interested in exploring why they are upset. She wants them to focus on what she is thinking. She is more interested in solving the problem than listening to an emotional rehash of it. She is furious when people don't follow her mandates. Her harsh and critical approach ruffles feathers. She is childishly petulant when she does not get her way. She doesn't give praise or respond to it. She explodes with anger at inappropriate moments. She takes opposition as a personal attack.

What: River prefers to ponder things more than talk about them. She consults her intuition. She is able to read the emotions, feelings, and morality of other people. She usually keeps her findings to herself. She understands the emotional cost of complete honesty. She has a vivid imagination and excellent memory. Her strong "feelings" leave the thinking types cold. She relies on her gut, but her hunch may be wrong. She believes strongly in what she accepts as true. She rejects information that counters her beliefs. She cannot handle criticism or conflict and withdraws at the first sign of them. She negates anything that doesn't fall in line with her ridiculously high standards.

Who: River has few friends. She does not trust easily and only listens to the few she respects. Her secretive nature makes her suspect. She holds a grudge and drops everyone who offends or disappoints her. She may end up isolated. She communicates naturally with River, Wynn, Cam, Taylor, and Shelby. She argues most with Kelly.

How: If pushed, River gives her opinion. It may not be what the person wanted to hear. She tells you what she feels, asks for and delivers sentiments, and is focused on whether the information is good or bad. She wants you to agree with her. It doesn't matter what the topic is, she wants you to understand how she feels about it. She wants you to acknowledge that she is upset. She is more interested in rehashing the emotional impact of the problem than solving it. She isn't interested in praise. She is a good listener, but her advice is not objective. She communicates better on paper than in person. She is cutting and sarcastic to those who argue with her. She blames other people when things go wrong. She represses her feelings and lashes out at the wrong moment.

Ways to Warp Your Mannequins

Peacemakers: Wynn, Nevada, Blair, Dallas, Hadley, Shelby, Taylor, and River take other people's feelings into account. They keep the peace at the cost of saying what needs to be said. Modern society attributes this as a feminine trait. However, there are twenty-six males and thirty-three females in this category. They make up fifty-nine percent of the population of Tinker Town. They are reluctant to offend other people.

They persuade people by appealing to their emotions. They become physically animated when confronted. Their blood boils and seethes. Their emotions rub off on those around them. Crowds are fed by this emotion. They win by making the other person feel bad. They turn personal, disparaging the other person rather than the facts. If pushed, they yell until they get their way. They strike in heat and repent at leisure. They are seen by the other half as illogical bleeding hearts.

ALT Logicians: Francis, Arden, Joss, Kelly, Greer, Cam, Morgan, and Lee tell it like it is no matter how anyone feels about it. Modern society considers this a masculine trait. There are twenty-eight males and thirteen females in this category in Tinker Town. They make up forty-one percent of the population. They say whatever makes the most sense, regardless of how it makes anyone feel. They are regarded as cold and brutal in their delivery. They persuade others by convincing them of the logic and the efficacy of their ideas. They make fun of frothing emotions.

They internalize their physical reaction when confronted. Their blood seethes too, but they temper it by becoming rigid and withholding. They view an emotional crowd with distaste. They retreat and walk away. They look for opportunities to prove they are right, leaving the emotional person to his rant with a smirk. They are master of "I told you so." Retaliation is best served cold.

ALT Consensus: Opposites struggle to reach consensus about what should be done in a household, a government, or a planetary council. The best course usually lies somewhere in the middle. To show growth, emotional characters need to consider objective facts. Logical characters need to consider the emotional impact of their words. The two coming together could solve the overall story problem and probably achieve world peace.

ALT Different Drums: Characters gather conflicting information. Two characters can gather the same information, but draw two different conclusions. They can look at the same evidence and decide to accept or ignore different parts of it. There might not be enough evidence to draw a firm conclusion. They listen to different people. Their confidants may not concur with the majority opinion. These obstacles create conflict at the scene level.

Approach: Characters have different styles of communication. Sometimes it's not what they said, but how they said it. It's not the request, but how they couched the proposal. Characters use different styles in different circumstances. Extreme situations force them to speak in ways they normally wouldn't. A logical character can lose his temper and offer an emotional tirade. An emotional character can be doused enough to deliver a cool parting shot. A furious character must bite his tongue when dealing with a toddler, an uncooperative patient, an elderly caregiver, or a world leader.

Aggressor: An aggressive communicator makes a good antagonist or foe. At his worst, any character could be driven to aggressive communication. An aggressive communicator believes everyone should be like him and he is never wrong. He has all the rights. He is closed-minded and a poor listener. He has difficulty seeing another person's point of view. He interrupts people mid-sentence and monopolizes conversations. He gets what he wants out of an interrogation, or a conversation, at the expense of others. He wants people to agree with him, not challenge him. He is condescending and sarcastic. He infringes on the other person's space or grasps them in an unpleasant way while talking. He points and shakes his finger, frowns, and squints. He is master of the stare-down.

If you oppose him, he gets louder in an attempt to shout you down. He speaks in fast, short sentences. He is verbally abusive. He threatens and bullies when he wants something. He always wins, or thinks he wins, an argument. It is fun when the reader realizes this character didn't win, but the character thinks he did. The verbal bully does not like his authority questioned. He is motivated by anger, hostility, frustration, impatience, and low self-esteem. When confronted by an aggressive communicator, a character's only real option is to walk away because he won't win or gain what he needs.

Sometimes your character can't help the urge to fight back, even when he knows it is pointless, because bullies really make him angry. The aggressive communicator inspires subtle acts of defiance, sabotage, and revenge. During a conversation, a character may pacify or agree with the aggressor to end the conversation so he can leave. A character might lie or cover something up to protect himself or other people in the moment. He can later exact revenge by making the verbal bully appear stupid or wrong. Readers like seeing the bully one-upped.

ALT Obstructer: A passive communicator has his own set of issues. He rarely says what he means. He avoids conflict and won't verbally disagree, even when he mentally disagrees. He won't offer an opinion, unless it reinforces what the other person just said. He is quick to cave in and change his opinion. He answers a question with a question. If you want or need a straight answer, he is maddening. He is apologetic. He doesn't trust himself or the foundation for his opinions. He rarely begins statements with "I want" or "I feel". He allows other people to put words in his mouth. He rarely succeeds when he is sent to find out an important piece of information or interrogate someone.

He sighs a lot. He agrees with both sides of an argument because he doesn't want to offend anyone. If he is offended, he clams up. He asks permission before proceeding: "May I say?" "Excuse me, I don't mean to intrude, but ...". He complains about a problem to everyone, except the person who can fix it. He offers complex, meandering justifications and explanations rather than a simple "yes" or "no." He often nods, smiles, and says "okay" to avoid conflict.

If he needs something, he whines, begs, or pleads. He hints and alludes and expects the other person to grasp his meaning. He is frustrated when the other person misses the hint. He won't look you in the eye. He speaks in a soft tone that is fast when he is anxious and slow when he is unsure. He often prefaces statements with a phrase that discounts or questions the validity of the statement: "I'm not sure but..." or "I'm probably wrong, but ..." The passive communicator procrastinates to avoid unpleasant conversations. He is quiet and withdrawn. He asks for advice often and doesn't trust his instincts. Strangely, he also wonders why he doesn't receive credit for anything. At the pathologic end, he is not well liked. His boundaries are too squishy.

[ALT] **Negotiator**: A healthy communicator makes a good protagonist. Every mannequin at his noblest is a healthy communicator. He has a healthy sense of self. He is assertive without being pushy. He is interested in sharing or gaining information, not winning. He is an effective speaker and active listener. He clearly states limits and expectations without labels or judgments. He is direct, honest, and uses "I feel" or "I want." He is tuned in to the feelings of other people. He makes statements about behavior instead of judging it. Instead of saying, "You always" or "You never," he says, "In this instance…" He trusts himself and trusts others. He is confident and self aware. He has a playful sense of humor. He is decisive, proactive, and takes the initiative. He subtly leads a conversation where he needs it to go. He is realistic and fair.

A healthy communicator uses open, natural gestures. Facial expressions reflect his attentiveness. He uses direct eye contact and a modulated tone. He varies his rate of speech. He is open to options and alternatives. When confronted, he negotiates, bargains, and compromises so both sides win. He takes care of issues as they crop up. He tries to leave the conversation on a positive note. He is even-tempered and enthusiastic. He makes others feel heard and understood and lets them know where they stand.

Passive-Aggressive: A healthy communicator can be pushed toward aggressive when dealing with a passive person or pushed toward passive when dealing with an aggressive person. Females tend to be more passive than aggressive due to cultural conditioning. However, there are aggressive females and passive males. When they defy stereotypes, they become more interesting. Every character is aggressive if he needs a decision quickly, the situation is an emergency, or he doesn't have time for an argument or consensus. This is true of police officers facing down criminals, a teacher controlling a classroom, or peacekeepers controlling a mob. If your character is threatened by a monster, he doesn't have time for niceties. If a character is right and the fact is crucial, he becomes aggressive to get his point across.

A character is passive when an issue is minor and he doesn't want to fight about it. He is passive when the consequences are greater than conflict itself. He can use a passive approach to calm emotions when emotions are running high and everyone needs to take a break and rethink. He becomes passive when placed in a position of lower rank or power. He is passive when the situation, rules, or other person is impossible to change. If he has a difficult mother, shouting at her won't make her less difficult. If he has an obstinate child, shouting at the child won't make him more cooperative. Spanking him might, in the moment. Long term, he is not helping the situation. If he is dealing with someone feeling irrational, shouting at him won't make him more rational.

ALT Crossed Purposes: Conflicts in communication occur when what a character says isn't what he means. Double entendre and coded messages fall in this category. A character might not shout, "Maniac standing next to you." He uses conversational shorthand:

"You remember that time you woke up and there was a spider on your sleeping bag?"

"What spider?"

"The big, black, hairy one. You screamed like a girl. Remember? We were in that tent in Kazakhstan."

"Oh, that spider."

If the other character knows him well, he understands the reference or the shorthand. Make sure your readers get it too. Cue them in with action and reaction so they are in on it with you. You don't have to stop action with a flashback to the past incident. You don't have to spend a previous chapter illustrating the incident in the tent in Kazakhstan. If the characters react and answer appropriately, the meaning is clear.

⌨ Setup and Payoff: It is fun to use this technique in dialogue several times throughout the story. Two characters can repeat the same word, phrase, or conversation multiple times within the same story. Key words and repeated phrases resonate with the reader. Use them wisely and sparingly. This tactic is effective in Comedy, but can feature in any genre. Each time the item is used, it can take on a different meaning.

⌨ Context: Conflicts in communication occur when something a character says is taken out of context or misunderstood. He can have the best intentions in the world. It won't matter if the character he addresses is having a bad day, feeling overly sensitive, or the words strike him at just the wrong angle. Small misunderstandings create big wounds. Characters all have their issues and sensitive moments. A character experiencing heightened emotions can be triggered by an innocent comment.

Characters reveal information they didn't intend to under these circumstances. Characters have triggers imbedded in their primitive brains. Innocent, or malicious, comments pull those triggers. The character perceives someone's comment as a blow to his pride, honor, integrity, intelligence, generosity, or belief system. A casual comment, even if it was meant to be funny, could result in a massive blowout. If a character intentionally says something knowing they'd strike a nerve, that's a higher level of conflict.

Muddled Meaning: Characters hear things wrong, interpret things wrong, and relate information filtered through their experiences and personal preferences. A character repeats things that are said to him. He may believe what he is saying. That does not make it true or accurate. Two characters can talk about separate things, but think they are talking about the same thing. It is fun when they, and the reader, realize they have been talking at crossed purposes. Misunderstanding happens between couples who have been together a long time. They develop a type of shorthand. They also stop listening to everything that comes out of the other person's mouth. You can have fun when a character talks to someone who is not paying attention. That person might agree to something and not realize it. He could confirm a piece of information and not know it. He could answer a question he didn't realize was asked. Misunderstandings set the stage for mild annoyance, misdirection, calamity, or hilarity.

Missing Steps: Sometimes a character launches a topic, but forgets to set it up first. He assumes the other person is privy to the thought process that led up to the topic. He expects the other person to read his mind. A character might be thinking about taking a trip to Hawaii. He starts talking about luaus and hula dancers and the other character has no idea why. He can interrupt another's reverie and receive a response that doesn't make sense. Miscommunication that interferes with what the character needs to find out is good dialogue conflict. If a character drops in during the middle of someone else's conversation, he might misunderstand what they are talking about.

An investigator can spend time researching a false clue. A spy might show up at a rendezvous and end up in a difficult position. A character might think her lover is planning a terrific surprise for Valentine's Day and realize her error when the day rolls around and he leaves to watch his favorite sports team with his buddy. A character can eavesdrop or overhear a conversation that doesn't mean what he thinks it means. Eavesdroppers rarely hear good things about themselves. A character might overhear something that deeply wounds him, angers him, or makes him take the right steps to correct a situation. He may have heard correctly or incorrectly.

[ALT] **Red Words:** Some words are "fighting words." There are ways of handling a conversation that guarantee a fight. A reader won't stop and think, "Wow, that word ignited a firestorm." Rather, the conversation sounds true to life because we've all had those moments. When two characters are on opposing sides of an argument or thematic premise, they can discuss the issue in a healthy way. They can make it personal and attack the other person's actions or behavior instead of the concept. The necessary conversation nosedives. It is almost impossible to get the exchange back on track. Accusatory statements often start with "You" as in: "You aren't listening...," "You don't know what you're talking about...," "You always...," "You never...," and "Who are you to tell me..." Use these zingers and the fight is on.

[ALT] **Red Flags**: Generalizations and exaggerations are red flags. Anytime a character utters words like "always," "never," or "every time," he is subconsciously picking a fight. When he introduces astronomic figures, he enters the realm of the ridiculous. "You've said that a million times," is clearly a lie. It goads the other person to counter the statement. People react badly to exaggerations that are invalid or demeaning, particularly if the flag is waved in front of other people. Flipping this cape at his domestic partner during a dinner party starts a domestic war. The innocent jab about her cooking becomes mutual mudslinging. It is a great way to derail a conversation that your character needs to have. Whatever he hoped to achieve, he blew it and has to try again later after the other person cools off. He must change his tactics.

[ALT] **Quicksand**: Sometimes the conversation gets mired in what happened in the past rather than the issue at hand. Rigid people keep a list they refer to when defensive. They switch focus to the the past. Others like to rehash things that are beyond their control instead of focusing on what can be fixed. When the issue at hand opens an old wound, the gloves are off. The character can forget whatever he hoped to accomplish by the conversation. Shifting to argue a past event interrupts the flow. The exchange devolves into a blame game and never ends well.

These arguments often begin with: "Remember when you...," or "The last time you..." This tactic is used to manipulate the other person's emotions. Making someone feel bad or inferior shames him into going along with, or changing his mind about, the topic. These conversations can reveal important backstory, reveal clues, reinforce characterization, or illustrate thematic conflict.

Hot Pokers: The best defense is a good offense. Some characters use this tactic without being aware of it. Others manipulate the conversation intentionally. These defensive statements start with: "It's all your fault...," "If you had just...," or "I can't believe..." These red-hot pokers force the other person to defend himself or retreat out of guilt. A well-adjusted character won't take the bait and returns to the original question or request. A passive character doubts himself and makes excuses. An aggressive character insults him, punches him, or storms off. Beginning conversations with "Are you absolutely sure?" implies a lack of trust in the other person's opinion, information, ability, integrity, commitment, or behavior. Even if the question is valid, the prod makes the other person defensive or aggressive in response. If the person is truly ignorant or incompetent, he won't appreciate having it pointed out. Using hot pokers when a situation is tense rarely has a happy result.

Laundry Pile: The confronted character deflects blame with layer after layer of justification. A character uses this technique to hide things he feels ashamed of. He turns the tables and projects his shame onto the other person. This response prevents a conversation from going further. The interrogator ends up defending the fact that he got drunk at a cousin's bachelor party ten years ago and denying he had sex with the stripper. A savvy protagonist resists rebuttal, calmly waits until the character is finished with his tirade, and returns to the original request or question.

⌨ **Pull the Trigger:** This tactic is effective with characters who bottle their emotions. Someone comes along at the wrong moment and makes a comment or asks a question that pulls his emotional trigger. The questioner becomes a target for the character's pent up anger and resentment. The character's emotional scattershot makes the questioner forget his original purpose. This happens often between couples. It also happens between friends, siblings, and at work. The character's emotional tirade may have nothing to do with the hapless questioner at all. He simply reached a breaking point and the innocuous comment tipped the balance. This interaction can reveal character change. It can release important information. It can keep an important piece of information from being revealed. If your character intentionally attacks another character's currency, the game is on.

⌨ **Sympathy Loves Misery**: A well-meaning attempt by one character to appear supportive can backfire. Try hugging a cat that doesn't like being picked up, the effect is the same. Offering unwanted reassurances or positive comments angers the person instead of making him feel better. A character with low self-esteem or one who hears criticism where none was intended are perfect examples. He decides he is being patronized or condescended to. Continued attempts to rephrase intent are met with increasing anger and resistance. Even though the reassurance or positive comment was well intended, it was ill received. The character's angry response often sparks a "You never..." or "You always..." accusatory rehash of past events.

⌨ **Advice Bombs:** Some mannequins feel the need to offer advice when it is neither requested nor desired. Giving advice places a character in a one-up position and implies he knows something the other person does not. The receiver reacts in a hostile manner, even if the advice is well intentioned, rational, or much needed. The merit of the advice doesn't matter. It's the way the advice is delivered and the state of mind of the person receiving it. To avoid conflict, it is best to ask the other person if he would like to hear a suggestion. Leave this step out, or approach someone at the wrong time, and the fight is on.

Bait and Switch: It is never a good idea for a character to start a conversation with a comment that sounds condescending: "I absolutely insist...," "There is no way you...," or "I am positive ...." These statements come across as arrogant. The other character stops listening to work out a way to refute the statement or the character's authority. The original point is lost in a cloud of contention. The instigator attempts to bring the conversation back to the topic and meets resistance. If the receiver disagrees with a character's original statement, he usually won't listen to the supporting evidence either.

Flattery: Confidence is a good thing when demonstrated in a healthy way. Confident statements suggest that the other person is equally competent and the conversation goes well. Conversations that begin with, "As you know," or "Like you said before," appeal to a character's sense of competence. You usually get what you want. This is particularly effective when the character's currency is competence or admiration. Characters like to talk about things they know about or think they know about. Encourage them and they tell you more than you wanted or needed to know. This is a good way for a character to get information out of someone. Flattery results in success if applied in the correct way and if the flatterer has the required amount of personal charm. If the character lacks charisma, flattery comes across as false. A flattering statement fails when it is clearly a lie, particularly with a logical character. If the target of the flattery is arrogant or not self-aware, he might fall for flattery and give the character the information or assistance he needs.

[ALT] Rate the Request: A character creates conflict by the way he asks or doesn't ask. A character is often open to a suggestion if someone asks rather than tells. Most mannequins don't like being ordered to do things, particularly the highly independent ones. Commands inspire them to do the opposite. Orders imply the other person has the right to tell them what to do. Commands work if a character is in the armed forces or in a situation where he is programmed to respond to commands without question. Commands work well with a character who looks to authority for guidance. Commands are ill-received by everyone else. A character may order a two-year-old to do something and get away with it. It's better to ask a twenty-year-old.

[ALT] Velvet Glove: Sometimes a character must convince someone who disagrees with him. Some temperaments are better at convincing than others. Some characters are more open to suggestion. Most want their point of view to have equal consideration. If their opponent adopts defensive or offensive tactics, the conversation death spirals. A character might resist because he has a knee-jerk response to every request. He might actually agree with the proposition or be willing to accede to the request, but enjoys making it tough for the person doing the asking.

ALT **Interrogation**: Questions are used to gather information. They can be used to build consensus and harmony. Too many questions make a character feel attacked. He worries the interrogator is trying to trick him, particularly if the interrogator doesn't appear to be listening to the answers. An interrogator effectively uses questions to show he is in control of the conversation. He allows or prevents the other person's response. Asking "why" makes the character defend his position or behavior. The interrogator may have no ulterior motive. A guilty person views innocent questions as accusatory. A character who hears criticism where none is intended feels attacked. A character can obscure a statement by phrasing it as a question. Statements that begin with, "You don't actually believe…" are fighting words.

Questions can also be about something else. The real question underlying a question can have long-reaching effects if not answered correctly or to the interrogator's satisfaction. Questions within questions create tension. A character may ask her spouse's opinion on something superficial like their weekend plans. The underlying question is, "Do you love me enough to spend time with me?" or "Are we okay as a couple?" An emotionally oblivious character misses the real question. It is important to use this tactic in a way the reader picks up on. If it is delivered in an obscure way, it won't have the impact you desire.

ALT **Trojan Horse**: Innuendo and insinuation are remarks or questions that deliver an implied or veiled suggestion. They are red flags and serve to insult or accuse. Taken literally, the words are innocent. The subtext is suggestive or malicious.

Insinuation, if the target catches on, sparks anger and aggression. Applied cleverly, it derails a conversation in a hurry. The attacked character defends or goes on the offensive. The original goal of the conversation is forgotten. Innuendo, if the recipient is open to it, becomes an invitation. If not, it's harassment. If the innuendo is directed at someone who doesn't pick up on it, the effect is comic. A character might use it to be cruel.

Prick the Hide: A character can make assumptions about the other person's thoughts and feelings. Characters that are prone to paranoia do this often. The conversation ends badly if the assumptions are wrong. Telling another character he understands what he is thinking or feeling can be a sign of solidarity or empathy. Taken the wrong way, or used with the wrong person, the tactic is insulting and patronizing. Statements that begin with: "I know, you think (feel, need, want)…," start a fight. No one likes being told how he feels. A character might not like being analyzed, particularly if he dislikes the analyzer. A friend might get away with a comment a foe won't.

Covered Ears: Characters interrupt, sigh, and rehearse what to say next while the other person is talking. It's impossible to get someone to understand your point of view if he isn't listening to it. There are many reasons why a character won't listen. He deflects information he finds uncomfortable. He is offended by the tone of the conversation. He stops listening to stories he has heard before. He dislikes the person speaking. He disagrees with what is being said. Something else captures his attention. He may be wrestling with an internal conflict of his own and what the other person is saying isn't important. If a character isn't listening when someone needs him to, it can work in his favor or cause him to fail at scene level. What a character wants to say is of primary concern to him; it might not be to someone else. If a character isn't listening, the results can be catastrophic.

FACTS, FANTASIES & LIES

This category of communication deserves special attention. When something has been proven, it is considered a fact. However, things that were once considered "facts" have been disproven. We know the sun does not revolve around the earth and the earth isn't flat. People were willing to kill over those "facts" at the time.

A character may lie, cheat, steal, or kill to prove that a belief or an opinion is true. Debating relative truth can be an overall story problem, a thematic argument, or a scene obstacle. The conflict can end with the character finding out what he believed is false, has elements of truth, or can't be proven either way.

When a character accepts something as true, he stops asking questions. He rejects information that counters his belief. The protagonist might have to investigate something he thought he had the answer to and realize he was wrong. Friends and foes re-evaluate the accuracy of things they thought they knew or someone they believed in. Prejudices, conceits, and commitments are re-examined in the light of new information. A character's willingness to re-evaluate data is affected by his temperament.

FACT VERSUS FANTASY

Characters all fantasize occasionally. Writers fantasize a lot. Daydreams are a form of fantasy. When a character fantasizes about something long enough, it starts to feel real. In a positive way, he grows and changes by picturing what he wants to become or to accomplish. He works to make his fantasy a reality. Fantasies allow your character to ask, "What if?" A sleuth solves the mystery because he is able to hypothesize, "What if?" A fantasy inspires a scientist to build a life-like robot. Fantasies have inspired great leaps in technology.

The dark side of fantasy is focusing so much on it that the character loses sight what is real. A mentally ill character may construct elaborate fantasies or suffer from schizophrenia, drug-induced hallucinations, or grandiose delusions. When a character believes a fantasy is real, he is confused when confronted by information that negates the fantasy. If a child believes his imaginary friend is real, it may keep him from having real friends. If the invisible friend is a ghost, it makes a great Horror or Fantasy tale. A serial killer lives in a dangerous fantasy world of his own making. In a horror story, a protagonist can be caught up in a fantasy gone wrong. Characters have sexual fantasies that create conflict. Fantasies of becoming a billionaire can lead him to invent a new product or conduct criminal behavior.

REASONS FOR LYING

Everyone lies at some point about matters small and large. Humans say they expect honesty and dislike liars. Lying is considered wrong, a sin, or a crime. Consistent lying makes a person untrustworthy. Lying breaks the bond of trust and trust is the glue that holds relationships together. Lies are a form of betrayal. Ironically, characters are lied to everyday by profits, preachers, marketers, politicians, manufacturing companies, doctors, lawyers, policemen, teachers, reporters, pundits, and history books. The truth is, people are sometimes lied to for their own good or to gain their compliance. There are degrees of lying and times when a lie is better than the truth.

Lies can serve as a thematic argument, overall story problem, personal dilemma, or create conflict at scene level. Lies are a form of knowledge obstacle. There are many reasons why a character lies.

[CTRL] Protection: He lies to protect himself. He pretends he does not have the information requested. He professes to not know how to do the task required. He may lie about money, especially if he is in financial trouble. He covers up his weak side. If the mannequin is poor at execution or follow through, he lies to cover up the fact that the task was left undone or the deadline not met.

He lies about why he is late. He lies to justify ignoring rules or defying authority. He lies about impulsive spending or actions. He lies about why he wants to stay home instead of go out. He lies about what he was doing while he was out if it goes against his partner's value system. The mannequin who loves a grand gesture might lie about how much a gift cost, or where he got it from, when his partner objects to the expenditure.

[CTRL] Protector: He lies to protect someone else from harm or harsh judgment. If a character doesn't have time to fully explain, a lie is sometimes quicker. A lie can keep a situation from getting worse. Lies of omission can cause as much conflict as telling an outright lie. If a character knows a loved one did something wrong, he might not rush out and tell the police about it. A character might forget to mention that he saw his boss screwing his secretary on Tuesday if it would cost him his job.

Blame: He lies to deflect blame, to avoid punishment, or dodge reprisal. He hides behaviors other people disapprove of. Everyone has secrets or things they are ashamed of. He lies to a bully or abusive authority figure. Characters make excuses when they fail to live up to certain expectations in an attempt to reduce their personal responsibility and avoid punishment. There are short and long-term effects of making excuses. Blaming others and telling half-truths that are not believable cast doubt on a person's character. A character that constantly makes excuses is seen as self-absorbed, unreliable, or downright stupid. When things go wrong, half of the mannequins blame someone else. The other half don't care who did it as long as it gets fixed. They are impatient with excuses. Apologies followed by an excuse, such as "I'm sorry. I forgot. It won't happen again," can diffuse tense situations temporarily. The excuse must be credible, show that the character is trying to fix the problem, and maintain good will. It can offer a character a short-term reprieve from conflict and setup a future scene for continued conflict.

Discomfort: He lies to avoid confrontation. A character pretends he didn't eat the candy bar that blew his diet. He mentally shaves off a few pounds when he steps off the scale to avoid arguing about it with his partner. A character hides a new pair of shoes or a designer handbag from her partner. A character may not want to discuss for the one-hundredth time why he plays golf every Saturday from ten until two. A character lies to avoid telling her partner she isn't interested in sex with him anymore. Some mannequins are better at confronting. Others do everything possible to avoid it.

CTRL Gain: He lies to gain something he wants or to prevent something he doesn't want. Cutthroat competition can inspire a rational man to lie about, or to, his coworkers or teammates. He lies about a product or service for financial gain. He lies about his qualifications on an application. He lies about the number of investors who back him or the quality of the cocaine he imports.

CTRL Kindness: He lies to avoid hurting someone's feelings. White lies are uttered in attempt to make someone feel better, avoid saying something unflattering, or to keep the peace. They are intentional or unintentional. Brutal honesty isn't pretty. The truth offends a character when it is something he doesn't want to hear or when it counters his belief system.

CTRL Pride: He lies to make himself look or feel better. A character lies to cloak the negative aspects of his shadow self. There may be parts of his personality he feels aren't admirable. He carries shame over small transgressions. He carries shame passed down through his upbringing or religious indoctrination. He exaggerates to shore up his self-esteem or make something seem less important than it was. He may inflate his financial status to earn someone's affection or respect then have to lie to keep that person from realizing it isn't true. He might invent elaborate stories about his past or brag about achievements that never happened. If he makes decisions or takes actions that support the lie, the situation grows complicated fast.

[CTRL] Authority: Characters assume people with authority are telling the truth because they are honor-bound to do so. The higher the position of authority, the deeper the societal wound when the character is caught lying. Characters are irrationally disappointed when they raise people up only to find they can't live up to their pedestals.

[CTRL] Power: He lies to appease someone with more power or to gain power over someone. A character can cover for someone. That someone then owes him a favor. He might overhear a discussion among strangers or speak to a mutual acquaintance and discover a secret someone thought he had well hidden. With the proliferation of cell phones, cameras, and computers, this happens quite by accident. People on cell phones talk loudly and don't seem to care who overhears them. People leave laptops open in public places. Everyone is armed with a camera. They capture things intentionally or accidentally. When they do, they have a powerful weapon.

[CTRL] Misinformation: A character can be coached or set up by someone else with false information. Misinformation is as bad, or worse, than lies. It is used as propaganda and a strategic counter terrorism tactic. Misinformation is used to manipulate the masses. It is used at scene level for good or ill. It can function as an overall story problem.

[CTRL] Pathology: He is a true pathological liar. If this character says the sky is blue, you have to look out and make sure. He lies about everything no matter how inconsequential. His logic is poor. He has difficulty keeping up with his constant lies. He leaves a trail of destruction wherever he goes. A pathological liar may actually believe his lies. He can get so lost in his version of reality that it blinds him to the world around him. He loses touch with reality. He makes a good foe, but a poor antagonist. Antagonists are usually more focused. When they lie, it is with intent and they remember the lie.

Memory: A character may not realize he is lying because his memory is faulty. Five siblings all remember their childhood differently. A child remembers traumatic moments more than the happy hours. His view of the past may not accurately reflect what happened. He remembers through his prism of wants, needs, perceptions, and prejudices. He remembers the slights and moments that made him feel insecure more so than winning the big game, making a new friend, or falling in love for the first time. He alters his "memories" when he relates stories from the past. He unintentionally embellishes the details, supplies forgotten ones, or represses negative ones. Adults remember perceived betrayals by friends, coworkers, and strangers.

Conflicting memories serve as an overall story problem or an obstacle at scene level. Two siblings, friends, coworkers, or witnesses can remember the same event differently. Five witnesses each record different impressions about an event. If they have heard news reports that contradict their impressions of an event, they adjust their memory to incorporate the news report. Characters talk following a traumatic event. By talking to each other, they reinforce certain parts of it, even if what they "remember" is wrong. Diseases from amnesia to Alzheimer's affect memories. It may be hard for the character to know what the truth really is.

[CTRL] **Justification**: Justifications allow a character to reconcile exceptions to what they know to be true while not acknowledging that they were wrong. They offer valid reasons for doing something that others think is wrong. Justifications create blind spots that keep characters from solving their dilemmas. A character may refuse to give up a point of view that isn't working for him.

[CTRL] **Dissonance**: When a character realizes his attitudes, thoughts, or beliefs are inconsistent with each other, it is called "cognitive dissonance." His mind rationalizes the dichotomy by inventing a comfortable illusion to account for it: "the devil made him do it" (true in a Horror story), "he was abducted by aliens" (perhaps true in Science Fiction), or he claims temporary insanity when accused of murder. A character may claim he didn't do something when he is the only person around who could have done it. He blames everything from the family pet to ghosts (true in a Paranormal story).

[CTRL] **Rationalization**: When a character expects his behavior will result in personal cost or punishment, he comes up with an artificial reason to deflect blame. The reason has to make sense and be plausible. It could actually be the reason, except it isn't. It might work initially, but is later proven false. Future conflict stems from his attempts to keep whatever he is hiding from coming to light. A character can rationalize everything from spiritualism to suicide bombing. A character rationalizes luxury purchases as investments. He rationalizes when he says things like:

"I didn't see any need to tell you, since I didn't think anyone would notice."

"Why expose the malpractice if the patient is going to die anyway?"

"Why tell them when it would only make them feel bad?"

"It was their fault. If they weren't so (fill in the blank), it wouldn't have happened in the first place."

"I did everything I could to make her happy. It isn't my fault if it didn't work out."

[CTRL] **Resolution**: Admitting a lie is better than being found out. By admitting he has done something wrong, a character takes ownership of it. This is healthy. By refusing to admit it, he compounds the breach of trust. Coming clean about a lie as soon as possible is the best way to repair the breach. The longer it takes him to 'fess up, the deeper the damage. Confession can serve as the thematic argument of a story or cause conflict at scene level.

[CTRL] **Shifting**: When your character asks a friend or lover to support his lie, he shifts part of the burden. The resulting stress can topple any relationship. The closer the relationship, the more of an imposition it is. The friend is forced to modify what he says and does. The friend eventually feels compelled to tell someone, even if the consequence is death.

[CTRL] **Revelation**: The truth rarely remains hidden. Lies are revealed in myriad ways and through the most innocuous and convoluted methods. The truth is: people talk. Most criminals are caught because they talked to someone. They might not be dumb enough to brag about it (some are), but they have to tell someone. That someone has at least one person he shares it with. And so on. And so forth.

HOW TO SPOT A LIAR

A liar either ignores that he will be exposed at some point or believes he won't get caught. Lies deflect the crisis of the moment, but create greater crises in the future. Carrying around a lie is exhausting. The bigger the lie, the more a character worries about being exposed. Anxiety causes him to respond in ways that are out of proportion. Whatever his normal reaction to anxiety is, lying amplifies it. He may withdraw, become hypercritical, or impulsive. He might start smoking or drinking to combat the stress. He must think before he speaks and acts. This is naturally difficult for some of the mannequins.

Some of the mannequins are natural lie detectors. They pick up nonverbal cues and body language. They hear what is not said. Let's explore how to catch a liar.

In terms of body language, lying curls the body inward. It is retracting and deflective. He uses objects as shields and distractions. Honesty expands and pushes the body forward. It is revealing and inclusive. He removes barriers. A liar rarely looks you in the eye. The pitch of his voice rises and tightens. His rate of speech increases. He hems and haws as he invents the story. He turns away, covers his mouth or eyes, and fidgets. The interrogator may have bad breath or the interviewee might just need to pee or be suffering a case of the hives. Assuming a character is lying based on body language alone is a conflict too.

👁 A liar gives too little information. In the course of normal conversation, a character says enough to express his idea or answer the question and no more. A liar cuts his response short because he does not have the additional information. If pressed for details, he invents them as he goes. He is caught when the details don't add up or he can't produce them in sufficient quantity.

👁 A liar over-embellishes to fill in the missing information. His answer becomes verbal vomit. He offers "too much information." Sometimes he does this intentionally as a deflection tool. In other situations, his anxiety forces him to ramble. If you try to organize the threads of his story, it falls apart. If pushed, a liar panics because he can't remember what he has just made up.

👁 A liar can't recount a situation backwards. He rehearses or invents information in chronological order. He struggles to relate it in reverse order. He says, "I went to Mike's, then we had pizza, then we played Nintendo, then we watched a movie." If you ask, "What did you do before the movie?" He might answer, "Ate pizza," leaving out the Nintendo part. If you ask about the Nintendo part, perhaps ask what game they played, he becomes flustered and defensive.

👁 A liar uses facts that are clearly wrong or exaggerated, particularly if he has scanty knowledge of the topic. A character claims he went bowling. When asked what his score was, he answers, "300." This is a perfect game and nearly impossible to achieve. If you continue to ask questions about it, he comes up with more lies or uses another tactic to abort the conversation.

👁 When a character lies, his logic or facts don't add up. When you probe to clarify, he becomes defensive, even hostile. Motive is important when a character lies. His reasoning does not make sense. He retaliates with, "Because, I just did, okay?" When the other character points out that his "why" doesn't make sense, the justifications fly or he changes the topic.

👁 A liar is vague on details. He omits key information. He says "my friend" instead of "Bob." He says "a coffee shop" instead "the Starbucks on the corner of Main and Fifth." He might give a sincere accounting of an event, leaving out a crucial piece of information. When confronted with the omission, he makes excuses: "I forgot" or "I didn't think it was important." Push a character who is omitting information for details and he gets defensive fast. He'll utilize a deflection technique to change the subject.

👁 A liar avoids having conversations he does not want to have. He hides in his office or workshop. He comes home late. He leaves early. He avoids being alone in a room with the person he is lying to.

👁 A liar is anxious. If your character withdraws, confronts, criticizes, explodes, turns passive-aggressive, or becomes erratic when anxious, his response is magnified when he is lying. His heart rate races. His body sweats. His skin grows warm and itchy. His face may flush or blanch.

A liar assumes other people are lying. If your mannequin naturally assumes that the world is suspect, the trait is magnified when he lies. He becomes paranoid and hyper-vigilant. He assumes everyone has an ulterior motive. He fears exposure. He becomes highly judgmental about other people's behavior to keep the light from being shined on his.

Diana Hurwitz

ABILITY OBSTACLES

Once a character knows something, and has pondered it or talked it over, he has to do something about it. Ability obstacles are created by a character's need to decide what to do, form a plan, and take the necessary action.

✖ A character lacks the strength or expertise to perform a physical or mental task.

✖ He struggles with forming a plan and seeing it through.

✖ He does not have enough or has too much time to think it through.

✖ Characters differ in their approach to the problem.

✖ His natural approach fails and he must rely on his weak side.

✖ He tries the opposite approach and it backfires.

✖ He invests effort in the wrong solution and fails.

✖ He is uncomfortable deciding or unhappy with the plan.

✖ He decides too soon or too late.

✖ He resists taking action or takes the wrong action to get it over with.

Every mannequin has strengths and weaknesses. He has areas of expertise and areas of ignorance. When action needs to be taken, different mannequins handle it in different ways. Some are able to make a plan and stick with it. Others prefer to wing it. Some make quick decisions. Others dither. Pairing opposites to get the job done creates conflict.

Deciding: Wynn waits for authority figures to make the decisions. If forced, she measures her options against her personal value system. She worries about how her actions appear to others. She considers the impact on those she cares for. She doesn't want recognition or expect it. Extenuating circumstances modify the rules. She is loyal and looks for consensus. She follows clues and ignores hunches. She notices details others miss, but loses sight of the big picture. Her approach is weak when the evidence is murky or points to the wrong solution. She isn't worried about the outcome. She becomes rigid and dismisses input she doesn't agree with when anxious. Logic goes right out the window when making life-altering decisions. She listens to emotionally charged arguments and is caught up in the heat of the moment. She makes snap judgments that can prove disastrous. Her weakness is gullibility. She is embroiled in efforts she otherwise wouldn't be if people play on her values or withhold important facts.

Planning: Wynn's primary goal is to be of use. She works quietly behind the scenes to make sure things run smoothly for the people she supports. She meets deadlines and is irritated by delays. She has a backup plan for the backup plan. She is reassured by safety nets. She expects things to happen again in the same way and prefers to do what worked before. She develops plans based on her experience, sees to the details, and handles the follow-through. Once she chooses a course of action, she doesn't question it. When the situation changes drastically or she hits a dead end, revising the plan makes her anxious.

Implementing: Wynn does what feels right, even if it isn't logical or the best answer. She acts alone only when pushed. She finds it hard to improvise and adapt. She dislikes supervising or relying on other people. Working with strangers or people she dislikes makes her anxious. She is horrible at delegating. Assign her a specific task, and it's done the way it has always been done. She focuses on the problem at hand, not those coming down the pike. She tackles the challenge head on and doesn't stop until it is completed. She doesn't care if it's done perfectly; she just wants it over.

Wynn changes direction only when her choice proves to be a bad one. When things go wrong, she focuses on the details of what happened and who was responsible for it. This limits her when the obstacle requires her to ignore what caused it and focus on what to do about it. She is better at working behind the scenes to help figure out how to keep the problem from happening again. She leaves it up to someone else to troubleshoot in the moment. Wynn's services are of a practical nature. She stays out of the limelight and makes sure things are done properly.

Deciding: Francis withdraws to ponder the situation; he may not have the luxury of time. He makes impartial and rational choices, regardless of the consequences or their popularity. Francis follows the evidence and ignores hunches. He wants facts not impressions. He isn't moved by emotional arguments or hype. He makes snap judgments before all the facts are in. He focuses on details, but loses sight of the big picture. He relies on his experience and that of the few people he respects. He looks to authority figures and laws for guidance. He imposes limits which others hate. He is always right, even when he isn't.

Planning: Francis thinks first and acts second. He comes up with a detailed plan, carries it out, and deals with the outcome. He has a backup plan for the backup plan. He is systematic and painstakingly thorough. Francis expects disaster to occur. He anticipates and plans for obstacles realistically. Surprises and last minute changes make him anxious. He likes to have control over the outcome. He maintains the status quo. He clings to a plan of action no matter what the proof points to or how drastically the situation changes. He risks all to prove he is right. He isn't interested in predicting what could happen in the future.

Implementing: Francis prefers to act alone and tackles obstacles head on. He wants the thing done so he can forget about it. He won't the leave a problem alone until he figures out what caused it. He wastes time when what caused it isn't as important as what needs to be done about it. He hates working with people he doesn't like or respect. He bows before authority and follows the rules, period. Improvising makes him anxious. Anxiety makes him controlling. He resists change. Once a new course has been set, he sees it through. Delays frustrate him. He changes tactics only when he hits a dead end. He won't admit to being wrong. He blames something or someone else for the failure. He wants to prevent it from happening again. He stubbornly stands aside or gets lost in the blame game, forcing someone else to resolve the emergency at hand. Francis takes advantage of opportunities to further his goals, despite the cost to others. He is an enforcer, no matter which side of the law he works work on.

Deciding: Nevada goes where the evidence leads and ignores hunches. Give him the basic facts and leave out your impressions. He notices details, but misses the big picture. He trusts his experience and the experience of others. What happened before will happen again. He isn't interested in what comes next. He wants to be viewed as responsible. He wants to do "the right thing" and fears disapproval. He looks for consensus and the reactions of the group to bolster his resolve. He calculates the human cost, particularly to people he cares about. He may cover up a friend's misdeeds to protect him. Nevada is swayed by emotional arguments. He makes expedient decisions to get it over with, even if his choice isn't popular. He follows the rules, but allows extenuating circumstances to modify them.

Planning: Nevada can craft a plan, see it through, and deal with the outcome. He likes a backup plan for the backup plan. He persuades others to support his plan. He anticipates other people's concerns and handles them with warmth and efficiency. He won't revise a plan even if he receives contradictory information or the situation changes. This is a problem when his plan makes the situation worse.

Implementing: Nevada takes charge, but wants backup. He delegates and organizes people. He is a nurturing presence and works well with others. He gets the job done correctly and on time. He takes rational action first and thinks second. He focuses on the task at hand, not those coming up the conveyor belt. Improvising makes him anxious and anxiety makes him intolerant. His quick temper interferes with his effectiveness. He anticipates danger and likes to rescue people. He sticks with the plan until it is carried out. Delays annoy him. He refuses to change tactics until he hits a dead end. He may spend more time blaming than fixing. When things go wrong, he focuses on what happened and who was responsible for it. This is a problem when there are immediate consequences that need to be dealt with. He imposes limits that enforce the consensus.

Deciding: Arden makes decisions that uphold his integrity and work ethic. He goes where the evidence leads and ignores hunches. He wants facts not impressions. He notices details others miss, but can't see the big picture. Arden values the input of people with experience. What happened before will happen again in the same way. He anticipates and plans for obstacles realistically and struggles with unforeseen variables. Arden makes impartial, rational choices. He won't care if they are popular or what the consequences are. He isn't moved by emotional pleas. He may place his interests first. He wants to control the outcome. He makes snap judgments and overlooks necessary information in favor of crossing the problem off his list.

Planning: Arden is detailed and likes understanding the rules so that things are done correctly. He is disciplined and regimented. He develops a plan, follows it through, and deals with the aftermath. He expects deadlines to be met. Once the plan is made, it is set in stone. He doesn't waver from it, even if new information is introduced or the situation drastically changes. If his plan fails, he has a second and a third.

Implementing: Arden is a rescuer. He isn't afraid to get dirty to get the job done. He likes working with people he considers equals. He respects experience not status or rank. He can take charge, but resists acting alone. He can be forced to act alone to uphold the rules. He prefers to gain consensus before proceeding. Delays annoy him. Improvising makes him anxious. Anxiety makes him hypercritical and controlling. He sticks with the selected course of action and hopes for the best. He acts hastily and wants the thing done. He meets challenges head on and sees them through unless he hits a dead end. When things go wrong, he gets caught up in whether the rules were followed or if the situation was fair rather than fixing the problem. He struggles to recalculate. Arden criticizes other people. He enforces rigid rules and isn't kind to those who refuse to fall in line.

Deciding: Blair goes where the clues lead and ignores hunches. She wants details not impressions. She projects what will happen based on what has happened. She chooses at the last minute and only when forced. She never feels she has enough information and relies on other people's opinions. She is confused when their opinions vary. She wants consensus before acting. She considers the impact on her happiness and personal freedom. She gets caught up in emotional arguments. She struggles when there are multiple paths and she can only choose one. All options are given equal consideration, which wastes time when the clock is ticking. Her approach may keep her from focusing on the correct choice. Choosing in a split second paralyzes her. If she procrastinates long enough, the decision is taken out of her hands or the action becomes unnecessary.

Planning: Blair feels internal resistance when asked to plan. She prefers to improvise on the fly. She isn't attached to a course of action and switches easily. She is terrific at coming up with ideas. She is weak at setting up the plan, ensuring that it runs smoothly, or dealing with the outcome. She is strictly an idea generator. She needs a detailed partner to plan successfully. If idea A doesn't work, she'll whip out a last minute idea B. She commits to a plan, then ignores it or adapts it at the last minute.

Implementing: Blair hates acting alone and isn't interested in herding other people. She may never reflect. She faces the problem at hand and isn't worried about what could happen later. She modifies the rules to fit the extenuating circumstances. She adapts as things change. She gets the job done, but at the last minute and just good enough. Deadlines are suggestions. She rebels when pushed. She is adaptable, but less capable of sustained effort. External compression is required to make her follow through. When things go wrong, she looks for someone to blame instead of focusing on how to fix it. Imposed limitations make her anxious. Anxiety makes her passive and withdrawn. She avoids taking action altogether to keep her options open.

Deciding: Dallas goes with her gut and ignores facts. She listens to the opinions and impressions of her inner circle. She wants them to reinforce her decision. She wants to be adored and chooses a course of action that makes sure she remains so. She is swayed by emotional arguments. She may have the correct information, but draw faulty conclusions. She is guilty of making hasty, unwise judgments. She's so busy thinking ahead, she ignores the problem in front of her. She misses details in her focus on the big picture. She chooses only when she can't avoid it and is never happy with her selection. She modifies the rules to fit the extenuating circumstance. All options are considered relevant, no matter how impractical. She forces people to reconsider an option they already dismissed. She could overcome the scene obstacle or waste time.

Planning: Dallas comes up with plans. She doesn't stick with them. She isn't interested in setting the task up, making sure it is done correctly, or sticking around to deal with the fallout. She is innovative and focuses on the potential of the idea. She is persuasive and gains consensus. If idea A doesn't work, she comes up with idea B. Her enthusiasm is contagious. People get caught up in her schemes and are disappointed when she disappears and they have to carry them out.

Implementing: Dallas anticipates catastrophe and lives poised to respond. She prefers working with people. She is comfortable being in charge. Deadlines are a suggestion. She takes calculated risks. She never does the same thing the same way twice. She is hypersensitive and alert. She assumes everyone else is like her. She needs minions to enact her creative solutions. She becomes passive-aggressive when pushed. She gets the job done, but at the last minute and just good enough. She is a master of subversive retaliation and usually has allies to pull it off. If she procrastinates long enough, the decision is taken out of her hands and the action becomes unnecessary. When things go wrong, she doesn't care what happened or who is to blame. You can't change it. You might as well move on. However, someone has to fix it and it usually isn't Dallas. She focuses on whatever draws her attention, which could be dangerous. She leads people into quicksand and leaves them there.

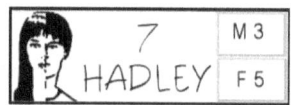

Deciding: Hadley decides first and thinks if she must. She goes where the evidence leads and ignores hunches. She wants the basic facts not impressions. She relies on experience. If it happened before, it will happen again in the same way. She focuses on details and loses sight of the big picture. She is swayed by emotional arguments. She looks to other people to reinforce her decisions. She likes to keep her options open and is never quite satisfied with the decision.

She chooses only when coerced. She wants someone else to make the decisions, particularly if it means being the bad guy.

Planning: Hadley is responsible. She recognizes what needs to be done. She won't make it happen or deal with the outcome. She encourages people to work together toward a solution. She isn't attached to a plan and discards it when someone comes up with a better alternative. This is a problem when she should have stuck with her original plan. She is never happy with any course of action and resists limitations. She is acutely uncomfortable when faced with multiple plans and limited to one. Hadley displays a surprisingly protective side when it comes to people she cares about.

Implementing: Hadley prefers working with people, but doesn't want to be in charge. She focuses on the tasks in front of her, not the tasks she'll have to face tomorrow. If she procrastinates long enough, the action becomes unnecessary. She modifies the rules to fit the extenuating circumstances. She takes calculated risks. She gets the job done at the last minute. She does not voluntarily go the extra mile. Details are forgotten or glossed over. Deadlines are suggestions. She views exertion as inconvenient but necessary. She has a self-protective streak. When things go wrong, she looks for someone to blame instead of fixing it. She becomes excessively impulsive when pushed. Stress makes her unreliable. She acts just to shut people up and that is where the danger lies.

Deciding: Shelby deliberates first and acts second. She values hunches over the evidence. She listens to other people's opinions based on her estimation of their intelligence. She looks to other people to reinforce her decisions. She hates having her options limited, but panics when faced with multiple options. All options are considered, no matter how irrational they are. She makes decisions based on how they affect her and those she cares about. She puts other people's welfare before her own. She gets caught up in emotional arguments. She is never quite satisfied with her choices. If she procrastinates long enough, the decision is taken out of her hands. She chooses only when she can't avoid it.

Planning: Shelby feels internal resistance when asked to plan. She relies on herself for guidance. She is innovative and imaginative with solutions, but weak at making them happen. She is more fascinated by the idea than the execution of it. She effectively gains consensus. She isn't attached to a plan and is willing to accept someone else's. This is a problem when the original plan would have worked better.

Implementing: Shelby focuses on potential difficulties more than the problem in front of her. She focuses on the big picture and loses sight of the details. She improvises and adapts on the fly. She modifies the rules based on extenuating circumstances. She changes tactics when the situation requires it. She gets the job done at the last minute and just good enough. Deadlines are suggestions. She takes calculated risks. When things go wrong, she isn't interested in what happened or who caused it. She focuses on what needs to be done. She would rather act alone than rely on someone else to do it. She wants to ensure that it gets done correctly. This trips her up when she truly needs help. She is highly emotional and critical when pushed.

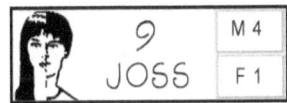

Deciding: Joss wants the facts. He isn't interested in impressions or debates. He relies on his own experience and the input of the few he trusts. If it happened before, it will happen again. He focuses on the details and isn't interested in the big picture. He makes impersonal choices no matter the consequences. All rational options are considered relevant despite the facts. Emotional arguments bore him. When the stakes turn personal, he prefers to keep his options open and is never quite satisfied with a decision. If he procrastinates long enough, the decision is taken out of his hands. He isn't hampered by this at work.

Planning: Joss doesn't give the order or design the battle plan. He accepts the order and knows what needs to be done without planning. He is that good. He discards a plan if it isn't working and calmly moves on to the next. He embraces the objective and gets it done in the most efficient method. He never has long-term plans; he has moment to moment plans.

Implementing: Joss prefers acting independently and rarely stops to ponder. He isn't interested in herding people. He works endless hours to achieve his goal. He is a master of his craft. He blocks out distractions to focus on what needs to be done. Physical challenges thrill him for the sheer high of it. He finishes what he starts. He is usually successful. He changes tactics when the situation requires it and takes calculated risks. He improvises and adapts to the situation at hand. He won't care what happens next. He'll deal with it when it happens. He follows the rules to the letter. He struggles when there are multiple courses of action and he must choose one. Deadlines are suggestions. He follows orders, but modifies the order if needed. He is unpredictable, unstable, and impulsive when pushed. When things go wrong, he rampages over what happened and whose fault it was.

Deciding: Kelly goes where the evidence leads in spite of the facts. He respects other people for their experience. He looks for backup for his decisions and makes them at the eleventh hour. If it happened before, it will happen again. He focuses on the details and loses sight of the big picture. He makes impersonal, rational decisions. He isn't swayed by emotional arguments. He follows the rules he agrees with. He prefers to keep his options open and is never satisfied with the option he chooses. If he procrastinates long enough, lesser mortals either decide for him or the action becomes unnecessary. He struggles when there are multiple courses of action and he has to choose one. He considers all options, even the ridiculous ones.

Planning: Kelly feels internal resistance when asked to plan. He prefers to make a plan happen instead of coming up with it. He isn't attached to his plan and adopts someone else's on a whim. They might not appreciate his modifications to it. He is great at coming up with solutions, but weak at seeing to the practical details of making it happen. He doesn't stick around to see how it turns out.

Implementing: Kelly makes things happen even when he shouldn't. He gains consensus and rouses people to follow him. He likes being in charge and being the center of attention. He relies on gut instinct, timing, and luck. He gets the job done, but at the last minute and just good enough. Deadlines are a suggestion. He changes tactics when the situation requires and takes calculated risks. His quickness and flexibility allow him to select the most efficient route to accomplish what needs to be done in the moment. He likes to be where the action is. He isn't known for being subtle. He becomes excessively impulsive when pushed. He makes mistakes when pressured and never justifies his actions. When things go wrong, he is more interested in finding someone to blame for it than dealing with the fallout.

Deciding: Greer goes with his gut and ignores evidence. It is important to him to look competent. He needs to be alone to think things through. He prefers open-ended solutions. He delays decisions about interpersonal matters so as not to offend or injure. He may not accept what other people deem as true. He trusts his own opinions and listens to projections by those whose intelligence he respects. He focuses on the potential of the idea. He isn't interested in what happened or who caused it. He concentrates on the solution. He considers the obstacles ahead more than the one in front of him. He sees the big picture, but misses details. He makes impersonal, rational choices, despite the consequences. He isn't swayed by emotional arguments. He prefers to keep his options open and only chooses when he has to. He is never happy with his choice. He needs other people to reinforce his decisions.

Planning: Greer comes up with innovative and creative solutions then leaves others to make them happen. He isn't attached to a plan, so he'll take on someone else's or modify it. They may not appreciate the changes. He won't care, especially when it works.

Implementing: Greer is fiercely independent and likes working alone. He blocks out distractions and gets lost in a task. He is oblivious to his environment. He isn't interested in herding people. He follows the rules that work. He changes tactics when the situation requires it and takes calculated risks. All options are considered relevant despite the facts. He improvises and adapts. He gets the job done in his way and on his schedule. Deadlines are suggestions. Greer's concern for others is intense if naive. He rushes in to avert chaos and destruction. He becomes withdrawn and resentful when pushed. He prefers to go around an obstacle rather than confront it head on.

12 TAYLOR M 1 F 2

Deciding: Taylor goes with her gut and ignores evidence. She focuses on the difficulties ahead rather than the problem before her. She relies on other people's opinions and listens to their projections if she admires them. She isn't interested in what happened or whose fault it was. She wants the bare facts and focuses on what comes next. She grasps the big picture and is fuzzy on the details. She makes personal, emotional choices based on how they affect everyone. She listens to impassioned arguments. Taylor hates making decisions because it cuts off her options. She decides by not deciding. Some of her decisions undermine her integrity and reputation. Once she decides, she's done, even if she obtains new evidence or the situation changes.

Planning: Taylor plans and makes sure deadlines are met. She comes up with innovative and imaginative solutions. She easily gains consensus for her ideas. She comes up with new ideas when her idea fails. She implements the plan once someone sets it up. She sees it through and deals with the consequences. She likes her day to be planned, but not boring. She is organized without planning.

Implementing: Taylor prefers helping and rewarding people. She likes being in charge. She thinks on the fly and likes a mental challenge. Rules are modified by extenuating circumstances. Delays annoy her. She wants the challenge crossed off her list. Taylor multitasks. She is more focused on the people factor than the procedural details. She is more concerned with the effect of the task than the task. She changes tactics or course only if she hits a dead end. She consults others before she decides on a new tactic. Anxiety makes her irritable and rigid.

Deciding: Cam goes with his gut and ignores evidence and emotional arguments. He makes decisions without consulting anyone. He likes closure. He is more interested in the tasks ahead than the one facing him. He respects the opinions of those he deems intelligent. He listens to their projections not their impressions. He isn't interested in what went wrong or whose fault it is. He wants the basic facts and focuses on how to fix it. He sees the big picture and may miss details.

He makes rational and impartial decisions, despite the consequences. He makes snap judgments and sticks with them, even if they end up being wrong. He comes across as arrogant by the less decisive. He lets you know immediately if he can help you or not and, if so, how.

Planning: Cam comes up with innovative ideas and knows how to implement them. He offers the outline. What people choose to do with it is up to them. If he is responsible for a task, he unilaterally makes plans, sees them through, and deals with the consequences. He discounts the effect on, and the opinion of, other people. He prefers a backup plan for the backup plan. He meets deadlines and is irritated when others don't.

Implementing: Cam resists improvisation, but is capable of it. He prefers to work independently. He isn't interested in herding people. Assign him a task and it gets done. He follows the rules that work. Since he doesn't respect authority, status, or rank, he considers suggestions. He won't humor people. Delays make him irritable. He changes course only if convinced it is necessary. He finishes the task, even when he has lost interest, so he can move to the next. Cam uses tactics that pay off. If a method doesn't work, he discards it, no matter how hard others cling to it. He works unsparingly and expects others to do the same. He seizes opportunities others haven't noticed. Anxiety paralyzes him or makes him overly structured. Structure helps him work through an unpleasant task and makes him effective in an emergency.

Deciding: Morgan goes with his gut and ignores evidence. He makes decisions on the fly and adapts as he goes. He rarely second-guesses himself. He listens to the opinions and projections of the people he admires. He looks to other people to reinforce his decisions. He isn't interested in what happened or who is to blame. He sees the big picture, but is fuzzy on the details. He makes impersonal, rational choices despite the consequences. He isn't interested in emotional arguments. He is never quite satisfied with a decision and likes to keep his options open. If he procrastinates long enough, someone else decides or the action becomes unnecessary.

Planning: Morgan feels internal resistance when asked to plan. He comes up with innovative solutions. He isn't interested in the procedural details. He considers the potential of the situation. He may not stick around to see if the solution worked. He isn't attached to a plan and modifies it or casts it aside in favor of someone else's.

Implementing: Morgan likes working with others and takes charge. He follows the rules that work. He likes being able to walk away from a situation. All options are relevant, no matter how ridiculous. He decides at the last minute and adapts as he goes. He struggles when faced with multiple courses of action and he is limited to one. He gets the job done at the last minute and just good enough. Deadlines are a suggestion. He changes tactics when the situation requires it. He takes calculated risks. Don't tell him something can't be done. He'll do it just to prove you wrong. He tries to juggle too many tasks. Morgan becomes scattered when stressed. He cuts corners if it is expedient. He hates routine and bureaucracy. He isn't interested in moving mountains, unless they are in the way of something he wants.

Deciding: Lee wants recognition and needs to look good. She goes with her gut and ignores evidence. She trusts the opinions of the few she respects. She works with the basic facts. She listens to future projections. She isn't interested in what happened or whose fault it was. She has no patience with whining, excuses, and emotional pleas. She focuses on the tasks ahead more than the one in front of her. She embraces the big picture and loses sight of the details. That's what minions are for. She makes impersonal, impartial, and rational decisions, regardless of the consequences. She decides quickly without questioning it. She rarely stops to consider the outcome or the effect it has on other people. She sticks with it, even if additional evidence is admitted or the situation changes drastically.

Planning: Lee generates innovative plans. She sets the task up, sees it through, and takes care of the consequences. She delegates and bludgeons others into doing it her way. She has a backup plan for her backup plan. She isn't happy when people ignore her deadlines.

Implementing: Lee is the first to lead the charge. She hates being challenged. She becomes argumentative and squelches the challenger with her steely gaze. She resists improvising. She enjoys ordering people around. She follows the rules as long as compliance gains her what she wants. She chooses a plan of action and barrels through it. She just wants it done.

She doesn't flinch, even if it turns out to be the wrong action. She steamrolls and insists she was right. She only changes course when she hits an irrefutable dead end. She becomes hypercritical when stressed. She never admits culpability and looks for someone to blame.

Deciding: River consults her psychic intuition and ignores evidence. She may rely on faulty data. She struggles when there is no happy solution. She weighs the potential of the idea. She trusts the opinions of her inner circle. She works with basic information. She focuses on the tasks ahead more than the one in front of her. She sees the global picture and has trouble with mortal details. She makes personal, highly emotional decisions based on how they impact people. She is soft hearted and easily swayed by emotional arguments. She ponders the situation before she takes action. She isn't comfortable with snap decisions. She can't ignore a problem once she is aware of it. She sticks with a decision once she makes it, even if evidence refutes it or the situation changes dramatically.

Planning: River comes up with intuitive solutions. She sways people to her side. She makes plans and respects deadlines. She likes a backup plan for her backup plan. She develops the plan, sees it through, and deals with the outcome. She struggles with the burden of responsibility. She finds trusting other people difficult. She needs the plan to have a benevolent outcome.

Implementing: River resists improvising. She prefers to face challenges head on to get them over with. Changing plans and shifting priorities make her anxious. Anxiety makes her critical and self-absorbed. She is horrified if she realizes she took the wrong action. She is willing to risk everything to prove she is right. She takes the path of least harm. She works tirelessly and consistently at tasks that she feels have merit. When things go wrong, she isn't interested in what happened or who is to blame. She wants to heal the situation and the people who were injured.

Ways to Warp
Your Mannequins

ALT **Special Talent:** In the end, the protagonist uses his secret weapon (ability) to solve the overall story problem. Utilize his natural preference as the special talent. Present him with obstacles and a story problem that require his natural approach to solve them. Overcoming smaller obstacles with his approach moves him toward the overall story goal. If he has a talent for taking the necessary action, make him the only one capable of doing so in the final hour. If his strength is deduction, have him succeed at several scene goals and the final story goal by using his mental prowess. The protagonist and antagonist can have equally matched skill sets, but different methods. The antagonist's special ability makes the protagonist's goal harder to achieve. Friends and foes utilize their abilities to help the protagonist or antagonist. If they have goals of their own, their special talents allow them to succeed.

⌨ Critical Flaw: Utilize the protagonist's natural preference as a weakness that trips him up as he goes along. Obstacles that play against his strengths keep him from obtaining scene goals. The antagonist's flaw eventually trips him up so the protagonist can win. Give them oppositional strengths that set the hero up to succeed and the antagonist up to fail. Antagonists and foes can have inflated opinions of their skill sets and thought processes. They attempt things they aren't actually capable of. This is the flaw that cements their failure. Friends and foes may have goals of their own. Their flaws keep them from succeeding.

⌨ Opposites Plan: If they plan a vacation, the planner designs the trip in exquisite detail down to the number of stops made, where, and when. He prefers an organized tour as opposed to a self-directed tour. The freedom-loving partner wants to meander, go with the flow, and do whatever feels good in the moment. They make each other crazy. They threaten each other's security and perceived needs. They'll either kill each other or wish they could. The stakes are higher if they have to work together to save the world or each other. When planning a heist, one comes up with a plan and won't alter it. His direct approach may miss the target. The other has a hard time focusing on one course of action and his efforts are erratic. His scattershot approach may hit the target.

⌨ Opposites Decide: One dithers while the other grows impatient. Use the method that solves the scene goal to move the plot forward. Use the method that fails to put on the breaks. Forcing oppositional characters to come to a decision together creates interpersonal tension. By reaching consensus, they make the right choice or kill each other in the process. One character wants to change his mind, the other stays steadfast. Only one of them can be right.

[ALT] Opposites Act: Obstacles force characters to utilize the physical and mental tools they have in their tool kit. Some characters are more aggressive than others. They might use a drill when a screwdriver would have sufficed. One pushes too hard; the other doesn't push hard enough. If an alien ship lands, the thinking character says, "Let's blow it up." The feeling character argues, "Let's find out what they want first and evaluate their weaknesses." The emotional character ignores efficiency for the sake of making it easier for everyone. The thinking character won't care who is in the way of the most efficient solution. The difference can cause mild irritation or push a character over the edge of rationality.

[ALT] Opposites Respond: One character attempts to sidestep a complication to the point of pretending it doesn't exist. The other tackles it head on, which causes further conflict if his aim is misplaced. One prefers to adapt to the situation rather than change it. The other wants to alter the situation to suit himself. One partner wishes to ignore the problems in the relationship and sublimates his needs to make the relationship work. The other one challenges his partner, argues, and fights until he improves the relationship or kills it off. Two characters can differ on how to deal with an oppressive regime or a corrupt corporation. Running and hiding is a good thing when confronting a fire-breathing dragon. It isn't good if he needs to confront his partner with her infidelity.

⌨ **Procrastinate**: A character can decide to leave things in the hands of fate. A story can end with the protagonist finding out there was no correct answer to the thematic argument. If a character leaves a scene obstacle unresolved, it comes back at more inconvenient time. If a protagonist knows a friend is lying, and chooses not to call him on it, the friend's lie crops up later and makes things difficult for them both. A character might not feel he has enough information to make a decision. This is a positive thing if options A and B are both wrong answers. By not choosing either option, the character avoids a trap. He may need to wait to make a decision until he has more information. This is good if he is solving a mystery. It's bad if the alien ship shoots first and asks questions later.

⌨ **Magnifying Lens**: A character can be so intent on preventing a problem, an argument, or a situation that he creates a bigger problem. If he takes steps to build defenses against something that doesn't end up happening, he has wasted a lot of time. He might be so afraid his lover is going to leave, he undergoes plastic surgery, dyes his hair, or starts dressing like a twenty-year-old. His efforts turn his partner off instead of on. People pleasers are often like that. They try so hard to please that they drive people away. This conflict applies to more than relationships. It applies to an alien ship that lands or a bubonic plague threat.

⌨ **Caution Flag**: Some characters are risk averse. They want to be certain of a thing before they try it. If they encounter the slightest resistance, they back off. Cautious friends serve as speed bumps in the protagonist's plunge toward the story solution. Caution is the yellow light at the intersection. A cautious character can talk the protagonist out of the correct solution. A naturally conservative protagonist may have to take risks to solve the story problem. If an antagonist hesitates, he loses.

Deep Dive: Some characters dive into shark-infested waters without considering the consequences. They often get eaten. They drag the protagonist into deeper trouble. With this kind of friend, you don't need an antagonist. Risk-taking is often the antagonist's critical flaw. It could be the protagonist's secret weapon. He may be willing to boldly go where no man has gone before, because he doesn't stop to weigh the consequences. He is willing to cut the green wire, because he doesn't care if he blows up with the bomb if it saves other people.

Elimination: Errors in deduction generate plot twists. Some characters reach a conclusion about how to solve the story problem or scene obstacle by the process of elimination. It can't be A, B, or C, so it must be D. Friends and foes come up with counter theories or poke holes in the protagonist's and antagonist's theories. A character may not have considered all the possibilities or have all the facts. Some characters stop looking for alternatives once they have made a decision. A sleuth might think he has narrowed down all the suspects then find out the one he thought "dunit" didn't do it. A concerned character might chip away at all the possible causes for his partner's inattention until he settles on a reason. When he confronts his partner, he finds out he was right or could not have been more wrong.

Opportunity Knocks: Present the same opportunity to two different characters. One takes it. The other passes it by. If it ends up being wildly successful, the one who passed is resentful. Have it end badly, and the one who took the chance pays the price. The one who passed says, "I told you so." A character can only take advantage of an opportunity to get a new job, win the girl of his dreams, or find the cure for the virus if he is open to new opportunities.

A story problem in a Comedy could be about a hapless guy who goes through life blind to opportunity after opportunity and finally "sees" at the end. An opportunity embraced or dismissed offers conflict at scene level. Taking advantage of an opportunity is the cornerstone of success. If a character invents something, the right opportunity to introduce it to the world may never come if he isn't focused enough to see it or brave enough to make it happen. Many creative types can do the groundwork. When it comes to launching the product or marketing it, they lack the charisma or the motivation to pull it off. A character can have a great idea for a business. Unless he knows how to run a business, it fails. He needs to rely on other people's expertise to make it work. These conflicts make great story problems. What if he must rely on someone and that character disappears?

[ALT] **Sudden Success**: A character may be muddling along and the right door opens. He goes through it and changes the trajectory of his life. His success alters all of his relationships. Money and success change everything. An opportunity to take a job in another state, country, or planet could cause conflict in a Romance, a Historical novel, or Science Fiction. If the opportunity to form a colony on planet Zircon comes along, some want to go, others don't. You have a terrific overall story conflict. Who stays? Who goes? Who and what do they have to leave behind? If opposites are romantic partners, the stakes are higher. Many stories explore the price of fame.

Moral Story: Present the character with an opportunity to help or hurt someone he resents. The way he handles the opportunity creates internal conflict as well as interpersonal conflict. Opportunities create moral crucibles. Self-interest is often thought of as a bad thing. There are times when putting self first is the best thing. A character from an abusive or chaotic family, or an oppressive political environment, may need to break free. A character who places his needs ahead of others, even if it is a healthy option, creates conflict. Self-interest leads to innovation. It can lead to revolution. It can lead a protagonist to separate from bad friends, leave a relationship that isn't working, overcome a dysfunctional family, or overthrow a corrupt government.

Immoral Story: The dark side is the "opportunist" who takes advantage of circumstances despite the immorality of it. Opportunists are the scam artists who prey on other people's vulnerabilities, the hackers of the computer world, the telephone spammers, and the fraudulent bankers. They aren't intrepid enough to attack people directly. They prefer to strike from the shadows. Despots are self-interested. Those who surround despots operate on the principle of self-interest as well. Opportunists take advantage of other people's mistakes, weaknesses, or distractions. They get ahead because of someone else's folly. Opportunists put personal gain over the gain of the group. Fields, such as politics, research, sports, and sales, are cutthroat. Those who rise to the top are driven by self-interest.

Remove the Watchdog: Characters behave differently when they think no one is looking. This has been the topic of multiple psychological studies from watching children to see if they eat a forbidden cookie to finding out how prison wardens behave when they think the cameras are turned off. A child who thinks he isn't being watched might eat the forbidden cookie. A prison guard who thinks he isn't being monitored, and will suffer no consequences, turns sadistic. The idea that he won't be caught, or won't suffer consequences, changes a character's motivation.

If a bundle of money falls out of an armored truck in the middle of a downtown area, one character collects it by the armful and runs. Another gathers it up and calls the police. The character who took the money isn't the type to enter a bank with a gun. However, when the opportunity for "free" money came along, he didn't hesitate to take it. The guy with a strong sense of morality wanted the cash returned to its rightful owners. This dynamic is an overall story problem or a conflict at scene level.

A character makes a small decision about attending or not attending an event he doesn't want to go to. He decides to pick up a quarter on the street, not realizing it has a bug in it or a microchip embedded with sensitive spy information. He takes home supplies that were just gathering dust in the storeroom at work.

Self Preservation: Most characters go to great lengths to save themselves, even at the expense of others. Does that make them bad or is it a biological imperative? In an airplane scenario, they tell you to put the oxygen mask on your face first so you can help others. In this instance, self-interest is a good thing. If there is only one parachute and you take it, are you wrong? This kind of decision makes terrific and terrifying thematic arguments. On a smaller, more subtle level, it creates scene conflict.

⌨ **Impossible Choices**: There are many psychological studies done on impossible moral choices. If you can divert a train, do you let it hit one person, or move it to the track where it kills ten? If you know, especially if you love, the one person, will you divert the train to kill the ten? These situations create rich thematic arguments and can create conflict in any story. Two characters driven by self-interest make great protagonist/antagonist combinations. Friends and foes act out of self-interest as well.

⌨ **Mistakes and Bad Choices**: There is a difference between a mistake and a bad choice. A mistake is doing something unintentional without realizing the consequences. A bad choice is intentionally doing something knowing full well what the consequences will be. Mistakes and bad choices complicate the overall story problem, create interpersonal friction, and create internal conflict within the conscience of the character. He doesn't have a conscience if he is a sociopath. Characters make decisions based on differing criteria. They may not have all the facts or they may interpret the facts incorrectly.

⌨ **Misunderstandings**: Characters with oppositional traits often invest each other with motives they don't have. They assume the oppositional approach is intended to wound. If someone dithers, the decisive partner thinks he is deliberately withholding support. The ditherer thinks the decisive character is cutting off his options to intentionally suffocate him. When the careful collide with the careless, and the freedom lovers encounter the rule makers, they strike each other's security centers. When they overcome their differences, or stop taking their differing methods personally, they move toward overcoming interpersonal obstacles. When they become further entrenched in their method, and the tug of war reaches toxic levels, they fail.

EXTERNAL OBSTACLES

Physical obstacles prevent movement, communication, access to a person, the retrieval of an object, or necessary exchanges. Physical distance prevents access. Time limits increase tension. Physical obstacles come in the form of:

A physical barrier, like having to break into a safe or out of a cell.

A situational barrier, such as trying to enter an area that is off limits.

Physical restraints, like being stuck inside a car, a plane, or a train.

Missing the boat, train, or airplane.

Limited mobility due to a temporary or permanent physical disability.

Misunderstanding the timeframe involved or not having enough time.

Actual physical distances that make accomplishing the task difficult or impossible.

Being misled about the correct time.

Being given an impossible deadline.

📷 Physical impediments to navigating between point A and point B.

Ways to Warp
Your Mannequins

⌨ **Countdown**: A countdown increases anxiety and mistakes. Some characters faced with time constraints are calm, motivated, and more creative. They fall apart after the crisis is over. Others freak out and have to be coerced into getting it together to focus on the task. A character can make things worse and only see things clearly in retrospect. Wynn, Francis, Nevada, Arden, Taylor, Cam, Lee, and River respond better to deadlines or time constraints than Blair, Dallas, Hadley, Shelby, Joss, Kelly, Greer, and Morgan. A ticking clock can be applied to escaping a sinking ship, heading off a nuclear attack, or deciding on a life-saving surgery. It affects the character's ability to meet a work deadline, catch a killer before he kills again, or decide what to do when a vacation plan is thwarted. In either case, there is pressure to meet the goal before the time is up.

⌨ **Acceleration**: A rushed character overlooks important details or does not listen effectively. Rushing raises the internal stress level of Blair, Dallas, Hadley, Shelby, Joss, Kelly, Greer and Morgan. Delays frustrate Wynn, Francis, Nevada, Arden, Taylor, Cam, Lee, and River. The tension heightens their emotional or mental response.

Trip the Tongue: The character may not have enough time to say what needs to be said or to fully dissect or explain the situation. Blair, Dallas, Hadley, Shelby, Joss, Kelly, Greer, and Morgan resist committing or saying what they have to. They shout, "Stop pushing me!" Wynn, Francis, Nevada, Arden, Taylor, Cam, Lee, and River say things to get it over. They shout, "Stop slowing me down!"

Bombs: A bomb can be literal or a subtle tactic only the reader is aware of. Knowing that something is brewing, or hiding around the corner, increases the suspense of the scene. The reader knows the truth and is waiting for the character to catch on or see it for himself. The reader knows who the antagonist is, what the truth is, or where the danger lies. The reader worries that the character won't find out in time. If a reader knows a character has cancer, he chews his fingernails waiting for the character to tell his partner or decide on a treatment plan. If the reader knows that a monster lurks in the belly of the dark cave, he flinches as the character steps inside. If a reader knows the suspect is lying, he impatiently waits for the sleuth to catch on.

Borders: Physical boundaries are actual or perceived. Characters erect fences, warning signs, hedges, and walls to define physical boundaries. Sports fields have painted boundaries. If someone at work consistently encroaches on the character's personal space (or work responsibilities), your character dreads going to work. He asks to switch offices or quits. He might escalate the territory war until the other character gives in or quits. If a sibling encroaches on your character's side of the room, he complains to the caregivers. If that doesn't work, it escalates into border skirmishes with petty acts of retaliation until one or the other wins, they agree to a truce, or the caregivers step in and separate them. Roommates, couples, or characters who share a desk, a room, a house, a school, or a planet engage in border skirmishes all the time. The battle can escalate and end badly for one or both. The battle could result in learning to share.

Killing Fields: A thematic argument could debate that geographical boundaries are perceived. Humans are willing to kill over scraps of land, even if the land lacks water, a food supply, or clean air. Step across the border from North Korea to South Korea and you have conflict. Step across the border between Israel and Palestine and you may be shot on sight. Enter a country that requires a passport or visa without one and you are arrested. Battles over physical borders figure in every genre. It could also serve as a problem at scene level if a character needs to enter a geographic area to gain something and can't go there. He may have to find a way in that is subversive or get someone else to go there for him. He may be trapped behind enemy lines. If kidnapped by terrorists and he escapes, he needs papers to cross the border to safety. If he does not have papers, he must find a subversive way to cross the line.

Hijack the Plan: If your character is physically prevented from taking a necessary action at scene level, he must attempt it again later or scrap the plan and start over. His temperament plays a part in how well he handles the upset and how easily he recalculates. Francis, Arden, Joss, Kelly, Greer, Cam, Morgan, and Lee already have a backup plan and move on easily. If step A isn't possible, they take steps B, C, and D. Wynn, Nevada, Blair, Dallas, Hadley, Shelby, Taylor, and River struggle to come up with a new plan or rely on someone else to tell them what to do next.

They gather their allies together to discuss the situation. Make opposites work in tandem and the results are hilarious or tragic. Have them balance each other and they succeed.

[ALT] Minority Rules: Dallas, Shelby, Greer, Taylor, Cam, Morgan, Lee, and River are the silent minority, coming in at only 30% of the residents of Tinker Town. They plan for catastrophe and try to avert it. They trust the flashes of inspiration or insight when they have them. They shoot from the hip and don't care about rules, facts, or statistics. They want to know how the other character reacts in a given situation. They aren't inhibited by protocol. Their approach might not hold up in court, but solves the overall story problem. Their decisions are rash and result in further problems. Being oblivious to the data can result in disaster if they don't pay attention to where the data leads. They become stalled.

[ALT] Majority Rules: Wynn, Francis, Nevada, Arden, Blair, Hadley, Joss, and Kelly gain cooperation because they make up 70% of the residents of Tinker Town. They prefer hard evidence. They don't trust hunches. They trust data, studies, and statistics. They are systematic and thorough. They conduct an orderly investigation and follow protocol. Their fact gathering might hold up in court or ultimately solve the story problem. It can also waste time.

[ALT] Mix and Match: Put these opposites together to solve a problem and you have conflict. They fight over how to gather evidence and process it. One comes up with ideas; the other shoots them down. One is conservative in his approach; the other is a renegade. These conflicts work well for friends and foes as well as hero versus villain. The protagonist is one way, his sidekick the other. Each strongly defends his methods. They waste precious time while they do so.

ORGANIZATIONAL OBSTACLES

Organizational obstacles relate to bureaucracies, companies, or groups that offer resistance in the form of:

🏃 Conflicting goals.

🏃 Inefficient practices.

🏃 Needing consensus or permission from a superior to move forward. The character must find ways around the authority or convince him to change his mind.

🏃 Lack of funds, policies, or procedures to implement the plan.

🏃 An action or decision counters a religious or political agenda.

🏃 Prejudices against people, places, things, and behaviors prevent solving the story problem or achieving the scene goal.

🏃 Moral restrictions enforced by society based on the time and place in which he lives or needs to overcome the obstacle.

🏃 Taboos are social restrictions that forbid the action or decision and result in fatal or highly unpleasant consequences.

🏃 Police enforce the legal rules of the society your character lives in.

🏃 Rulers are charismatic, whimsical, and downright dangerous to cross. They set the tone and hand down the mandates for the world they control.

We've discussed how receptive to people's opinions our characters are and what it would take to convince them they are wrong. Now we take a look at how they view society's restrictions as whole and whether they respect or dismiss the authority figures in their world. A character's safety relies on interpersonal rules and regulations and societal rules and regulations. How far is he willing to sacrifice his personal safety to overcome the obstacle?

Wynn relies on her own thoughts and opinions and does not care about consensus. She prefers situations where rules are well defined and traditions are upheld. She isn't politically or morally controversial. She hates confrontation. She sails along with the prevailing wind. She obeys the laws and societal expectations, unless something comes along to convince her the lawmakers are harmful to the greater good. She works in a quiet way to depose those who have lost her trust.

Francis readily accepts and supports the given hierarchy. He doesn't care if a rule is popular. He has a firm sense of right and wrong, particularly in his area of expertise or responsibility. He desires freedom of thought and movement in his personal life. He either fervidly embraces a belief system or holds himself apart. He works within the laws of the land and societal expectations, unless something comes along to convince him they are abusive. If he loses respect for authority, he works hard to overturn them. If he respects them, he has no trouble being an enforcer.

Nevada likes being in charge and believes that seniority rules. He looks for consensus, so he would never rebel alone. He embraces the prevailing religion, conservative politics, and conforms to society's expectations. He makes decisions and takes actions that follow the existing rules or current mindset. He takes swift action when he catches a wrongdoer then feels the need to rescue the perpetrator from his own folly. If convinced that an authority is abusive, he could work against them to rescue others. He might cling to the belief system, but insist on a change in management.

Arden places high value on consensus: politically, socially, and legally. He enjoys being in charge. He only respects characters who have some authority of their own. He enjoys enforcing rules handed down from up above. He thinks power, position, and prestige must be earned. He is materialistic and upholds rules that make material success possible. If those in charge lost his respect, he would turn against them as long as he had other people to back him up.

Blair lives by her own code of conduct, which she is quite passionate about. Her code may not fall in line with anyone else's. She values tradition, but rules and limitations make her feel dead inside. She seeks harmony and isn't one to intentionally rock the boat. She chafes under restrictions and engages in quiet acts of rebellion, particularly if she finds the authority figures abusive. She dismisses a rigid authority's right to be in charge. She struggles with societal restrictions.

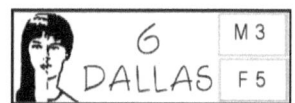

Dallas respects authority figures and attributes them with more power and insight than they possess. She does not like to be dependent on other people and does not want them relying on her. Unfortunately, her charisma draws followers. She aims to please her caregivers, authority figures, and friends. She is influenced by their opinions. She may embrace the prevailing belief system or find it boring. She could be nominated an alternative authority by those who surround her. She finds rebellion uncomfortable.

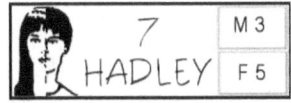

Hadley embraces the rules, on the surface. She is the first one to break them if they cramp her style. She isn't interested in running the show or telling other people what to do. She hates overly strict people because they kill the party. This is true of policemen and priests alike. She indulges in the prevailing philosophy so long as it doesn't overly restrict her. She might outwardly comply and inwardly rebel. She challenges any authority figure she considers unfairly restrictive. If an authority becomes abusive, open rebellion and flouting conventions are not a problem. She'll gather followers.

Shelby evaluates authority based on her principles and belief systems. If she embraces the belief system, no one can convince her it is wrong. She challenges authority if she feels the authority does not have the best interest of people in mind. She is firmly on the side of good. Her version of good might not be in the best interest of all people. She has no problem with open rebellion if she feels it is the only course of action against a despotic regime or religious figurehead. She may cling to the system, but reject those in charge of it.

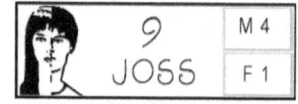

Joss responds with annoyance when his life and work are interfered with. If the rules don't impact him, he doesn't waste time thinking about them. Put an authority figure in his way and he circumvents them. He has a natural disregard for rules and authority. He'll trample over a system that infringes on his freedom. He ignores laws or moral arguments if they aren't applicable to his task and even if they are. He isn't interested in fitting in. He won't crusade against a belief system, but he isn't fully invested in one either.

Kelly admires and respects any authority that bests him at his own game. Everything is a game. Rules make him feel dead inside. Anyone who tries to rein him in is considered hostile. He is clever and capable of manipulating the rules to his benefit. If that doesn't work, he undermines the authority or has them removed. He uses subtle rather than overt tactics, but the result is the same. He conforms to societal expectations only as a method of manipulation. He goes along with those he needs to as a means to an end. He isn't attached to a particular belief system.

Greer is impatient with bureaucracy, rigid hierarchy, and politics. He views everyone as an equal or less than. He isn't interested in leading or following. A title does not make someone an authority. He is more interested in what they know than what they are called. He has no trouble ignoring or overthrowing an authority he disagrees with. He isn't one to protest for change. He may go along with a belief system that doesn't interfere with his life. He might rebel if it does.

Taylor assigns a high value to those with status of some form. Taylor goes along with the prevailing belief system and societal expectations. She obeys the rules. When she doesn't, things usually go horribly wrong. She is influential. If she flouts authority, she has a posse to help her. If an authority figure fails her in some way, she turns on him. She has no problem leading the charge to unseat someone she considers brutal or unfair. She may cling to the system and work to remove the figurehead.

Cam discounts any authority other than his own. Rank, titles, accolades, celebrity, and status are meaningless. He conforms to the rules that are useful and ignores the rest. He is free from the constraints of convention and sentiment that bind other people. He expects people to do what they are supposed to and is annoyed when they don't. He doesn't care what they believe. He only cares what they do about it. He doesn't interfere unless it affects him personally. If those in authority are viewed as malign or incompetent, he has no trouble working behind the scenes to uncover or destroy them. His views are not popular.

Morgan ignores the restrictions of authority and tradition. He does what he thinks best in all circumstances. He is impervious to societal pressure to conform. If what he thinks falls in line with the majority, things are fine and good. If it doesn't, he ignores them. He won't arrange a protest. If he gets push back, he finds subtle ways of getting around the rules. He is often cleverer than those enforcing the rules. It amuses him to be subversive. He considers rule-makers petty annoyances. He isn't interested in open rebellion because stupid people aren't worth his energy.

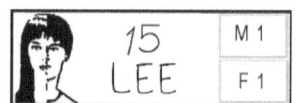

Lee prefers to be in charge. She respects policy more than regulations. She rarely acknowledges any authority over her own. She is materialistic and status conscious. She plays the game in a way that gains her what she wants. That usually means embracing the prevailing thought tides, on the surface. If she is put in charge, she makes sure the rules are followed. Once she buys in, she is in. She ignores someone else's authority, unless it is a means to an end. If an authority stood in her way, she'd plow them down without a backward glance.

River isn't interested in power or glory. She champions the oppressed and downtrodden. Her belief system is fixed and may not be entirely rational. Her mystical bent either reinforces a religious system or runs alongside it. It may not be traditional. She won't entirely reject the prevailing belief. She modifies it to fit her bias. She upholds the rules she agrees with. She works quietly to overturn the rules she disagrees with. She weighs whether the authority has a right to enforce the rules. She evaluates the rules based on whether or not they are best for the people involved. What she considers best may not be good for everyone.

Security: How far is someone willing to go to ensure his safety? A character can lie, cheat, steal, or kill to ensure physical safety in wartime, psychological safety in a relationship, or perceived safety in almost any aspect of his life. A character that doesn't feel safe, won't make the healthiest decisions. He needs to feel safe when he walks out the front door. He can't do that in high crime locations or if vampires are waiting to bite him. Children can't feel safe in abusive families. Citizens can't feel safe under a despotic regime or in a country at war. World wars and small acts of rebellion are inspired by a person's need to feel safe.

Chaos: Members of a chaotic family or society feel insecure. Some characters thrive on "chaos", others can't handle it. Chaos places stress on relationships between friends, coworkers, neighbors, groups, and family members. Some mannequins draw chaos to themselves like bees to honey. The other mannequins hate it. Addicts and criminals threaten their loved-ones' security. In their search for the next fix or next gambit, they don't think about anyone else. A chaotic character could be the overall story problem in a Literary story or the personal dilemma in any genre. They are friends and foes that complicate the overall story problem.

Money: Characters desire financial security. How much money is enough? It varies. Some characters are happy with a cabin, a horse to ride, and food on the table. Others aren't happy unless they have a Mercedes, a McMansion, and a stock portfolio worth millions. Money changes everything. Disparities in income and access to money harm relationships. It creates one-up hierarchies. What happens to your characters if they don't have enough money? What are the restrictions imposed by their world? Do they have money? If not, what is their currency?

Dependence: If the intent is benevolent, the receiver struggles to receive it in a positive way. If the intent is malicious, it becomes a breaking point. Who has the money, hence the power, in your story world? What if your world isn't ruled by money? What is it ruled by? Who is your character indebted to? Whom must he appease?

Cheaters: When a character commits financial infidelity, he strikes at the heart of his partner's need for security. When a ruler commits financial infidelity, he threatens an entire population. Trust and fidelity are keys to any successful relationship. Remove them and the relationship crumbles. When a ruler lies to his subjects, it is betrayal of the highest order. Who does your ruler trust? Who does he listen to? Who lies for him?

[ALT] **Ambulance**: Characters prey on victims of accidents or disasters. When fires, tornadoes, tsunamis, hurricanes, or earthquakes strike, some characters risk their lives to save others. Some prey on the victims. Others go to inspiring lengths to help people rebuild. Some start looting to make sure they have the necessary items to survive. Others randomly steal stuff they didn't have access to before. The chaos following an accident or disaster makes characters insecure. They revert to hoarding things to ensure their supply of food, clothing, and shelter. Normally law-abiding citizens are driven to lying, cheating, stealing, and killing. Apocalyptic tales explore the theme of what happens after the bombs go off. Science Fiction explores what happens when a planet dies. Natural disasters can function as a story problem in Historical, Western, Thriller, or a Literary tale.

[ALT] **Predictions**: When a character feels insecure, he builds defenses against threats both real and imagined. Real danger may or may not exist. His insecurities become the danger or blind him to real danger. He projects his negative experiences onto seemingly innocuous situations. He expects disaster, so he creates disaster. Worriers encourage the protagonist to avoid unknown situations that might result in substantial rewards or drive him away from efforts that actually solve the story problem. On the positive side, a worried friend or foe can motivate the protagonist to prepare for the worst when the worst approaches. If the worst doesn't happen, the protagonist is sidetracked by efforts that were unnecessary. This can delay the resolution of the story problem or solve it.

Weapons: Characters that fear the external world carry weapons. They use them unwisely. If there have been a number of cop killings, a cop may shoot first in a dark alley and ask questions later. A character might move to a gated community or build a "safe room" and find out he isn't safe after all. A fearful character retaliates against those who threaten his sense of security, whether they deserved it or not. He antagonizes characters who could help him. He makes a good foe and could potentially serve as an antagonist.

Opposites Attract: Bring two characters together with different social expectations, cultures, or traditions. How far is their community willing to go to keep them from upsetting the status quo? How do their differing beliefs keep them from seeing the solution to the problem? How does it hinder them from taking the necessary action? Is it legal for them to be together? How do they help each other grow?

Alliance: The reverse side of belonging is the sense of ownership or alliance. Many tales hinge on divided alliances. Alliances involve characters in gangs, criminal activities, and wars. Members belong to their religious congregations and sports teams. Citizens belong to their city, state, or country. Plots turn when those organizations, cities, states, or countries place unreasonable demands on the people they feel they "own." Organizations are benevolent or menacing. Characters can force others to belong to their group. Characters can try to escape a group. People who belong to a group are shunned, punished, even murdered if they try to leave. People are willing to lie, cheat, steal, and kill to belong to an exclusive club. Characters behave in ways that are detrimental in order to "belong". They accept unpleasant circumstances and tolerate unpleasant people in an attempt to "fit in." They sometimes humiliate and harm themselves to be included in cliques. Cliques surround rock stars, actors, potentates, scientists, lecturers, and popes.

Diana Hurwitz

DISUNITY OBSTACLES

Disunity obstacles relate to characters that offer resistance to another character's scene goal or overall story goal in the form of:

🏃 Competition.

🏃 Jealousy and resentment.

🏃 Gossip, rumors, and backbiting.

🏃 Blackmail.

🏃 Differing goals and needs.

🏃 Dislike, hatred, or anger.

🏃 Love for something or someone.

🏃 Friendship and loyalty.

🏃 Oppositional methods of negotiating the world.

🏃 Shallowness versus depth of connections.

Next, we consider what kind of friend our mannequins are, who they are drawn to, and who they dislike on first meeting. If the prospective pool of friends is vast enough, and the character's access to them ready enough, they select friends based on their native inclinations. If not, they make do with those they have access to.

1
WYNN

M 4

F 9

Wynn puts her faith and her family above her friends. She is valued for her warmth, dependability, and depth. She truly enjoys her friends and often discusses her problems with them rather than her family. This is bad if she should be discussing the situation with her partner or if her partner feels violated by her oversharing. She relies on her friends' opinions when making decisions. Her partner may resent that. She is a people watcher. She is drawn to a diverse group, but relies heavily on close confidants. She is reserved outside her inner circle. She is hurt when her friends ignore the plans they have made. She takes it as a sign that they are disappointed in her. She is naturally drawn to Wynn, Francis, River, Nevada, and Blair. Her complete opposite is Morgan.

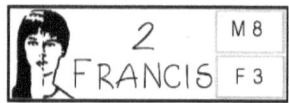

2
FRANCIS

M 8

F 3

Francis is selective. Time spent with friends falls below time at work, with his family, and community service. The few friends he manages to make, he values. He pencils them in when he can. His social outings become rituals. He is drawn to people who have similar interests and views. He has no patience with those who are vastly different or those who live outside the bounds of propriety. He occasionally lets loose and has a little fun if dragged there by an extroverted friend. A highly extroverted friend eventually wears on him. He can get along with almost anyone for a little while. He usually tells them how wrong they are once too often. He is naturally drawn to Francis, Cam, Wynn, Arden, and Joss. His opposite is Hadley.

Nevada places the needs of family before friends. He is a social creature and values loyal, like-minded souls. He invests in close personal relationships. He is let down if others don't value their relationship as much as he does. His friends appreciate his genuine interest and kind-heartedness. However, he doesn't give anything freely. He expects something in return, even if it is praise for having given it. He refuses to believe anything negative about his friends. He is drawn to a variety of people. He makes his friends feel good. He enjoys throwing parties so he can show off his possessions. He is service-oriented and invested in the happiness and satisfaction of those around him. He is naturally drawn to Nevada, Arden, Taylor, Hadley, and Wynn. His opposite is Greer.

Arden puts work and family above social ties. He enjoys the time he spends with friends. He seeks people who have the same personal standards and interests. He may be drawn to sports or athletic activities. He socializes with family and those involved in his community or church, even if they aren't compatible. He desires status and respects those he feels have achieved a high degree of success. He is less controlling with those he views as powerful or authoritative in their field. He has no patience for people he deems flighty or unconventional. They find his rigid adherence to rules off-putting. He can display a sharp wit. He enjoys telling jokes and stories. His friends view him as steady and dependable. He is very opinionated and likes to be in charge, but softens those tendencies when around others of his temperament. To the feeling types, he comes across as rude and insensitive. Arden is naturally drawn to Arden, Lee, Nevada, Kelly, and Francis. Arden's opposite is Shelby.

Blair takes her commitments seriously. She is drawn to life-long friendships. She is intensely private. Her friends might be surprised by how strong her opinions are. She defers to others, which creates problems if her friends are unaware that she actually has needs or opinions. She grows resentful when her friends aren't as attentive to her as she is to them. She feels overlooked, discounted, and used. She gives up on relationships that don't meet her needs, even though she never stated her needs. She expects the other person to be psychic. She is caring and supportive of her friends' dreams and aspirations. She hates conflict and avoids confrontation. Her currency is being seen and understood. She gets along with most people. She is reserved around people she does not know well. She gravitates toward those who share her interests and values. She is highly territorial of her personal space and repelled by the intrusive. She is naturally drawn to Blair, Joss, Shelby, Hadley, and Wynn. Her opposite is Lee.

Dallas is highly social and never boring. She is considerate, nurturing, and invested. Her interpersonal skills work in her favor. Her enthusiasm is catching but exhausting. She is a terrific ally and a potentially troublesome foe. She makes other people feel good. She is usually well liked. She is loyal and dedicated as long as her friends share her values and aren't overly critical of her. She collects friends from all walks of life, but only has a few that she trusts. She drops them as soon as they bore her or violate her belief system. Dallas is naturally drawn to Dallas, Hadley, Morgan, Shelby, and Taylor. Her opposite is Francis.

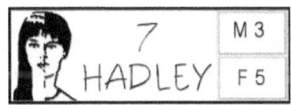

Hadley is bubbly and popular. Almost any type could be drawn into her orbit. The more serious, single-friend introverts are hurt when she moves on. She isn't interested in the intellectual types or devil's advocate debaters. She draws the ire of people who find her too flighty. Others are insulted by her blunt honesty. She is drawn to other extroverts who live in the moment. Her love for the friends she admires and trusts runs deep. She is very warm and caring. She offers comfort and concern when needed. She is quick with her brand of advice. She lives for a good time and ensures her friends have one too, perhaps too much of a good time, be it food, alcohol, or frolicking. She goes out of her way to be nice. When she loves, she loves mightily. She isn't good with long-term commitment. If a character thinks they are best friends forever, she is hurt when Hadley dumps her. Hadley is naturally drawn to Hadley, Kelly, Dallas, Blair, and Nevada. Her opposite is Cam.

Shelby is warm and caring. Once trust has been established, she is devoted and true. She is perceptive and usually gets along with everyone. She holds herself in reserve except with a select few. She comes across as somewhat aloof to those who don't know her well. She cares deeply, but is easily offended. She is perceptive and aware of what other people are feeling. She needs space and respects her friends' need for it. She may have unrealistic expectations. This makes maintaining friendships difficult if the friends can't measure up to her standards. She is naturally drawn to Shelby, Blair, Greer, River, and Dallas. Her opposite is Arden.

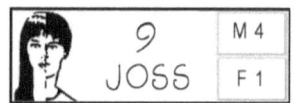

Joss is an exciting catalyst. He encourages others to embrace his risk-taking hobbies. He has an affinity for sports, but also an artistic appreciation. He is tolerant of most people. He is valued by friends. They are confused and hurt when he drops them without notice or explanation. He isn't good with long-term commitment. He won't tolerate anyone he perceives as boring. He is drawn to whoever shares his passion of the moment. He has many different sets of friends. No one is an intimate friend. He is often found with extroverts because of his leisure activities, but they quickly tire him. He doesn't have time for navel-gazing introverts. He makes day-to-day efforts to keep a friendship going, as long as it is interesting. He is naturally drawn to Joss, Greer, Kelly, Blair, and Francis. His opposite is Taylor.

Kelly isn't invested in long-term relationships. He takes people one day at a time. He quickly moves on without a backward glance if the other person gets too needy or boring. When he is with you, he is truly with you, until the day he isn't. He tailors his behavior to fit in with all kinds of people. Friends are drawn to his charm and love of a good time. He wears them out. He is drawn to other extroverts. He enjoys sports and risk-taking hobbies. He is on the move, not sitting around pondering the meaning of life. He is usually popular. Few feel they know him well, if at all. He is inspired by the concept of brotherhood, but lacks the commitment it entails. He is naturally drawn to Kelly, Morgan, Hadley, Joss, and Arden. His opposite is River.

Greer chooses a trusted few who share his interests. He enjoys intellectual conversation. He has little patience with mushy feelings and woo-woo stuff. He finds it hard to step out and connect with other people. He isn't interested in belonging to groups of any kind. The few he allows access appreciate him. To have a relationship with him, he has to deem you worthy. He banishes people who lose his confidence and trust. He values intelligence and rationality and isn't drawn to overly emotional characters. He is a blunt straight shooter. He isn't interested in manipulating people or playing games. He would not appreciate being toyed with. He is naturally drawn to Greer, Joss, Morgan, Shelby, and Cam. His opposite is Nevada.

Taylor is a social butterfly. She wants to make her friends happy. She is the life of the party and is often a hostess of one. She turns against anyone she sees as a false friend. Because she shifts to accommodate other people, many different people consider her a friend. She has a real problem with characters who resist consensus or don't work toward the collective good. Her self-worth is tied up in the closeness and quality of her relationships. She is needy and resentful when she does not receive the positive affirmations she craves. She is momentarily vicious if crossed, but returns to being all sunshine a moment later. At her worst she is suffocating. She is naturally drawn to Taylor, Nevada, Lee, Dallas, and River. Her opposite is Joss.

Cam is hard to get to know. He has a low need for connection and belonging. He has a few, quality friends. He cares for his inner circle deeply and is their greatest ally. He would be surprised by the high regard those outside his circle have for him. He is serious some of the time and fun the rest. He appreciates the finer things in life. He has a caustic, self-deprecating wit. His extroverted friends encourage him to get out more; otherwise, he is a loner. He only spends time with people he respects and enjoys. He may be seen as snobbish because he is reserved and quiet. He is naturally drawn to Cam, River, Francis, Lee, and Greer. His opposite is Dallas.

Morgan gets along with most people. He avoids dull, plodding people. He is a fun-loving wild card of a friend. He embroils them in adventure and leaves them there. He loves a good debate and that grows tiring. His penchant for playing devil's advocate irritates the most balanced character. He is competitive. His need to be one-up intimidates and offends some types more than others. If paired with another competitive type, the situation escalates to comic or tragic effect. He doesn't mean any harm and is useful to know. Those who take objective statements as criticism find him contentious. He is naturally drawn to Morgan, Dallas, Kelly, Greer, and Lee. His opposite is Wynn.

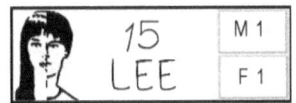

Lee is social and energetic. She is interested and interesting to those she deems worthy of spending time with. She loves a good intellectual debate. She impresses with her vast knowledge base. Her friends are never in doubt where she stands on any topic. She is a fierce ally and woe betide those who land on her bad side. She makes characters with low self-esteem, even those with self-confidence, insecure. She grills rather than banters. She isn't happy with glib statements. She tears apart an argument if her opponent doesn't have a firm understanding of the topic. This drives many potential friends away. She is drawn to those those who share her interests. She has little patience for touchy-feely types. She is attracted to other powerful people, even if she doesn't agree with them. She ends friendships that grow stale or don't stimulate her intellectually. It takes a strong individual to stand up to her confrontational communication style. She is friends with Lee, Taylor, Arden, Morgan, and Cam. Her opposite is Blair.

River puts her family and spiritual needs above those of friendship. She isn't an overly social creature and is drawn to a few, well-trusted friends. She cares deeply for those she forms attachments to. Those who admire her intuitive, almost otherworldly, demeanor are protective of her. She spends most of her free time with her family if she has one, her inner circle if she doesn't. She is highly involved in her religious or spiritual community. She drops anyone she considers dishonest or corrupt. She isn't interested in flighty, slightly dangerous extroverts. Friends admire her dedication to humanity and her high personal standards. She isn't interested in being famous and doesn't care what other people think of her. She is naturally drawn to River, Wynn, Cam, Taylor, and Shelby. Her complete opposite is Kelly.

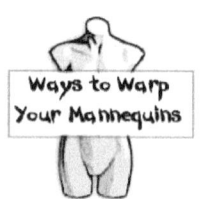

Friendship is a bond that links people together. Even baboons in zoos have specific baboons they prefer to hang out with. Animals cross species to make friends. Humans are trickier, though characters can cross racial and social divides to make friends.

[ALT] **Mismatch:** There could be things about their upbringing, politics, religious leanings, or socioeconomic status that keep them from seeing eye to eye. If one characters violates another's core value, it is a deal breaker no matter how harmonious they seem. Total opposites don't think, feel, or navigate the world the same. Characters that butt heads at three trait levels find it hard to reach common ground. Characters that share three trait levels have the most common ground and leave a little room to help each other grow. When they differ in two major areas, they have a lot in common and an equal degree of difference. When opposites make plans, the one who expects a commitment to be honored is hurt by the friend who blows them off. Enforcers are upset when their friends break the rules. The free-flowing character is irritated by the imposed restrictions of her orderly friend.

Those who have identical temperaments are not necessarily friends. They share the same desire for social interaction, though it could vary slightly and vary on any given day. One character may like hobbies and sports the other can't stand. One character may have a circle of friends the other can't stand. They both either prefer to question or uphold the status quo. That does not mean they agree with the way everyone in society does everything. They could still be highly critical of different aspects of the status quo while desiring to maintain harmony. If they both favor facts or hunches, their facts and hunches may not be identical or correct.

[ALT] **Tenuous Connection:** Characters have different connection needs. Some characters are happy with one best friend, others aren't happy unless they have twenty. Put someone who values one good friend with someone who thinks everyone is his best friend and you'll find heartache. It leads to jealousy and resentment. It leads to one of the friends feeling trapped or restricted. A spouse with many friends might not understand the partner who prefers one. If a spouse views his partner as his best friend, he might not understand why she needs so many other people to fill her time. Introverts and extroverts are often drawn to each other. They exasperate each other when one wants to go out and the other wants to stay in. The introvert might not like the extrovert's wide circle of friends. The extrovert may not like the introvert's close circle of friends. Extroverts make introverts leave the house. Introverts help the extrovert settle down. Extroverts explain to introverts the social impact of their behavior. The introverts help the extroverts see that they don't have to please everyone. These character pairs usually work and play well together with minimal conflict. Extreme introverts are most lonely in a crowd of strangers. Extreme extroverts are most lonely when alone and resist solitude.

[ALT] Solitary Confinement: Most characters feel the need to belong somewhere and to someone. If they don't, they are susceptible to loneliness, social anxiety, and depression. A compelling protagonist arc could take a hero from feeling isolated to feeling connected. When there are fewer people, they rely on each other more. Such is the stuff of Westerns and Literary pioneer stories. When people died, especially in large numbers due to disease, famine, or drought, it preyed on the basic fear of being alone. If the population of a planet is dying, you have an overall story problem. If a character feels alone in his marriage, it is a personal dilemma. If introverts are best friends and one decides to move, it is a painful transition for both and they try to stay in touch. The extrovert is less affected and may not stay in touch. When communities are very small, characters make friends with people they normally avoid. It creates uneasy alliances. A character must overlook differences to have some form of human connection.

[ALT] **Stranded:** A situation in a dark, spooky mansion is heightened if the character is alone. A perfectly normal forest is scarier when he is alone. A planet would be very scary if he was the only astronaut left on it. The smaller the population, the higher the stakes of survival and the more claustrophobic the situation becomes. Put ten thousand people in a city and a character is easily lost in the throng. That makes a good Mystery. Putting ten people in a space station makes a great Science Fiction story. Killing them one by one makes a great Thriller or Horror story. Post-apocalyptic stories explore our fear of being alone and the desire for survivors to find one another. Science Fiction stories explore our desire to not be alone in the universe.

How far is your character willing to go to not live alone? He might marry someone he does not love, become friends with someone he wouldn't otherwise, build a robot so he has a companion, join an organization he does not agree with, or draw a face on a football so he has someone to talk to. How far is someone willing to go to live alone? A character might rent a cabin in the Dakota badlands or buy an island and find out he needs people after all. Characters in psychic pain withdraw from the people around them. Some do it for a week, others a month. At the most extreme end, they withdraw from life entirely. Standing alone could be a strength.

[ALT] **Unraveled**: Ownership is tricky business. One of the first things a child learns to say is "Mine!" Children think they own shared toys because they had them first. We all think we own things that are tangible and intangible. Characters think they "own" their friends. Friendships form and dissolve due to life circumstances, misunderstandings, different belief systems, geographical restrictions, boredom, boundary violations, and a variety of other reasons. Friendships can last a lifetime, perhaps longer than romantic entanglements. Shifting friendships cause conflicts in any genre. Literary stories follow the rise and fall of a friendship. Friendships cause complications in a Romance. When a friendship ends for no apparent reason, it leaves some characters with an anxious need to understand why. The character who prefers closure may secretly worry that he did something wrong. If a friend simply disappears, stops returning his calls, or moves with no forwarding address, it can inspire a character to go to drastic lengths to find out why.

[ALT] **Grave Digging**: Contacting old friends and lovers has become an obsession in the internet age. What if a character contacted an old friend who didn't want to be contacted? He might realize the old friend was better left alone. He might learn a horrible secret about why the friendship ended as an overall story problem. If a friend doesn't call back on a specific day or in response to a specific request, it can cause anxiety at scene level. It is a cool dose of reality to find the friend simply walked away because he was bored or didn't like the character very much.

[ALT] **Transplants**: When communities are so large you don't know who your neighbors are, finding people you have an affinity with is difficult. Characters who relocate often have trouble making new friends and maintaining long-distance friendships. It's harder for an introvert than an extrovert. This makes a good literary tale, especially a coming of age tale. Relocation can feature in a Western where the Irish protagonist has to make friends with Swedish immigrants. Being a fish out of water or the "new" guy causes friction. The new cop proves himself by solving the mystery. The new quarterback has to fit in to an existing team. The boss's nephew has to prove he got the job due to talent not connections.

ALT **Narratives**: Friendships are based on trust and commonality. Characters meet, share their personal narratives, find similarities or joint affinities, and want to know each other better. It's important to know why your characters are friends. Best friends know as much about each other as they are willing to share with another person, sometimes more than their spouse. The intimacy between friends causes conflicts with those around them, especially if their partners feel excluded. Belonging to the same group can cement friendships, so can having similar dreams, goals, political or religious views, or children of a similar age that play together. Hearing the same old stories over and over can end a friendship.

ALT **Frenemies**: Friendships run the gamut from mutually supportive to mutually destructive. Friendships interfere with relationships and make great conflicts in a Romance tale. Most protagonists have a least one good friend in the friend and foe mix. This character often acts as his sounding board. Friends help the protagonist achieve his goals and cheer him on when he succeeds. A jealous friend can resent it when the protagonist achieves his goal. A friend might pretend to be supportive, but secretly undermine the protagonist. Even an antagonist can have a friend or two.

An obnoxious friend can cause difficulties with the protagonist's relationship, other friendships, family, or work. A friend could monopolize the protagonist's time and interfere with the other compartments of his life. A friend's self-destruction can force the protagonist to make difficult choices. In some cases, it's harder to end a friendship than it is to end a romantic relationship. A Literary tale can focus on an unusual or especially tight friendship, or it can follow a friendship as it unravels. In a Comedy, friends meddle and complicate each other's lives in hysterical ways. In a Mystery, the friend is a complication in solving the case or a suspect.

[ALT] **Confessional**: It is assumed that females are more likely to ask other females for their opinion. Women supposedly talk about deeper issues and share the dark corners of their souls more often than men. Understanding temperament turns that stereotype on its head. Some males have strong ties to friends. They have strong bonds of honor and teamwork, even if they aren't soldiers or policemen. A man can have the temperament type that talks to everyone about everything. A woman can have difficulty maintaining friendships and find it hard to share her inner thoughts and feelings.

You can use friendships to cause interesting dilemmas in your story world.

LOVE, SEX & HATE

Characters all need to be loved by someone. Healthy love brings out the best in people. Unhealthy love destroys them. A character can go to ridiculous, sometimes self-destructive, lengths to find and keep the object of his affection. This pursuit is the heart of a Romance novel. It also provides complications in every other genre.

Communication, common goals, trust, respect, and personal balance create successful partnerships. One's strengths can make up for another's weakness if they acknowledge their differences and work together. Fortunately, for fiction writers, they most often can't or won't give up their point of view and methods and conflict ensues.

Exact temperament pairings have minimal conflict. Sometimes friction is sometimes needed to ignite passion. Partners with exact temperament matches might muddle along for a while, but end up boring each other. Truly well-balanced characters of all temperament types manage to stay together and weather the tempests in their own special ways.

The pairing of opposites can result in a balanced relationship where one's strengths make up for the other's weaknesses. For the purposes of a romance novel, this works. If you use a character's relationship as a complication in another genre, the differences in personality add the friction to fiction.

Currency: Wynn needs to feel appreciated for being a good person. If she feels unappreciated, she grows resentful. She works hard to make her partner happy and expects him to reciprocate. If her partner is distant, or skips cards heaped with praise, she won't feel the love.

Priority: Wynn's relationships take precedence over everything else, with the possible exception of her spiritual life. She seeks a permanent, committed relationship.

Approach: Wynn is emotionally intense, but guards her heart. She is happy with the traditional role assigned to her. She puts the comfort of her partner at the top of her to-do list. She is caring, empathetic, and willing to gloss over minor indiscretions. Her habit of keeping things to herself to avoid conflict leads to inappropriate scatter blasts of anger and resentment during a confrontation. She often says things she can't take back. She becomes rigid when anxious. Those tactics won't have the effect she desperately needs. She has difficulty leaving an abusive relationship and accepting that a relationship has ended. She blames herself and obsesses over what she could have done differently, especially if she feels she has been faithful and kept up her side of the bargain. She might remain faithful to the memory of a deceased partner.

Deal Breakers: Wynn's selflessness puts her at risk of being taken advantage of or steamrolled. She hides her distress and bottles her resentment and anger until something comes along to uncork them. If she feels unappreciated, she leaves mentally or physically. It takes a lot of provocation to push her there.

Desire: Wynn views sex as a way of strengthening the emotional bond. It is her duty to make sure her partner is happy. She is affectionate. She may not utter loving affirmations, but needs to hear them. She shows her love through gifts and small actions.

Growth: Wynn must place her needs higher up on the priority ladder. To show growth, she must learn to address problems as they arise, without taking criticism as a personal attack.

Love Matches: Wynn is naturally drawn to Taylor, Arden, and Nevada. Her opposite is Morgan.

Currency: Francis is more interested in being right than being happy. He hates challenges to his authority and viewpoints. All is well as long as his partner accedes to his point of view and decisions.

Priority: Francis is true blue and committed. He wants a permanent relationship. He takes the "until death do us part" vow literally.

Approach: Francis goes through the tradition of dating and wooing because it is expected, not because it is what he would like to do. He struggles with huggy-touchy stuff. He is supportive and cares for his partner. If his partner points out he isn't meeting her emotional needs, he does his best to meet them. He feels love passionately, but struggles to express himself. He is faithful and loyal. He wants his home and family to run smoothly. He struggles with chaos and family members who don't behave as they should. He imposes restrictions on his partner. He meets what he considers his obligations, which may not be the priorities his partner values. If his partner berates him, he listens to the part that addresses functional points: "You need to take the trash out on Thursdays." He ignores the emotional context: "You work too hard and are never home when I need you." If he marries one of the feeling types, he could wreck her self-esteem.

Deal Breakers: Being right is very important to him. His partner may walk away if her point of view is never considered. He isn't threatened by constructive criticism. He can handle conflict without taking it personally, as long as he isn't called wrong. Leaving Francis requires a really good lawyer, or a shotgun.

Desire: Francis views sex as a physical release and his duty more so than an expression of emotion. He expects intimacy to occur on a scheduled basis. He brings home flowers and chocolates if he has been told it is expected, not out of inspiration or because he felt like it. He thinks his actions should speak for themselves. Working hard every day should count. He gives positive affirmations if his partner asks for them, even though he doesn't need them. He deflects his partner's attempts to praise him. The female version of Francis goes along with whatever her partner wants, though she is uncomfortable with anything out of the ordinary.

Growth: Francis becomes a slave to routine and needs to learn to loosen up a bit, especially when friends and family need him to. He needs to accept that other people have the right to do things a different way. He needs to consider opposing viewpoints and learn how to process other people's feelings.

Love Matches: Francis is naturally drawn to Arden, Cam, and Joss. His opposite is Hadley.

Currency: Nevada's currency is appreciation. He craves loving affirmations for working hard and providing for his partner.

Priority: Nevada takes commitment seriously and believes in living up to his obligations.

Approach: Nevada avoids confrontation at all costs. He considers criticism, and the need to discuss a problem, a personal attack. He is prone to depression and low self-esteem. He is overly concerned with appearances and expects his partner to maintain them. He is good around the house. He takes care of things that need attention. He is cautious with money, because he thrives on security. He works hard to make life secure. He needs to belong: to institutions and his family. This makes him very social. He throws parties and attends events at work, social club functions, and community events. He expects his partner to participate. Pairing him with an introvert who hates parties is problematic.

Deal Breakers: Nevada needs a lot of positive reinforcement from his partner and resents it if he doesn't get it. He is passive-aggressive in response and often does the wrong thing to elicit the appreciation he craves. He won't quit easily.

Desire: Nevada is warm and loving. He invests a lot of time and energy in making his partner happy. He views sex as an opportunity to express affection and considers withholding a deliberate insult. He is highly traditional. He is eager to please his partner, but resists anything too out of the ordinary for fear that someone might find out.

Growth: Nevada can be a little too needy and uptight. He tries to overcompensate and takes over tasks he shouldn't to prove his usefulness. He needs to relax a little. He needs to share responsibilities with his partner. He needs to stop feeling let down just because his partner didn't thank him for cutting the grass or going to work in the morning.

Love Matches: Nevada is naturally drawn to Arden, Dallas, and Wynn. His opposite is Greer.

Currency: Arden's currency is gratitude and appreciation for his integrity. As long as his partner feels grateful and appreciates his hard work, things go smoothly.

Priority: Arden fulfills what he sees as his commitment to the full extent of his capacity. When he chooses a partner, he plans to be with her forever.

Approach: Arden likes to be in charge and is controlling. He works hard to provide financial security with a focus on the material things that signify success. He provides a secure home life, but makes room for fun and leisure. He schedules vacations. He expects his partner to do the right thing and be a good example in the community. He sees himself as a guardian. He freely gives positive feedback when he is impressed by his partner's behavior or accomplishments. He is open and honest with his thoughts and opinions. He expects his partner to take part in the social requirements of his job and the community. Don't pair him with an introvert who hates going out or there is war. A feeling character is hurt by his perceived criticism and overwhelming expectations. If his partner firmly, factually, and preferably unemotionally, expresses her unmet needs, he does his best to accommodate them. He wants to do what he is supposed to and takes care of details.

Deal Breakers: Arden would not consider divorce lightly. Problems arise if he doesn't feel appreciated. His job is to shield and protect. He can carry that too far and infringe on his partner's autonomy. His partner might not appreciate his instructions or guiding hand.

Desire: Arden is a lively lover. He tends to be traditional and may be rather regimental in his expectations. He sees sex as a physical demonstration of affection rather than a spiritual communion. He may not remember to use sweet words. He expresses love through hard work and dedication.

Growth: Arden needs to learn that his partner's methods and opinions have merit, even if they are different. He needs to relax and let things be. He needs to understand that, for some partners, sex has an emotional component.

Love Matches: Arden is naturally drawn Francis, Nevada, and Wynn. His complete opposite is Shelby.

Currency: Blair's currency is affection and admiration. If she isn't praised for being wonderful, she deflates.

Priority: Blair places her relationship on top of the list. She wants a long-term commitment. She struggles to choose, but sticks with her choice forever if possible.

Approach: Blair loves deeply, but is slow to warm up. Her partner may not understand just how much she cares. Few people know her extremely well. She is secretly intense while appearing outwardly light-hearted. She is vulnerable and easily hurt, though she won't tell her partner. She expects him to "see" he has hurt her. She is disappointed when he doesn't. When hurt, she withdraws. She hates conflict and goes to great lengths to avoid it. She is an easy-going partner. She doesn't ask for, or expect, a lot. She is traditional and organized and takes care of what needs to be done. She wants to be adored for it.

Deal Breakers: Blair feels attacked when an argument gets heated. She releases all the negative impressions and feelings she has repressed. She isn't likely to leave, even if her partner is dissatisfied. She stays and works it out if at all possible.

Desire: Blair is serious about sex. It is a sacred act that should be given the time and attention it deserves. She is sensual and enjoys the physical expression of love. She shows her love through this communion. She needs positive affirmations to feel good about herself, but doesn't offer them.

Growth: Blair needs to learn how to address conflicts as they arise. She needs to stop feeling injured when someone opposes her or when she does not receive praise for simply breathing.

Love Matches: Blair is naturally drawn to Hadley, Kelly, and Arden. Her opposite is Lee.

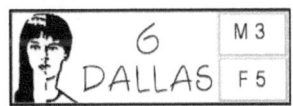

Currency: Dallas wants to be adored for being Dallas. She wants her partner to appreciate her sense of fun and adventure. Everything is fun until the party is over.

Priority: Dallas likes exploring all the options. Once she commits, she intends to stay. She might not if the situation grows tense. She always wonders if there are better bachelors behind other doors.

Approach: Dallas is passionate and fun loving. She cares about her partner's happiness. She is flexible and open to suggestion. She takes her partner's emotional temperature frequently, which irks some mannequins. Problems arise when she encounters conflict and confrontation. She takes criticism, even objective statements, as a personal attack. Conflict stresses her. She represses her initial response for the sake of smoothing things over, but continues to fester. She gives in to avoid a protracted disagreement. She ignores a problem until she can't. This just delays the inevitable.

Deal Breakers: Dallas is loyal and views it as her responsibility to fix things that aren't working. She isn't one to give up easily. If things get too intense, restrictive, or boring, she moves on. She finds it hard to do so and blames herself for the failure.

Desire: Dallas is playful and creative. She has a rich fantasy world, which she applies to sex. She sees sex as a natural expression of her love. She needs positive affirmations. She may fish for reassurance and compliments. If she doesn't get them, she lavishes them on her partner in the hopes of sparking them.

Growth: Dallas needs to learn that negative feedback or small disagreements aren't personal or the end of the world. She needs to remain present during the discussion and work through issues.

Love Matches: Dallas is naturally drawn to River, Shelby, and Taylor. Her opposite is Francis.

Currency: Hadley wants to be adored for breathing. Since she is adorable, her partner usually complies. If the adoration fades, trouble sets in.

Priority: Hadley isn't overly interested in being tied down. She places a relationship on the back burner. She struggles with long-term commitment and likes to explore all the bachelors. Hadley loves to be in love and struggles when the initial adrenaline rush tapers. She may overcome her desire to flit and settle down, as long as the relationship isn't too restrictive or her partner too critical.

Approach: Hadley loves to date and encourages her partner to enjoy life as much as she does. She is weak at planning and follow-through. She takes every day as it comes and wants to grab the gusto. If that means changing plans, she changes plans. She doesn't ask for much. She wants to be happy and wants her partner to be happy. She schedules a busy social life. She changes things to keep them from becoming dull, whether it's rearranging the furniture or their lives. She hates to miss out on anything she considers fun. She doesn't like vague promises or "we'll see" as an answer. If you stated it, you promised. She is bored by analyzing the past and worrying about the future. Tomorrow will take care of itself. She ends a necessary conversation. She would not deal well with someone who likes to debate for fun.

Deal Breakers: Hadley isn't good with conflict and lashes out angrily in the moment with words she can't take back. She retreats when criticized or restricted. A controlling partner sends Hadley off to find someone more fun to play with.

Desire: Hadley energetically embraces romantic love. She seeks out and enjoys intimate contact. She is tactile and sensual. She is generous, warm, and highly motivated to make her partner happy. She is lavish with loving affirmations. She isn't big on gifts, but can provide them when requested.

Growth: Hadley needs to restrict herself occasionally and learn to take criticism as constructive rather than personal. She could try to appear a little more invested.

Love Matches: Hadley is naturally drawn to Kelly, Blair, and Arden. Her opposite is Cam.

Currency: Shelby wants to be honored and respected. As long as her partner makes her feel respected, things are fine.

Priority: Shelby is loyal and committed. If she isn't in a permanent relationship, she continually searches for one. Once committed, she places her relationship at the top of her list. On a subconscious level, she feels vaguely dissatisfied with all of her relationships because they are never truly "ideal."

Approach: Shelby seeks a harmonious, loving relationship and works hard to make it a success. She may need reminders to do the bill paying and housekeeping. She often pushes routine tasks to the bottom of the priority pile. That annoys a partner who expects her to be on top of things. Once committed, she may romanticize a bad relationship in her own mind as a form of protection. She may attribute virtues to her partner that he lacks and place him on a pedestal. She struggles to reconcile the idealistic romance novel relationship with the demands of a real one. She overlooks imperfections for the sake of connection. She avoids conflict and confrontation. If she ends up with a partner that is all action, no talk, she grows resentful. She values personal space and the freedom to do her own thing. If her partner respects and supports her, she thrives. She is not the possessive or jealous type. She understands her partner's need to indulge in his own pursuits. She respects his privacy and independence. She rejects hints that something is going on and firmly defends her partner while secretly worrying that she has done something wrong to drive him away.

Deal Breakers: Shelby resents a controlling spouse. Her need to avoid conflict and criticism is a problem. No matter how a comment is presented, she takes it personally. She responds with irrational emotion. Her distress, and immediate assumption that she is somehow at fault, make her lash out. She manipulates her partner through guilt to obtain the positive feedback she craves. It is a very unhealthy dynamic. She would not leave easily, but will if things become unsatisfactory enough.

Desire: Shelby is slow in letting someone close. Once trust has been established, she embraces the opportunity to express her intense love and affection. She is affirming and affectionate. She values the romantic aspect over the physical aspect. She places her partner's pleasure above her own.

Growth: Shelby needs to learn how to handle conflict and understand it's better to tackle problems head on rather than let things fester. She needs to handle criticism.

Love Matches: Shelby's ideal mate is Dallas, River, or Taylor. Her opposite is Arden.

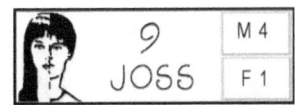

Currency: Joss wants recognition for his intelligence and skill. He usually gets it, in the short-term. His derring-do draws them in, but eventually drives them off.

Priority: Joss places a permanent relationship at the bottom of his list. He struggles with routine and commitment. He thrives on new experiences and new partners.

Approach: Joss is exciting and intense for short bursts. He is the ultimate hard-to-get partner. He is the man or woman of action and few words. He resists routine and strict schedules. He hates being controlled by other people, particularly his partner. He spends a lot of time exploring his interests without his partner. He is happy to provide basic needs and the kind of dating behavior that keeps a relationship humming along. He isn't free with his opinion, but open to someone else's. He listens in information gathering mode and evades answering questions by asking more questions. This frustrates his partner when she needs a direct answer. He doesn't feel he owes anyone an explanation and never asks for permission. He is protective of his emotions and avoids deeper feelings. His level of intensity can vary from day to day and that can leave his partner feeling unbalanced. He has problems with the traditional expectations of behavior.

Deal Breakers: All is fine until Joss becomes bored or the other person becomes too demanding or clingy. He won't stay to fix it. He remains in a life-long relationship by taking it one day at a time. His partner is never entirely certain he'll stay. His air of aloofness may draw his partner in, but could drive her away.

Desire: Joss views sex as recreation. He is sensual and enjoys experimentation. He is spontaneous, creative, and enthusiastic for as long as it lasts. He sets the mood and makes it fun. He loses interest if it becomes routine. He breaks up and makes up for the novelty it provides.

Growth: Joss needs to learn to hold on and open up. Being vulnerable would be very difficult, but might prove ultimately rewarding.

Love Matches: Joss wouldn't mesh with someone identical to himself. He is naturally drawn to Arden, Francis, or Lee. His opposite is Taylor.

Currency: Kelly wants to be admired for being the life of the party. He usually is, at first.

Priority: Kelly isn't looking for a permanent relationship. He has trouble honoring a commitment once he makes it. His relationship is on the bottom of his priority pile.

Approach: Kelly is enthusiastic. Life with him would be quite a ride, full of ups and downs, and lots of spinning. He is extremely charming and superficial. He offers his partner the world and she attributes him with a big heart. He loves life. He makes those in his orbit love life too. The problems start when his partner realizes he can't make a plan and stick with it.

Deal Breakers: He has a problem with commitment and behaves in ways that are detrimental to the relationship. He is shocked when his partner objects. As soon as he is restricted or bored, he finds someone else to play with.

Desire: Kelly considers sex a physical carnival ride. He makes things exciting. He is a sensual lover. He goes for the big moments, once in a while. He is oblivious to the emotional content. If his partner needs emotional closeness to feel loved, she probably won't get it. She may tell him and he may try, but he can't sustain it. He isn't good with positive affirmations. He won't grasp the neediness of a feeling partner. He is master of the grand gesture, but grand gestures aren't always enough.

Growth: Kelly needs to learn how to commit. He could learn to go through the motions that his partner needs. He could learn that loving is made up of smaller, more consistent moments.

Love Matches: Kelly would be good with someone exactly like himself. He is naturally drawn to Francis, Joss, and Hadley. His opposite is River.

11
GREER

M 3
F 1

Currency: Greer wants recognition for his competence. Since he is usually competent, he receives it. When he forgets to take care of things around the house, his competence might be questioned.

Priority: Greer isn't looking for a permanent love connection. He honors a commitment once made, but may not remain emotionally present.

Approach: Greer takes his relationship seriously and analyzes it much like he analyzes everything. He is low-demand and easy to get along with. His problems stem from the lack of emotional engagement and low need for social interaction. He isn't big on traditional trappings. He can't relate to high-needs people. He is straightforward and honest. He won't play games or manipulate his partner. It is hard for him to open his heart and he retracts at the first sign of danger. He feels passionately, he just can't verbalize it. Of all the types, he is the hardest to have a relationship with. It's a good thing he is a rare bird.

Deal Breakers: He usually runs at the first sign of messy complications. He avoids conflict and deals with it in an analytical way, ignoring the emotional component. He defends his commitment by saying, "Of course I love you. I'm here aren't I?" If his partner reads him as distant and disengaged, she might move on.

Desire: Greer is imaginative and loving, but not overly demanding. He is quick to sublimate his needs or loses track of them when focused at work or on his hobbies. His intense passion may not be apparent to his partner. He isn't in tune with his partner's emotional life. He misses the hints and emotional cues she exhibits. His displays of affection may be out of sync with his partner's desire for them. He isn't good with the positive affirmations and praise some types need.

Growth: If Greer is able to step outside his own head long enough, he could have a very tight bond with his partner. He needs to learn to love his partner the way she needs him to.

Love Matches: Greer pairs well with his temperament type. He is naturally drawn to Morgan, Cam, and Arden. His opposite is Nevada.

Currency: Taylor wants to be appreciated for her goodness and service. She usually is, unless her efforts become toxic.

Priority: Taylor considers a permanent relationship a high priority.

Approach: Taylor is warm and committed. She wants her partner to be happy. She sacrifices her wants and needs to make sure he is. She blames herself when things go wrong and criticism chips away at her self-esteem. If the relationship fails, she walks away thinking she was defective. She bounces back and tries again. She works hard to keep a relationship together. She is sensitive to her partner's emotional needs. She is very social and works to make her home a great place to entertain.

Deal Breakers: Taylor won't walk away unless a serious core violation occurs. She could walk away over it, but tends to stick with unhealthy relationships where she does all the giving. She hates conflict and ignores her partner's slings and arrows to avoid it. She gives in rather than extends the fight. Ignoring problems turns them in to bigger problems that eventually become explosive.

Desire: Taylor is enthusiastic and creative. She is warm and fun. She sees sex as a direct expression of her love. She works hard to make her partner happy and doing so makes her happy. She pencils it in as often as she needs to. She won't express her own needs. She needs loving affirmations, but won't ask for them. She is hurt when the sweet words aren't forthcoming.

Growth: Taylor learns to give her needs and wants equal priority and to verbalize them. She needs to accept that the world won't end over a disagreement.

Love Matches: Taylor fares well with someone just like her. She is naturally drawn to Wynn, Lee, and River. Her opposite is Joss.

Currency: Cam wants to be admired for his intelligence and competence. His partner usually admires that about him, until he forgets he has a partner.

Priority: Cam isn't looking for a permanent relationship, but honors his commitment once he is in one.

Approach: Cam is more focused on his inner world than the external one. He comes across as aloof. He is emotionally intense, but guarded. His partner is shocked by how deeply he experiences emotion. His quiet confidence and reliability are appealing. He possesses keen insight into what makes people tick. He applies that information to his relationships. He thinks more than acts. He has a hard time reconciling the way things should be with the way they are. His distraction sometimes limits his awareness of his partner's feelings, particularly if she doesn't express them. He becomes overly structured or paralyzed when anxious. He may get so involved in his projects that he forgets his partner for a while. He avoids interpersonal conflict, but loves to debate.

Deal Breakers: Cam does not need companionship enough to put up with abusive or unsatisfying relationships. He finds it easy to cut his losses and move on, having learned a valuable lesson. He may not express his distress. He represses negative emotions until he explodes.

Desire: Cam enjoys thinking about intimacy and ways to make it better. He is creative and intense. In a negative relationship, he thinks about sex more often than having it. He tends to show how he feels rather than talk about it. He offers loving affirmations and gifts if his partner desires them.

Growth: Cam needs to learn that his partner is sometimes right. Since he is open to a rational person's ideas, he is capable of it. He needs to keep in mind that his logical dissection of a situation has an emotional impact. He finds emotional neediness hard to grasp.

Love Matches: He partners well with someone with an identical temperament. He is drawn to Joss, Lee, and Francis. His opposite is Dallas.

Currency: Morgan wants to be admired for his intelligence and competence. That usually happens, at least until his behavior makes those traits questionable.

Priority: Morgan considers a relationship a low priority. He prefers variety to permanence. External compression forces him into a long-term commitment. His relationships are tenuous.

Approach: Morgan is easily bored. He needs a partner that constantly engages and challenges him. He treats his relationship like any other experiment by asking what works and what could be improved. His partner might not appreciate being "managed" in that way. He eagerly adopts new activities and plans, but drops them as quickly. He means well. However, his love of debate grows tiring. He carelessly throws out comments about what he might do. His partner might take him seriously. His risk-taking could create trouble for both of them. While invested, he is attentive, eager to explore, and enthusiastic. He neglects the relationship when a project takes over, whether it is an assignment at work or his decision to renovate the house. He isn't in touch with his feelings and may be oblivious to his partner's. If his partner states a need, he creatively attempts to fill it. He is prone to forgetting.

Deal Breakers: Morgan walks away if bored or restricted. His partner grows tired of his need to play devil's advocate instead of just focusing on what needs to be done.

Desire: Morgan is spontaneous and resists routine. He is open to trying new things. Sex is a physical release not an emotional bonding experience. He offers a grand gesture, but can't keep it up long term.

Growth: Morgan could learn to focus and finish what he starts. He could try listening more and talking less. He could get in touch with his emotions.

Love Matches: Morgan is naturally drawn to Greer, River, and Arden. His opposite is Wynn.

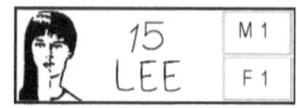

Currency: Lee wants recognition for her competence. She usually earns it. Things are fine until she steamrolls once too often.

Priority: Lee considers a relationship a low priority. She takes a commitment seriously once she has made it, but often loses touch with her partner.

Approach: Lee is emotionally aloof. She takes the lead and feels responsible for making things work. She has a lot to offer. She is dedicated, dependable, and hardworking. She holds herself accountable. She is creative and pushes her partner to explore his own dreams. If she decides something isn't working, she unilaterally changes the terms of the relationship. It puzzles and alarms her partner. She is steady financially and values a nice home and creature comforts. She may never be home long enough to enjoy them. If her partner tells her flat out that she isn't meeting expectations, she may try. Operating against her nature would not be easy. If there is conflict, she views it as a chance to learn and improve. She is confrontational by nature. If paired with a partner that avoids conflict and sees criticism as a personal assault, the relationship won't survive. She may learn to temper her approach with her partner in the interest of making it work. She finds it hard to share power. A relationship would have to be based on mutual respect. She has to view her partner as competent. She expects him to be independent and to develop his own interests.

Deal Breakers: If she finds a relationship unsatisfying or her partner boring, she ends it and abruptly moves on literally or emotionally. She could become an abusive bully to a weaker partner. She doesn't admire weak people enough to partner with them long-term.

Desire: Lee is creative and adventurous. She expects sex on a regular basis. She is self-confident. She has little patience with someone who is emotionally needy. She shows her love through her actions. Loving affirmations don't mean anything to her. She isn't interested in giving or receiving compliments or flattery. If partnered with a feeling type, it won't go well.

Growth: Lee needs to learn to share power. She needs to respect her partner's opinions and ideas even if she doesn't agree with them. She could focus less on being skilled and more on being warm and loving.

Love Matches: Lee is naturally drawn to Arden, Joss, and Taylor. Her opposite is Blair.

Currency: River wants to be admired for her wisdom and desire for harmony. She usually is admired, unless her desire to be worshipped becomes obsessive.

Priority: River seeks a permanent and perfect communion of souls. Her intensity drives some types away. She goes from relationship to relationship in search of the ideal. She is vaguely dissatisfied with every partner.

Approach: River feels intensely. She needs constant feedback and affirmation. She wants a perfect relationship and her excessive probing to find out what is wrong is wearying. She works hard to keep the relationship alive. She bonds permanently and deeply. She is good with loving affirmations. She is generous. She is drawn to deep and complex partners. She comes up with creative solutions to conflict and is highly aware of her partner's emotional state. She is protective and withdraws when she meets resistance. Her overly emotional approach irritates a thinking partner.

Deal Breakers: River becomes highly critical of her partner if he acts out or can't be trusted. She blames him when things aren't working. She represses her emotions and becomes vicious when she bursts. She stays in a relationship until she is sure it can't be repaired. She moves on easily when it is truly over.

Desire: River views sex as a spiritual communion. She is in search of a soul mate. She selflessly gives to her partner. She is tactile and sensual. She struggles to state her case in person and may resort to an emotional letter.

Growth: River needs to relax and stop taking her partner's emotional temperature every five minutes. She needs to stop elevating every encounter into a peace negotiation or worship session.

Love Matches: River is naturally drawn to Taylor, Arden, and Nevada. Her opposite is Morgan.

Growth: When it comes love, the reader roots for a happy ending. Partners overcoming their differences leads to a happy ending. Becoming more fixed in their opposition leads to a down ending. Growth involves appreciating their differences and reaching consensus. It means recognizing and developing their weak side. They stop telling their partner they are wrong. They stop correcting and micromanaging each other. They learn to state feelings and deal with conflicts as they arise. They accept their partner's different need for depth and space. Partners oppositional at four trait levels attract each other at first. They soon make each other crazy. Differences at three levels create high conflict partnerships. Differences at two levels balance them or break them up. Differences at one level can work, but the partners may be too similar. Even identical pairings are rife with conflict. Their opinions, plans, traditions, friends, work, and slight variations in their strengths create conflict.

Wholeness: A character is often drawn to that which he feels he lacks, the traits he is weak in, or those items buried in his shadow shelf. He picks someone who peels the scab from his childhood wounds in order to heal them. Who you assigned as your mannequin's caregivers is as important as who he chooses for friends and lovers. The same conflicts resurface at this higher Def-Con level. Nasty things arise from the shadow self. Fears, doubts, jealousies, and insecurities fuel the flames. They threaten the character's need to be connected (or distant) and loved for who he is. Sexual hungers and repressions are tossed in too.

ALT Brick Walls: Love is like playing the game Tetris. The game features different shaped blocks that float down from the ceiling. It is up to you to make sure they fit together to form a complete level. When a complete level is formed, the row disappears. The pieces move faster as the clock counts down. If you don't fit the blocks together fast enough, the wall quickly reaches the top of the screen. You lose and have to start all over again. Relationships are similar. Negative encounters add blocks. Positive encounters remove blocks. For every negative encounter your mannequins have with each other, it takes four or five positive encounters to erase them. When they make each other feel good and validate each other's currency, the pieces fit and a row of blocks is deleted. When the mannequins annoy each other, it adds a row. When they violate core values or invalidate their partner's currency, the bricks pile up faster and the clock ticks faster. They run out of time to offer the necessary positive encounters to delete the wall. A power struggle develops. Heated words get slung or partners withdraw to protect. When there are more negative encounters than positive, the countdown to total annihilation begins. The partners either make up and heal or break up and nurse their wounds. In modern day North America, partners pretty much come and go as they please. In other times and locales, it isn't so. In your Fantasy or Science Fiction world, you can make up any rules you like.

ALT Lock and Load: When wooing, characters use their best manners, bite their tongues, and smile when someone behaves differently. Then they move in together and share physical space, emotional space, mental space, and finances. The small quirks overlooked in the haze of lust begin to chafe. They revert to temperament. Opposite temperaments can balance each other. High oppositional pairings can turn a character into the worst version of himself. Every day there are small skirmishes or outright border wars, both physical and psychological. They argue over keeping the house tidy or sloppy, whether to invite people over or not and when, how they buy groceries, when they pay bills or don't pay bills. Some characters are neat and organized; others thrive on chaos. Some are thrifty. Some are spendthrifts. The planner is irritated by his partner's flightiness. The factual character is irritated by the fanciful partner's ideas. Some are workaholics; others can't stick with a job. Some prefer to think a problem through before making a decision; others make snap judgments. A character conditioned to not speak up might be attracted to the type who does, endlessly and about everything. It becomes grating.

ALT Connection: The introvert and extrovert argue about whether to go out or stay in. The one who consults others is irritated when his partner doesn't want anyone else's opinion added to the argument. Either could use friends to bolster his side of the argument. A partner who spends what the other considers too much time at work, with his friends, or riding in the Tour de France, creates tension. The introverted partner may be happy when the extroverted partner works out of town, goes on a hunting trip or spa weekend, or pursues solo hobbies. Time spent apart can be the relief valve the relationship needs or an excuse to leave it. An extrovert might be attracted to an introvert, thinking he will help her be more social. It might work. It might not. The introvert may be so exhausted by the extrovert's need for stimulation that she refuses to attend all the social functions her partner signs up for. The extrovert is irritated when introvert wants to stay home and read a good book. If you pair an introvert with an introvert and an extrovert with an extrovert, there is still room for trouble. The introverts might indulge in different solitary pastimes. The extroverts might have different circles of friends and never see each other at home.

Chapels: There are differing opinions on the validity of the institution of marriage. Some are for it. Some are against it. Some argue it's the commitment, not the piece of paper, that matters. Others argue that going through the ceremony of commitment and taking an oath of loyalty before other people makes the commitment more serious. The partners fight harder to make it work when there is a binding agreement. Some societies are opposed to divorce. Other societies don't see the point of marriage. Some tribes have polygamy. Some tribes endorse free love. Some characters feel the need to "parent" their partners. Divorce comes along and strikes at a character's deepest insecurities. His financial security is threatened. His home is threatened. His life might be threatened. The more intimate and closed in the cauldron, the more heat you generate. It's hard to create friction when both sides can easily move on.

Currency Exchange: There are differences in what characters value. Understanding each other's currency is crucial. Currency is highly individual. The marketers get it wrong half, if not two-thirds, of the time. Roses, jewelry, wine, and dinner at an ultra-expensive restaurant are promoted as signs of love. Those gifts fail to please if the character is allergic to flowers, would rather have a diamond bit than a diamond ring, doesn't drink, and hates gourmet food. There are difficulties when a character expects his partner to read his mind. A character might consider a gift invalid unless it is a piece of jewelry. If a characters buys his partner sweaters and ice cube trays, his partner hates it. The first time is an irritant. The fiftieth time is grounds for divorce. Until his partner states what she values, the character continues to do the wrong thing without knowing it. Meeting each other's currency brings couples together. Denying each other's currency drives them apart.

[ALT] Handcuffs: Marriage is a balance of power and creates the perfect battleground for conflict. Some characters have trouble sharing power. There are difficulties balancing individual freedom with connection so that both people are free to grow yet stay together. Lovers often weigh their need for romantic love with their need for personal fulfillment and independence. If one character is clingy and the other is fiercely independent, you have conflict. They need to reach compromises that leave both parties feeling heard and in control. Lovers struggle for dominance until they figure out that they are both equally important or agree to live with inequity. If they don't, the relationship fails.

[ALT] Money Matters: There are difficulties in balancing financial independence and the need to share assets. Financial infidelity destroys relationships. Partners lie to each other about how much they spend, what they spend it on, and why. Who earns the money? Who decides how it is spent? Disparity in income causes friction and imbalances in the power struggle. Separate banking accounts can save relationships. A couple may need to learn to pool their resources and share equally no matter who earns more.

⌨ Domesticity: One of the greatest challenges in a relationship is dividing up domestic duties and job responsibilities. They fight over inequities in the division of labor. It is assumed that females are natural homemakers and males aren't. Temperament theory turns that argument on its head. Some temperaments are naturals at organizing, planning, and following through on the things that need to get done. Others can't do it no matter how hard they try. Whether the mannequin is male or female is irrelevant, except when society assigns him a stereotypical role. Put a mannequin who isn't suited to the task in charge of the house or the children and chaos ensues.

⌨ Honeymoons: There are difficulties when a character agrees to things to please his partner. After a while, he wonders why the person he dated isn't the person he is married to. Lovers enter people-pleasing mode when dating and become more egocentric over the long haul. Things he was willing to do for a weekend, like watching sports or antique shopping, become items of contention after a character has done them a thousand times more than he ever wanted to. Personal narratives bring couples together. Hearing the same stories twenty times a year is grating. Some mannequins naturally sublimate their needs after the wooing has ended. They build up a volcano of resentment and blast their partner with it at inappropriate moments. That makes the wall higher.

⌨ Lie to Me: There are difficulties when partners lie about their pasts, particularly past relationships. The truth has a nasty way of making itself known. Lies can be small or large.

See the section on lying. Lying adds rows to the wall and could make it too high to breach.

Clingers: A child who is abandoned by a parent often has a desperate need to be loved. He goes to unhealthy lengths to obtain and keep that love. He may accept an abusive partner. An adopted child sometimes has an attachment disorder that leads to poor choices and irrational decisions. The damaged adult sabotages the relationship to fulfill the prophecy. One minute he loves her, the next he hates her. The push and pull wears his partner out. The partner usually leaves, because she can't heal this for him. The mannequin has to heal this wound himself. When the partner leaves, it reinforces his secret fear that he isn't lovable, even though he caused the exodus.

Renovators: A child of abusive or neglectful caregivers often tries to repair the object of his affection. He chooses someone who is "psychologically" broken or oppositional and sets about saving her or changing her. These relationships never work without intense therapy. Fixers and the broken often end up in codependent hell together. Temperament mismatches add brimstone to the fire.

Biology: Sex is a biologically driven need. There are many theories as to why and how we are attracted to other people, from the imago theory of unmet childhood needs, to differing DNA, to pheromones. There are opposing views on whether man was meant to be monogamous. There are deeply divided opinions on transexuality and homosexuality. These thematic arguments complicate any genre. Characters are stigmatized, discriminated against, even murdered for not following what a given society considers "the norm." Studies have shown that sexuality is more ambiguous than one might think. Biology is diverse. Psychology is diverse. Sexual needs are diverse. Have a character point that out to a person with a fixed opinion on the topic and the war is on. The other character probably won't listen to the supporting arguments if he has a deep-seated resistance to the idea. Sexual mores have shifted drastically over the centuries. Communities within the modern world differ greatly on what is considered an "acceptable" relationship. Characters are willing to lie, cheat, steal, and kill to enforce what they consider "normal."

[ALT] **Red Lights:** The dark side of sexual need is explored through thematic arguments over pornography, sexual exploration and exploitation, and prostitution. These topics are explored in Mystery, Thriller, Historical, Literary, and Western genres. Most frontier towns had prostitutes. Prostitutes followed armies all over Europe in some centuries. Debates over what should and shouldn't be allowed become extremely heated. Why can't someone sell a service he enjoys providing? Who is he hurting? The opposing arguments are equally virulent. He is hurting society as a hole. It marginalizes women. It attracts crime. It risks spreading disease. There are violent aspects to the environment that involve drug addiction, crime, and human trafficking. Different cultures have alternate views on the acceptable expressions of sexuality. Ancient Greece and Rome seemed to have a relaxed response. Ancient Hindus had the Kama Sutra. The Puritans were willing to shun or expel members from their communities for even a hint of what they considered impropriety. These endeavors involve vast amounts of money. Money corrupts. A character can be driven to desperate measures to obtain money to feed his children, satisfy his drug habit, or pay for the medication for an ailing parent. He may participate in those trades to provide his loved ones with basic needs. He may do it to fulfill exaggerated perceived needs for expensive cars and designer handbags. He may just view sex as recreation and not understand why society is so fixated on what he does with his body.

[ALT] Cuddles: Partners have differing needs for nonsexual affection. Some thrive on it, others are acutely uncomfortable with it. A partner who desperately needs it paired with one who doesn't creates a rift. The one feeling unloved often withholds sex. Withholding leads some temperaments to find someone else to play with. A character's nonsexual affection for a friend could add bricks to the wall. Two characters who aren't sexually attracted to one another could be friends, even marry, and have a life together. If one of them later becomes sexually attracted to someone else, the conflict begins. These make great thematic arguments and can provide subtle conflict at scene level.

[ALT] Infidelity: Sexual infidelity is an overall story problem or a complication in any genre. It strikes at a character's security center. It messes with his self-esteem. Jealousy motivates people to lie, cheat, steal, and kill. It is a prime motive in a Mystery. It is an overall story problem in a Romance. It is terrific motivation for an antagonist and can cause complications among friends and foes. There are huge debates about whether males and females can be friends without the undercurrent of desire.

[ALT] Hate: The flip side of love is hate. Hate is anger fueled by fear. Hatred is a character's most violent response to a person, place, thing, idea, or situation that threatens his sense of security. It is an irrational response to having a perceived need threatened or to a sense of betrayal or denial. Hate twists the heart of the most rational mannequin when his core values are transgressed or his perceived needs denied. Hate leads to divorce, custody battles, protests, murder, war, or genocide. Hate serves as motivation in any genre. The character can express hate as subtle passive-aggressiveness or rage extreme enough to harm others. Hatred and resentment eat away at a character's core until he is incapable of seeing the world clearly. Hate makes a great motivation for an antagonist. It can also motivate friends and foes.

[ALT] **Closed Minds:** Prejudices are fueled by fear and expressed as hatred. The object of the prejudice threatens a character's core values, perceived needs, or hints at something in his shadow self. Characters all have prejudices large and small. He can have a prejudice against a person, place, thing, idea, or situation. A story can examine what causes him to be prejudiced. It can follow the fallout from his hatred or the resolution of it. It can have a positive outcome or a tragic one when prejudice affects a relationship.

FINAL THOUGHTS

I hope you have enjoyed learning how to mangle your mannequins and that the information we explored will help you craft believable conflict. As an avid reader, I encourage you to keep writing. There are never enough good books to feed a book addict's habit.

Follow the companion blog, Game On! Crafting Believable Conflict at www.dianahurwitz.blogspot.com.

Diana Hurwitz

INDEX

Abandonment, 118
Ability obstacles, 12, 265
adulthood, 167
advice, 245
aggressive communicator, 235
Aim the projector, 115
androgynous names, 35
Arden, 43, 73, 97, 128, 150, 171, 189, 201, 218, 270, 306, 319, 338
astrologic signs, 25
Blair, 45, 74, 98, 128, 151, 172, 189, 201, 220, 272, 306, 320, 340
Bombs, 299
boundary violations, 119
Brick walls, 358
Cam, 61, 82, 108, 133, 156, 180, 193, 205, 228, 281, 309, 324, 351
CAREGIVING, 93
Childhood, 69
Clover Leafs, 18
cognitive dissonance, 258
Collisions, 20
Competence, 142
Critical flaw, 287
currency, 360
Daddy issues, 114
Dallas, 47, 75, 99, 129, 152, 173, 190, 202, 221, 273, 306, 320, 341
Dead-Ends, 15
Depression, 143
Detours, 16
Disunity obstacles, 317
enneagrams, 25
External obstacles, 12
EXTERNAL OBSTACLES, 297
extroversion, 27
fantasy, 252
Favorites, 86
Feeling, 30
Forks, 16

Francis, 39, 71, 95, 127, 149, 169, 188, 200, 216, 268, 305, 318, 335
Fusers, 117
fuzzy, 120
Gender confusion, 116
Ghosts, 86
Greer, 57, 80, 105, 132, 155, 178, 192, 204, 226, 279, 309, 323, 348
Hadley, 49, 76, 101, 129, 152, 174, 190, 202, 222, 274, 307, 321, 342
hate, 365
healthy communicator, 237
healthy relationships, 120
homogeneity, 36
Inferiority complex, 141
Innuendo, 248
Internal obstacles, 12, 23
Introversion, 27
intuition, 29
Isolators, 117
Joss, 53, 78, 103, 130, 154, 176, 191, 203, 224, 277, 308, 322, 345
judgment, 32
Justifications, 258
Kelly, 55, 79, 104, 131, 154, 177, 192, 204, 225, 278, 308, 323, 347
Knowledge obstacles, 12, 213
Lee, 65, 84, 111, 134, 158, 182, 194, 206, 231, 284, 310, 325, 354
liar
    how to spot a, 260
Logicians, 234
love, 333
LYING, 252
Midlife, 187
Mitigating Circumstances, 33
Mommy issues, 114
Morgan, 63, 83, 109, 133, 157, 181, 194, 206, 230, 283, 310, 325, 352

Nevada, 41, 72, 96, 127, 150, 170, 188, 200, 217, 269, 305, 319, 337

obstacles, 12

Organizational obstacles, 303

pantsers, 8

Pantsers, 12

passive communicator, 236

Passive-Aggressive, 238

pathological liar, 256

Peacemakers, 233

Perception, 32

personality types, 25

Physical obstacles, 297

planners, 8, 12

Psychological boundaries, 120

Questions, 248

Rationalization, 258

Red words, 242

response, 13

rigid, 120

River, 67, 85, 112, 135, 158, 183, 195, 207, 232, 285, 311, 326, 355

role model, 116

scene goal, 10

Self-esteem, 141

Sensing, 29

Sex, 363

SEX, 333

Shelby, 51, 77, 102, 130, 153, 175, 191, 203, 223, 276, 307, 322, 344

Special talent, 286

Speed bumps, 14

Stir the cauldron, 113

Stop Signs, 20

Taylor, 59, 81, 107, 132, 156, 179, 193, 205, 227, 280, 309, 324, 350

teenage years, 125

thinking, 30

Time limits, 297

Traffic Jams, 17

Traffic Lights, 19

Triggers, 115

Wynn, 37, 70, 93, 126, 148, 167, 187, 199, 214, 266, 304, 318, 334

young adult, 147

If you missed the first book in the Story Building Block Series, it is available through Amazon.com & Barnesandnoble.com in print and e-book versions. It is available through your local bookstore on request.

Diana Hurwitz

If you enjoyed Story Building Blocks II, you will enjoy Story Building Blocks II The Companion which features an in depth look at how each mannequin squares off with the other mannequins. To be released.

Story Building Blocks III: The Revision Layers.
Good writers compose sentences.
Great writers sculpt language.

Diana Hurwitz

ABOUT THE AUTHOR

Diana Hurwitz spent her childhood near Cincinnati daydreaming and writing poetry. She currently resides in Indianapolis with her husband, teen daughter, and two cats. She is a member of SCBWI, ALAN, Mystery Writers of America, and the Ladyscribes critique group.

For more information visit

www.dianahurwitz.com

Other Works include:

Mythikas Island: Book I Diana
Mythikas Island: Book II Persephone
Mythikas Island: Book III Aphrodite
Mythikas Island: Book IV Athena

Diana Hurwitz

www.ingramcontent.com/pod-product-compliance
Lightning Source LLC
Chambersburg PA
CBHW061333280526
45784CB00001B/8